Advance Praise for
The Audacity to be Queen

"What was once only for celebrities and royals is now available to every woman, thanks to Gina DeVee. *The Audacity to Be Queen* demystifies the mindset, ways of being, leadership style, and lifestyle secrets that will empower you to manifest your dreams without blowing out your adrenals. Let this book be your new source of confidence, grace, influence, and ease!"

—Katherine Woodward Thomas, *New York Times* bestselling author of *Calling in "The One"* and *Conscious Uncoupling*

"In today's world, where women are torn between conforming to society's standards or being who they know they are meant to be, Gina DeVee gives all women the permission to step up and be Queens. *The Audacity to Be Queen* is your guidebook to living a life so full of passion and purpose that you can only be jealous of yourself."

—Cynthia Pasquella-Garcia, founder and CEO of the Institute of Transformational Nutrition

"Gina DeVee is a modern philosopher who defines what it means to be a woman with sass, spirituality, and style. This book is a go-to bible for empowerment, divinity, and the exquisite, all at the same time. Let Gina take you on a powerful journey of renewal that brings the idea of self-care to a whole new level. You will find your deepest truth in this book and you will find, ladies, you can in fact have it all!"

—Lisa Cannon, TV anchor and producer of *Box Office*, Virgin Media Television

"Gina DeVee's fierce devotion to helping women own, earn, and most importantly enjoy their worth is unparalleled. Her coaching experience, built upon years in the trenches with clients from all over the world, gives her a unique perspective on what the modern woman really needs to rise. Brass-tacks practicality blended with a profound spiritual message, Gina's unapologetic message ignites."

—Jennifer Racioppi, author of the forthcoming book
Lunar Logic* and contributor to *Well + Good

"In a world where women are told to be powerful but not 'too much,' aggressive but not masculine, and beautiful but not to the point where that beauty intimidates other women, Gina DeVee's new book, *The Audacity to Be Queen* is a breath of fresh, lavender-scented air. Thoughtfully written for the everyday woman, Gina offers a generous roadmap to help readers elevate the everyday, become intimate with their intuition, and step into their most unapologetic selves."

—Cara Alwill, bestselling author of *Girl Code* and
host of the *Style Your Mind* podcast

"Gina DeVee is a true game changer. She has built a global tribe through female empowerment to help others find their passion point and live their best life. The fact that she is a Queen in an international arena and is sharing with others how they can also wear this crown will no doubt become a global phenomenon. I am proud to call her a friend."

—Tory Archbold, CEO and founder of
Torstar + Powerful Steps

"Gina DeVee eloquently and humorously demonstrates that you can be a Queen and have *both* success and spiritual awareness—in fact, your true role on this planet is to embody both facets. Highly recommend this book for any woman craving a deeper sense of purpose with the power of the feminine."

—Sahara Rose, bestselling author of *Eat Feel Fresh* and host of the #1 spiritual podcast, *Highest Self*

"Gina DeVee's book is a true work of art, here to help today's woman access her feminine power and rise to the Queen that she was always meant to be. Gina's authenticity, wit, and wisdom make this an inspiring guide for women around the world to dream big and make an impact. It's a must-read."

—Ashley Stahl, international career coach, TedEx speaker, author, and host of the *YouTurn* podcast

"The age of the Queen is *now* and Gina has created a life-changing book for women to give themselves permission to own their greatness. This is a book that every woman on the planet can read over and over again to remind themselves that we get to live the abundant, powerful life of our dreams and fulfill our true calling—on our terms!"

—Sarah Pendrick, founder of GirlTalk Network and TV show host

THE *Audacity* TO BE QUEEN

THE UNAPOLOGETIC ART OF DREAMING BIG AND MANIFESTING YOUR MOST FABULOUS LIFE

GINA DeVEE

hachette
BOOKS

NEW YORK

Information about global trends in women's wealth came from the following two sources:

The Economist Intelligence Unit, "The new face of wealth and legacy: How women are redefining wealth, giving and legacy planning," Royal Bank of Canada website, 2018, https://www.rbcwealthmanagement.com/us/en/research-insights/the-new -face-of-wealth-and-legacy-how-women-are-redefining-wealth-giving-and -legacy-planning/detail/

Carter, Shawn M., "More women are the breadwinner at home, but most still say men treat them differently at work," CNBC.com, March 23, 2018, https://www .cnbc.com/2018/03/23/more-women-are-breadwinners-but-are-still-treated -differently-at-work.html

Hachette Books
Hachette Book Group
1290 Avenue of the Americas
New York, NY 10104
HachetteBooks.com
@HachetteBooks
Twitter.com/hachettebooks
Instagram.com/hachettebooks

First Edition: March 2020

Hachette Books is a division of Hachette Book Group, Inc.
The Hachette Books name and logo are trademarks of Hachette Book Group, Inc.

The Hachette Speakers Bureau provides a wide range of authors for speaking events. To find out more, go to www.hachettespeakersbureau.com or call (866) 376-6591.

Print book interior design by Six Red Marbles.

Library of Congress Cataloging-in-Publication Data has been applied for.

ISBNs: 978-0-316-45879-5 (hardcover); 978-0-316-45878-8 (ebook); 978-0-306-84621-2 (library ebook); 978-1-549-18252-5 (audio downloadable)

Printed in the United States of America

LSC-C

10 9 8 7 6 5 4 3 2 1

For my King of a husband, Dr. Glenn A. Sisk,
whose empowered masculinity and unconditional
love cleared the path for me to be Queen.

CONTENTS

PART IV

The Fully Financed Queen

PART V

Queens Do Come True

INTRODUCTION

In every woman lives a Queen. She is smart, feminine, powerful, spiritual, generous, visible, prosperous, and usually has a great
sense of humor. Though she has, enjoys, and requires great material wealth, she doesn't bow to it, nor does she lord it over others.
Instead, she lives a life worthy of her calling.

Being Queen is about becoming the best version of yourself. A
Queen never denies her ability or her worth. She is confident. She
doesn't settle for crumbs or scrape by on the bare minimum. She
makes excellent decisions quickly and easily. Her boundaries are
intact and she's appropriately mindful of the boundaries of others.
She doesn't ask for permission, she gives it to herself, in spades.
Most importantly, at the center of a Queen's life is her spiritual
connection. A Queen's true power comes from her divine source.
That's why a Queen never fails to prioritize her time with Spirit
and time with herself.

Sadly, most women have become too familiar with putting
ourselves last, resulting in a half-lived life versus fulfilling our
glorious potential. We're expected to play the part of the perfect employee, wife, mother, daughter, boss—and all while looking camera-ready. When is there time to do what *we* want when
we're constantly tending to the needs of everyone around us?
Our true potential doesn't have a chance to become manifested
when unending amounts of work, dismal bank accounts, other

people's expectations, crushing stress, and our own limited beliefs of what we deserve have us trapped in life's straitjacket. Throw in a few wrecking-ball hits to our confidence along the way, and it's tempting to believe we're going to stay exactly where we are, *forever.*

What's happened is that women have been taught to strive for success the masculine way, being overly responsible and pitifully reasonable, working all the time, thinking that big results only come from *doing* rather than *being*, and looking more into spread-sheets than into our hearts. In the process, we've given up too much of ourselves and our natural feminine instincts, so that we end up never experiencing true success including the quality of life we crave. The result is that everyone suffers. I've seen it in myself, my friends, and my clients. If we're not aware, we can get stuck in a soul-sucking approach to life: hustling through our 9-to-5 (whether from a back cubicle or a corner office), wonder-ing why we don't have more interesting and supportive friends, still feel burdened financially, continue to live in the same apart-ment we've complained about for years, or haven't found the time or money for the eighth year in a row to cross St. Barths off our bucket list.

Speaking of chronic patterns, at the beginning of my journey, I noticed that my friends who were consciously in their feminine energy—women who prioritized their spiritual connection, lived for new moon circles, and wore flowy outfits with wings—were always broke. Simultaneously, I was pained to watch my smart, financially successful girlfriends blow out their adrenals as they worked twelve-hour days, playing by all the boys' club rules to prove themselves, and inevitably being seen by the world as lonely, hardened, or even "undateable." I didn't want to be part of either camp. So my internal question became, how can a woman be feminine while she is loved and enjoys life, *and* masculine while she creates wealth while accomplishing amazing results in her career?

Thankfully the solution is sexy and simple: Awaken the Queen within. Queenhood is an empowered approach to life that is a masterful blend of masculinity and femininity. The time has come for women to stop being the ones who disempower ourselves by unconsciously behaving as the Money Slave Girl, the Martyr, the Bitch, or the Princess. These are just a few of the archetypes stealing the crown that you'll meet throughout this book. Those personas don't lead to our fulfilled lives. Fortunately, when given permission, the Queen within is more than capable of reclaiming her throne.

The knowledge that I had the ability to be Queen in my life first appeared in my late twenties, when I read the true story of Queen Esther of Persia (Chapter 4) and finally understood what it meant for modern-day women to be Queen. Before that moment, I had read Bible stories as if they were only about *other* people: grand, exceptional heroes with miraculous powers like parting the Red Sea and surviving being swallowed by whales. I never saw stories like Esther's as my own.

Fortunately, that year, my spiritual understanding had grown. Marianne Williamson, the renowned spiritual teacher and bestselling author, had recently moved to my town. As a by-product of attending her lectures, I started to see these stories symbolically, metaphysically, and archetypically and discovered how to apply their wisdom to my own life. Through this new lens, I gathered some exceptional takeaways that changed my life immediately.

I became obsessed with studying all things Queen, devouring every relevant text on psychology and mythology, and signing up for every spiritual seminar within a hundred-mile radius. More illuminating than any one teaching was the process of putting all these lessons into practice. The more I deepened my femininity (I first had to unlearn and relearn what I thought it even was) and integrated spirituality into every part of my life, the more I experienced long-lasting transformation in all areas.

I started to realize that my desires are real and worthy of manifestation. Whereas previously I judged them as selfish or wrong, or only allowed them to surface in small doses if there was enough time or money left over, I now knew they were part of me and here to guide me to fulfill my purpose.

I started trusting and saying yes to my desires more and more. I said yes to having my gifts and talents used to positively impact the lives of others. I said yes to being visible as an industry leader. I said yes to marrying my soul mate. I also said yes to hiring a housekeeper for the first time in my adult life. I started saying yes to speaking on stages and later said yes to moving into my dream home in Malibu. And almost miraculously, after making the decision and taking the right actions, resources and opportunities showed up, and this elevated level of career, love, and lifestyle became my new normal. I also said yes to private travel, though sadly that one hasn't happened yet (#transportationgoals).

When I was a struggling life coach desperate to find my next client, I was denying my desires. I wasn't thriving, nor was I contributing to the lives of others at the level of my potential. Claiming my real power and Queenhood has turned all that around for me. It turned my startup into what is now Divine Living, a global, multimillion-dollar company dedicated to providing women's empowerment, personal development, and business trainings so women and their families can live in financial, emotional, spiritual, and lifestyle abundance. It has allowed me to give back and contribute to causes I care about as well as fulfill my dream of international travel and working globally. All of this has modeled to the women in my programs, who share these aspirations, what is possible for them.

Though it's meant for every woman, not everyone sees Queenhood as possible for themselves. Throughout the years, I've heard it all. "Who do you think you are?" Some are triggered by my personal choices. "How can you travel the world and work from anywhere?" "How can you charge that much?" "How can you take time off and shop like that? You're wasting your money. You need to save for a house. Aren't you worried about your retirement account? Shouldn't you be donating more to charity?"

In my commitment to studying what it means for us all to be Queen, I realized these women weren't asking the right questions. They were just judging my audacity to be the Queen of my life.

I understand why. Too many women have been shamed for merely admitting they know they are meant for something more *and* they want the best for themselves and their families. We've been told that our appreciation for the larger life makes us shallow, selfish, or irresponsible, and we've been instructed to squelch our dreams, work in jobs we don't enjoy, remain in loveless marriages, and save our latte money.

The truth is, most driven people have high-vibrational desires, and for a reason. What criticizers often fail to get is that although Queenhood includes a decidedly fabulous lifestyle, it's ultimately about a woman making her contribution in the world at the highest level.

If I had continued doing only what people deemed acceptable and sensible, my epic life, the one that has me waking up most mornings thrilled to be living out my true purpose, would have never happened. I had to stop giving power to other people's judgments and focus more on my contribution and my spiritual connection. Through prayer, meditation, reading, journaling, and working with mentors, I opened up to what *I desired*. I stopped asking for permission and started giving it to myself. It was liberating and it worked. I became Queen of my life.

WHY I WROTE THIS BOOK

Everyone from my friends and family to social media followers and clients are constantly asking me: What does it mean to be Queen? How can I be more feminine? How would a Queen handle this situation? How can I communicate to my beloved so that I'm heard? How do I know that's my Queenly intuition speaking? When do I set powerful boundaries?

I had these same questions, and after almost two decades of searching within, studying countless outside resources, working with thousands of women, and putting my learnings into practice, it's my great honor to bring together this compendium of Queenly wisdom that has worked miracles for me and my community, as well as women around the world.

The royal road is not an ordinary one, and that is music to our ears. Because we aren't ordinary. It's our great privilege at this time on the planet to be the generation of women who have been called to be Queen. This way of life is not for the faint of heart. Yet time's up for thinking someone else is meant to make the money, speak up, be on TV, own the company, or lead the nation. Time is of the essence, as the Age of Queen is *now*.

In becoming Queen, we take ourselves off the back burner: financially, romantically, physically, politically, and socially. This new empowered and feminine approach to life will lead us to knowing that we can be spiritually guided, create our legacy, *and* have a divine lifestyle. By giving our desires attention, we'll harness our natural talents and our connection with the Universe. By using our intuition to work smarter (not harder), we'll manifest the success that is meant for us individually and collectively.

Becoming Queen is about developing the fierceness to change our relationship with what's possible, having the power to see things not as they are but as they could be, and cultivating the audacity to say no to the status quo. It's unapologetically shifting into much bigger thinking that guides us to go on an adventure through India, launch that dream project, sign up for open mic night, run for office, volunteer for a meaningful cause, or finally reactivate that online dating profile. Stepping into this visionary mindset permanently changes how we all see what's meant for our lives, the world, and women's role in it. When a woman chooses to be Queen, everyone benefits.

If you're questioning whether you've got what it takes, I promise that you do. There is no such thing as a weak woman. If you just graduated from college and are looking for more than an entry-level job, if you're a business owner who's exhausted because your entrepreneurial dream turned into a nightmare, if you've got a 9-to-5 but fantasize about being your own boss, if you're an assistant and ready to do more, if you're in entertainment and longing for your big break, if you're a mom who needs more than discussing who's the best SAT tutor in town, if you just sent your youngest to college and refuse to spend your days watching *Judge Judy* from your La-Z-Boy, if you're killing it in corporate but fear spending New Year's Eve alone, or if you just retired and can't stand the thought of water aerobics, this book is for you.

Queenhood is the opportunity for modern women to embrace what is rightfully ours. To tap into the endless possibilities available to us, to own the true impact we are capable of, and to be completely confident claiming our most fabulous lives. Once you access the Queen within, everything in your life opens up.

Looking for clarity on your life purpose? Check. Confidence? Check. Ability to create wealth without burnout? Check. Self-worth to allow deep, committed romance? Check. Trustworthy intuition? Divine Guidance at your fingertips? A career based on passion? A life full of pleasure? Check, check, check, and *check*! Femininity never looked so good.

By the time you've finished reading this book, all your fears and excuses will be unraveled. In their place, you'll find someone to kiss when the ball drops, confidence that you do have what it takes, certainty in your spiritual connection, and the ability to cross St. Barths off your bucket list. It doesn't matter if you're just starting out in life or feel like you've lived nine of them. You are so much more powerful than you think you are.

PART I

Your Epic Life Is Waiting

one

QUEEN BY DESIGN

Growing up in the suburbs of Detroit, I didn't know any celebrities, and possibly just like you, I knew I wanted to be one. Similar to so many naturally enthusiastic little girls, I never shied away from the spotlight. I danced in ballet recitals, performed in all the school plays, and was wickedly talented on my roller skates. I even won first place for my *Lady and the Tramp* routine.

In addition to my desire to entertain others, one thing I cared about deeply was helping people. I remember in first grade, my teacher, Mrs. Schmidt, had our class create a compilation book on paper almost as tall as us seven-year-olds, strung together with yarn. It was titled "When I Grow Up..." We all drew with crayons what our best lives would look like for our future selves. Firemen, ballerinas, policemen, nurses, and astronauts were all represented. My contribution declared, "I want to be a counselor so I can help people."

I had a zest for a glamorous *and* meaningful life. My mother and father encouraged my natural instincts, instilling in me that the sky's the limit (or so it seemed) and that anything is possible. Yet I also received mixed messages from society and culture that said, "Just be happy with what you have. You have to work really hard for money. You need to be responsible and practical so that one day you can get married and have kids."

My parents were schoolteachers, and like most mothers and fathers, they wanted the best for their children. At home after school, my days were filled with playing tag with the neighborhood kids, finishing homework just in time to watch *Little House on the Prairie*, and practicing Pachelbel's Canon for my upcoming lesson.

My parents worked hard and stretched every dollar to provide my brother and me with a home in a district with great public schools, plenty of extracurricular activities, and fun summer adventures including camping trips and later attending Interlochen National Music Camp. They did all the "right things" parents should do. They instilled in me: be nice to others, go to college and get a job, and always return your library books on time. I was grateful. But secretly, I was preparing for something much *bigger* than a life in Troy, Michigan. I didn't realize it at the time, however; looking back, I can see that right from the very start, this world isn't set up for women like us to express our *full* selves. It's set up that either you're famous *or* you help others. You can make the money to enjoy a luxurious lifestyle *or* you can make a difference.

This either/or situation went against what every little girl before age seven knows is her deepest truth, that one day she'll be Queen and as Queen, she will lead an epic life. Presumably, similarly to you, I had envisioned playing a starring role on life's stage. According to my big imagination, I was destined for a world-impacting career, legendary romantic love, and a jet-setting lifestyle that would take me far beyond my sensible and conservative Midwestern upbringing.

Don't get me wrong, I appreciated my nice life in Middle America, it's just that some of the constraints and mentalities I knew were not for me, like shopping exclusively off the sale rack, only being able to afford in-state college, and the idea that a fancy vacation meant driving down I-75 for two twelve-hour days to get to Florida. Begrudgingly, I did all three. I followed all the rules and maintained good (enough) grades, allegedly my golden ticket. Imagine my despair when it only took me as far as Western Michigan University and a mailing address of Kalamazoo.

"This isn't me!" my soul screamed in protest. Living in what for me was the capital of mediocrity, getting my BA in communications because that was what the adults in my life told me I "should do," had me in tears for three solid years. "This cannot be my real life! I see myself with a meaningful profession positively impacting the lives of others plus attending galas in New York and operas in Vienna, wearing Versace and Valentino. Instead, I'm in a snowsuit trudging uphill with my ginormous backpack, wasting my time sitting through boring general education classes like economics and astronomy, and generally hating life!"

By my third grueling winter in Kalamazoo, I was done with the city rumored to have last seen Elvis. I could no longer ignore the red flags that I'd been thrown completely off course of living the epic life I had envisioned for myself. I didn't know what to do or who could save me from having no better options than going to basement grunge parties that annoyingly blared Kurt Cobain music. Just as I was coming of age and excited to step into my soon-to-be-glamorous style as a young adult, I realized this was the early '90s, a time when it was illegal to look like you might have taken a shower or put a brush through your hair within the last three weeks.

I needed a win, so I turned to the relationship I had always relied on during an existential crisis such as this. "Dear God, please help me," I prayed. "Show me the way to a magnificent life full of meaning. I'm asking for a miracle. I know you've created me for more than this."

And because "Ask and it is given...," a few weeks after putting my plea into the heavens, a childhood friend of mine from Interlochen "just happened" to call me to catch up. Abigail told me how much she was enjoying college life at American University in Washington, D.C., making new friends, going to fun parties, meeting interesting people from around the world, enjoying picnics on the National Mall, and having an absolute blast.

When I shared with her my bummer of a university experience, she encouraged me to join her in what sounded like the center of the Universe. Digging deep, tapping into those little-girl dreams of greatness, thinking bigger for myself, I decided to believe that a better college life was possible and immediately acted on what clearly was the answer to my prayers by submitting numerous applications for summer internships.

I was offered a position at a nonprofit organization, the National Center for Victims of Crime. I was thrilled to be of service in our nation's capital, which was filled with people who were up to big things and at the top of their game. For the first time, I felt that here my contribution could have purpose and meaning that would affect people on a grand scale. *Finally!* Not only did I enthusiastically get up every morning to go to work, I couldn't stop meeting fabulous new friends. My social life was thriving, nightly in Georgetown, on weekends at the beaches along the Atlantic Ocean, and midweek at fund-raisers where I mingled with other smart people who worked on the Hill, or for political action committees and think tanks.

I was loving my new life, and there was no way I was going to leave it just because the summer was over. By the fall of my senior year, I had secured a prestigious internship giving public lectures at the Supreme Court of the United States, and for my second semester I landed the holy grail of internships, working for the chief of staff in the first lady's office at the White House.

My idea of the epic life had just hit the jackpot! Queen by

design, here I am! Walking into the coveted, West Wing–adjacent Eisenhower Executive Office Building daily never got old. The women in Hillary Clinton's office were *amazing*. High-powered, smart, on purpose, generous, and fun to be around. Fully committed to making the world a better place, and all while treating each other and everyone in the office, including me, with the utmost respect. They'd let me peek into state dinners, attend helicopter takeoffs, even sit in on a few unclassified meetings just so I could watch and learn. It was glorious! These were my first up-front and close role models of Queens, who, to me, were living the epic life.

Then it was time to graduate. Upon receiving my diploma, I accepted a paid position with a private company owned by a political insider, who I quickly discovered didn't live by the ethics that had been modeled by my previous supervisors, so after a few short months, I resigned. I had witnessed the underbelly of what can happen in the political arena, while working for this egomaniac who wound up in an international scandal. Though his dealings were completely unbeknownst to me, I discovered what "guilt by association" meant by age twenty-one, which by definition had me *exiled* from life as I knew it. (We'll discuss more of what it means to be exiled in Chapter 4.)

Seeing no other options, in a haze and fog I moved home to Detroit, where I now was surrounded with twenty-somethings who thought going to rave parties in abandoned warehouses was cool. What a fall from grace. I felt like my professional life was over before it had barely begun. I sank into a depression.

PLAYING BY THE RULES

Without having my identity directly attached to prestigious positions at the world's most influential institutions, I was lost. But admitting that publicly? I couldn't take it. What I could take was signing up for graduate school so my life could sound impressive again. I had been going to therapy three times a week to "find myself," and after a year of inner exploration that even Freud would have been impressed by, I discovered a master's degree program in clinical and humanistic psychology. In my head, this would be a great excuse for a socially acceptable year of personal development.

During that program, I did more than find myself. I learned first-hand about human potential. I proved to myself that a woman who was willing to grow could create anything she desired, which ended up being the subject of my master's thesis, *Living Life Unlimitedly*. My inner child was roller-skating figure eights of joy in my heart.

The epic life was slowly coming back into clear view. Upon receiving my degree, I became a licensed psychotherapist, and now it was my turn to facilitate this exciting process of change and transformation for others. I was dazzled at the resilience of the human spirit. Women who had survived sexual abuse were healing. Marriages that suffered affairs came out stronger than before the betrayal took place. Children shaken from divorces made peace with a new definition of family. Teenagers who were angry, anxious, and even suicidal found inner joy and confidence. Active addicts experienced spiritual awakenings that led to sobriety. All of us were witnessing miracle after miracle as we tapped into the inner psychological and spiritual terrains. I was extremely grateful that I had been led to transform my own depression, pain, and professional exile into a deeply meaningful career. I enjoyed it so much that the pragmatic Midwesterner within could hardly believe I was getting a steady paycheck to do what I loved.

Surprise, surprise, two degrees deep and the legend of financial security had yet to be proven true. Mysteriously, after having done everything "right," I still found myself in $75,000 of student loan debt, with my credit cards maxed out, and on a first-name basis with Delores at HSBC, begging her not to charge the late fee *again*. Yes, I was getting paid, but not nearly enough. Despite my higher education and government experience, I was clueless about how to make any decent amount of money, let alone create major impact in the world and be the successful mover and shaker I'd dreamed I'd be.

How was this my "epic life"?! Again, I had followed all the rules (except paying my bills on time). I did everything right. I went to college, got the jobs, earned the degrees, and wasn't partying. (Sooooo boring, I know! Try being me at twenty-eight years old). I was willing to work hard, help others, and be a good person. And yet, fast-forwarding to age thirty, I found myself utterly disempowered, in debt, feeling alone and invisible, working seventy-five hours a week getting nowhere, unable to land a date to save my life, *and* (yes, it gets worse) living at home with my parents in Michigan.

WONDERING WHY LIFE ISN'T FAB?

I know I'm not the only woman in the history of the world who has had an era like this be part of her story. Maybe for you an epic life looks a little different, but the pain of feeling stuck is always the same. As women, if we're not consciously making the choice to be the Queen of our epic lives, we usually find ourselves working really hard, as we've been told to do, yet secretly sad because *nothing changes*, not really.

Need proof? Let's take a quick inventory. Since last year, how much of your life is relatively the same? Le muffin top? The lower-than-you're-comfortable-with bank account balance? The going-through-the-motions sex life (or lack thereof)? The same circle of friends still venting about unbearable bosses, complaining about unexpected expenses, and pathetically insisting that he's going to leave his wife this time (even though you know he's not)?

Family frustrations that have been reenacted since the Paleolithic Period? Tolerating the place we live rather than doing what it takes to move into a home we are inspired by and genuinely love? The demanding career that doesn't actually advance, leaving us hope-addicted that if we work hard enough, we'll hit it big "one day"? And then there's the wardrobe that hasn't been properly updated since Lincoln was in the White House.

Maybe if you're lucky, at least one area of your life has had a significant change for the better. Yet as a Queen, that is just not good enough for you.

If you're asking, "Is life meant to be this slow, this hard, this heavy? Where is the quantum leap? Did all miracles just exit stage left?" No, they did not. We stopped (or never started) believing in them.

Sitting at your kitchen table in last night's pajamas, scrolling around your laptop, burdened to get through unending amounts of work all day every day, is *not* how our lives are meant to look forever! The only reason they do is that we've fallen prey to a mindset of limited thinking. If before now you thought the biggest accomplishment you could have this year would be to complete the closet clear-out you started last summer, your epic life begins with a possibility mindset and looks more like launching your side hustle, healing an eating disorder, landing the promotion, running for office, running a marathon, or crossing *African safari* off your bucket list. And although you once thought you'd be lucky to go on a decent date twice in a row, your epic life comes with a legendary romance with your soul mate.

How did so many of us smart women get stuck settling for less than our full glory? We let *epic* get removed from our mentality. We've learned how to follow the status quo, pay and manage our bills online, read Jane Austen, and highlight our cheekbones, but we haven't been taught how to thrive. We've been programmed to be a "good woman," a "good wife," a "good mom," and of course a "hard worker." We've been taught to focus on the important assignments of pleasing our man, our boss, and the accounts receivable department at Amex, plus keeping a roof over our kids' heads, so we haven't really had the time or brain cells to think about how to answer our highest calling. Seriously, when's the last time someone asked you, "What do *you* want?"

More likely, we've been told by the other loud voices in society that whatever our spirit longs for is too unrealistic, expensive, and improbable to happen, so why even ask. Making others' voices more important than our own breeds self-doubt and self-abandonment. The first whispers of "You can't," or "What will they think," or "That's not possible" send our beloved dreams straight to the graveyard. It's as if unless there's a panel of judges celebrating our ideas in front of a stadium of cheering fans, we think our vision can't work.

Making matters worse, the world deems it irresponsible for a woman to take risks: to be wild, outrageous, passionate, and courageous enough to go for something big that inspires her—whereas Henry Ford went bankrupt twice, Walt Disney almost tanked his studio from going over budget on his first animated feature, and Steve Jobs got fired from his own company for being too visionary and demanding. Clearly they weren't worried about being called a bitch and didn't let refrains of "that's not possible" stop them from living their purpose, making millions, and changing the world.

And yet women are chastised, made fun of, and even crucified online when we dare to manifest something more, which dims our fiery nature. Just having the blasé energy of "sure, that'd be nice" is like Niagara Falls dumping on the fragile flame of our dreams.

Without passion, we don't stand a chance. No successful

woman got to where she is today easily. If you've ever thought, "Well, she could do it because she grew up in a prominent family, has better genes, maintains VIP connections, or got lucky," I get it. I'll give you that; some women who've already manifested their epic life and what you also desire may have had better resources to start with. Yet I'll promise you this: every woman has a story, and not one is an easy one. I'll also guarantee that many of those who have already manifested what you desire had equally challenging circumstances as you did, if not more so. Still, they decided not to self-abandon and figured out how to up-level their lives, just like you can and you will.

You may be thinking that even if your dream is possible, it'd be so much work, time, and money that it wouldn't be worth it in the end. The great news is that as you step into your Queenhood, you'll become your number one best advocate so that you never give up on your goals, and you will focus exclusively on manifesting them instead. Welcome to your feminine power.

Actualizing your desires doesn't have to be painful, slow, overwhelming, or exhausting, and let's get real, even if it was all of the above, and you did fulfill your purpose, wouldn't that be worth it? I see women go through absolute torture, experiencing the most severe pain they've ever felt, many having their bodies sliced open, all to joyfully and gladly bring new life into the world. And then, it's mere months later when you hear them say, "Let's do it again!" For some, again and again, and *again*. Not one woman has ever told me that the reason she didn't want another child was because of what she went through to give birth to the previous one. It's like they totally forget, or at least overlook the birthing process, because they're so lit up and focused on the goal of bringing their baby into the world.

And yet when it comes to our dreams, our big life, what we're also capable of, we'll stop at the mere *thought* that this might be hard. *Really?* Isn't the worst possible outcome to live and die with the regret that you didn't do what you came here to do? To look back and find that you stood by and watched others live the life that you know you were meant for? To have endured all this emotional pain anyway, and find that you let fear and self-doubt unnecessarily ruin your life?

Well, whatever's kept you playing small, thank *gawd* this stifling state of affairs is over for you, darling! Telling yourself you're not good enough, following other people's rules, and watching other women claim what's meant for you ends here.

THE DECISION TO BE QUEEN

Back in Detroit, my status quo certainly didn't have me thinking I was in the perfect spot to unleash my next level of superstardom. Especially that gloomy winter Friday night. After getting home to an empty house from another twelve-hour day of seeing clients and doing endless paperwork, I flipped on *Entertainment Tonight* (don't judge) and started to dream about what it'd be like to move to Los Angeles, the land of sunshine and the stars! I'd watch the features on Jennifer Lopez (my spirit animal) and her new album *and* movie *and* perfume; I'd see Jennifer Aniston walk the red carpet with her gorgeous boyfriend of the moment, or catch up on some behind-the-scenes clip where Julia Roberts was hanging at Clooney's Lake Como villa with the *Ocean's Eleven* cast. How were these fabulous women doing it? They weren't playing by the rules; they weren't "one of the guys"; they weren't saying, "Who am I to be wildly successful?" And they definitely weren't living in the fear, lack, and limitation that I had started getting used to.

Exuding femininity and strength, these women didn't dim their light by pretending to be any less smart, any less fierce, or any less worthy of making money so that those around them wouldn't feel threatened. They were doing it all; why couldn't I? I had accomplished the meaningful career part, but not the money for the luxurious lifestyle. These women made me realize *I wanted both*. At this point, I could have easily fallen into a comparison trap thinking it's okay for movie stars to live this way, but not people in the helping and healing professions, but instead I claimed my desire and let these women show me what was possible. I didn't want to be invisible and do exclusively what society said I was "supposed" to do. I wanted to live an epic life on my own terms, and unapologetically. I wanted to be feminine, powerful, wealthy, generous, and connected with the movers and shakers. Are you with me? I was as passionate about having a positive impact on others as I was to travel the world, live in a dream home, belong in a vibrant community, and give to causes I cared about. I wanted to experience it all.

Enjoying the microwave popcorn and my new dazzling awareness, right there during the commercial break, I decided it was time for a career change. Finding inspiration in superstar coach Tony Robbins's teachings, I saw a bigger vision for my life. Psyching myself up, I declared (sound the trumpets) that I was going to move to Los Angeles and become a life coach! No more struggling psychotherapist for me.

It was by no means the easiest decision I'd ever made. I loved what I did, I just couldn't take the financial constraint or hassles with the insurance companies any longer. I also had just wasted another $100,000 on a year of law school (don't ask) and was now choosing to kiss my expensive license as a psychotherapist good-bye.

Dedicated to my decision, I took on as many client hours as I could book and purchased the all-black, water-resistant restaurant-worker shoes necessary for my part-time night job busing tables at Morton's Steakhouse. I then mustered up all the courage and rolled quarters I could scrounge together and somehow saved up enough money to move out of my parents' house, fly across the country, and set up my new life in a little apartment in Santa Monica. I hung up my shingle, proclaimed myself to be a life coach *extraordinaire*, and my entrepreneurial journey began.

YOUR EPIC LIFE IS WAITING

Now it's your turn. Epic life, really? Yes! I know a lot of people tell you to "just be happy with what you have." And I also know how boring that sounds to you. Your life *is* good. And you *are* grateful. Yet you're craving more: clarity on your life's purpose, your own glamorous jet-setting career that contributes to the well-being of others, the extra time to draw a *lavande*-scented bubble bath and enjoy the latest issue of *Vogue*, inspiring new friends who invite you to their second home in Thailand, and the energy to have an orgasm more than twice a month. And all for a good reason.

You have a stunning, inspiring, and meaningful role to play on this planet and in this lifetime. You have more important things to be doing than merely existing, trying to keep up with your bills, household tasks, workout schedule, and the number of times your dog needs to be let out. Perhaps you never knew that as a Queen, your calendar could sparkle with pleasurable projects and appointments with delightful people.

Stick with this Queen concept and you'll never be forced to put on a navy blazer, name tag, or apron and go work at your monotonous job ever again. Nor will you resign yourself to the dull relationship that you're staying in for the sake of the kids, or be okay with living in the same zip code and never leaving town because that's where your family's from. Whatever your version of a "nice life," I know how soul-sucking any form of settling is for smart, vibrant, sexy, outrageous women like us.

THE WAY YOU ARE WIRED

Here's the proof. All life forms are naturally and spiritually programmed to thrive. It's how the Universe works. There is an Intelligence within, guiding all seeds of potential from the invisible realm to being manifested in physical form. The greats of history have all known about this vital force that lives within each of us and created their life's masterpieces in collaboration with it.

Aristotle was one of the first to put this idea into words. *Entelechy* (pronounced "en-TELL-eh-key") is the ancient Greek philosopher's term for the higher guidance embedded into every living cell, driving its development. For example, the entelechy of an embryo is to become a baby, and the entelechy of an acorn is to become an oak tree.

Emotionally, intellectually, and creatively, every human being also has their own entelechy in their cells that contains the path to their highest level of wisdom, success, love, and contribution. Our entelechy understands why we're here and who we're capable of becoming. It knows how to make use of our highest gifts and talents and turn our visions into our realities. So you see, we are all literally wired for optimum success, including *you*.

Meanwhile, living out of alignment or doubting the grandness of your entelechy is where frustration, stagnation, indecision, fear, and resistance set in. It's where late-night spinning (and I'm not talking about SoulCycle) shows up to ruin our lives again and again.

When you're conscious of your entelechy and connected with it, you're tapped into Divine Guidance. This is the Spirit that fuels masterpieces, inspiring the world's greatest contributions, from medicine to technology to art and beyond. Our entelechy is pushing us for constant growth.

This is why you and I are always desiring more, by the way, because we are literally programmed to continuously grow. Isn't it amazing how society has made us women feel wrong for wanting more when it's exactly how nature created us to be? There's nothing wrong with you. You're not crazy. You're not inept.

You may be following some really bad advice from some really well-meaning people. Or maybe you've been so overwhelmed that you've gone unconscious in constant "busy" mode. Either way, that's just because Queenhood and all of her glory hasn't been modeled for you, or at least not at the level you crave. And because we've believed in the limited ways that status quo conformists have instructed us to behave and think, we then feel wrong, guilty, or even ashamed for desiring what we've naturally been designed for.

If you're feeling unsure about how exactly to access this greatness within so you can make a difference in the world, experience financial relaxation, and live your bigger life, keep reading. You're exactly where you need to be.

HOW TO LIVE YOUR EPIC LIFE

It's time to start dreaming big again! And it begins with those little-girl dreams. What were they? For most women I know, these are the memories you can turn to that leave plenty of clues on where to begin today. The first step is to explore what your desires were and likely still are, whether on a hobby basis or full-blown life-purpose path.

Dreaming big is a mindset, and this mindset is the necessary foundation for you to live your epic life. What lit you up when you were young? What did you love doing so much that the time just flew by and you couldn't get enough of it? Who were you or weren't you around when you felt happiest? As you start to recall the people and places that have left traces and the meaningful moments that fed your soul, write them down.

Now take a look at how they can translate into your adult life today. Maybe you *loved* playing dress-up in Halloween outfits. That could be a sign to send out invites and host a themed dinner party or finally tell your parents you're quitting pre-med and enrolling in Parsons to pursue fashion design. Or if you were more of the artsy type and loved drawing, it's likely time to enroll in a painting class or, if you want to think even bigger, look up who's teaching watercolor along the Arno, treat yourself to that Tuscan experience next summer, and create the treasures that galleries will sell on your behalf.

Once you've gotten clear on some of your desires, next comes believing that something more is not only possible for you, it's actually meant for you. This is more than a nice thought, a hope, or a wish. It's having full faith that your entelechy is designed to support you in making your highest contribution in the world. Every woman must cultivate a deep belief inside herself that her desires matter and can be manifested, so that she can live her calling.

As Queens, we must become our own number one advocate on behalf of our dreams. Why? Because it's about more than just you. With every epic life comes a "double blessing." When you show up confidently, fully expressed and modeling what's possible, it by definition blesses you *and* those lives that you positively affect. Think about anyone you're inspired by or look up to who's living the epic life. Their lives are full of abundance and blessing, and as a result of them stepping into their greatness, you have been blessed too.

Lastly, for the epic life to move past fantasy and into reality, it takes not just the courage to think big but the audacity to take immediate action. Anyone can create a Pinterest board, but it's the Queen who decides to take inspired action in the direction of her dreams. This can look as small as buying an ice cream maker to start testing recipes or as grand as signing the lease on your brand-new gelato shop. If you don't know what you desire just yet, don't worry; trust that you have a calling, and know that if you commit to taking action on the steps in this book, you have the ability to discover what it is. It is the Queen within who has the answers for what your epic life looks like as well as *how* you will fulfill it. And you're about to meet her.

You too have been designed for greatness, darling. Don't you doubt that. No one else is more important, more talented, or more capable. The entelechy within you proves that. No one else has a grander destiny than you. I promise. You've been designed perfectly and for an extraordinary purpose.

YOUR ORDINARY LIFE IS OVER

What a relief to be reconnected with the truth: that you can be, do, and experience life in the extraordinary ways you've always known to be possible! It's important that you nurture, deepen, and maintain this stellar mindset, as it is your foundation for all that is to come. And until thinking big becomes your natural state and default mode, be compassionate with yourself.

You're human, my darling, which means that while you're creating this new way of thinking, it's normal to wobble in wondering if you have what it takes, and you may even temporarily plummet emotionally, thinking your task at hand is too hard. Queenhood will give you the skills that all your other attempts at transformation have been missing.

If the medicine from this chapter starts to wear off and you forget that miracles are possible or begin to doubt that you are meant to live your epic life, reread this chapter repeatedly to make sure it is deeply ingrained in you. Keep in mind that living a life of greatness isn't just about you experiencing life at its fullest, it's also about you contributing and making a difference in this world. Everything we build on together in this book from here on out will be rooted in the idea that *all things are possible*, not just for others, but for you as well.

No longer will you need to dim your light from your bigness, make yourself wrong for wanting more, feel insecure because others will think your idea is crazy, or hold back in any way from outlandishly playing full out in this one precious life you've been given. Wear the Versace at home in the middle of the day, raise your rates, value yourself enough to take out a loan and invest in your side hustle, ask for the promotion before you're 100 percent comfortable, don't answer the phone when your toxic black-widow mother-in-law calls, book the trip to see the blue lagoon in Reykjavik, have the break-up conversation lovingly yet unapologetically, and by all means, don't let another year go by without confirming your attendance at the Biennale in Venice. You've been designed for the epic life; it's time to claim it.

A PRAYER FOR THE EPIC LIFE

Dear God,

Please open me up to see what my potential is. Help me say yes to my bigger purpose and to believe in it deeply. Anchor me into my epic life so that I can contribute at my highest level. Please use my life to be a light in this world. Amen.

two

SPIRITUALITY IS YOUR SUPERPOWER

Speaking of the way you've been designed, it's time to connect with your Creator! I'll start by sharing my relationship with the Divine. We met at the gospel church downtown that my parents drove me and my brother to every Sunday morning, Sunday night, and Wednesday night. And let's not forget the random Holy Spirit rallies on Friday nights. Clearly, I was a card-carrying Christian by the time I was a toddler. By age five, I could recite the names of every book of the Bible, and by age twelve, I was speaking in tongues. The biggest "blessing" of being raised in a fundamentalist Christian church is that you develop a seriously close and intimate relationship with God right out of the womb. So to say that me and the Big Guy have been on speed dial since I could crawl is an understatement.

Throughout this book, you'll see me use *God*, *Spirit*, *Universe*, *Source*, *Infinite Intelligence*, and *Divine Guidance* interchangeably. Of course, feel free to insert the wording that resonates with you.

Though over time, some of the more dogmatic rules I learned from this era in my life have faded, my faith hasn't. My relationship with Spirit has always been my solid foundation, and for that,

I am deeply grateful. From manifesting my biggest desires to lifting me out of the gutter, God has always been there for me.

Have I gotten angry with the Universe? Of course. Have I been so depressed that I binged on Domino's pizza daily for two weeks straight instead of consulting God? You bet. Did I ever lose all faith that my soul mate exists and become temporarily convinced I'd never meet my man? Sad, but true. Have I been Sicilian-grade furious over child sex trafficking, global poverty, and plastic in our oceans? Yes. And have I gotten into the middle of the ring with Spirit fearing that the money wouldn't show up? Ahem, *maybe*.

Over time, I've personalized and transformed my relationship with the Universe, and today it is loving, guiding, benevolent, forgiving, unconditional, and highly communicative on both ends. My God is not angry, punitive, boxed in, or lacking compassion. He also isn't absent, hard to find, emotionally unavailable, or distant. I, on the other hand, have been *all* of these. Especially when I'm not nurturing my spiritual connection as the superpower it is. At the end of each of these sad and sometimes pathetic scenarios, I've always found my way back to Source, and thankfully, I'm immediately welcomed back every time and like BFFs, we pick up right where we left off.

The same can be true for you. Even if you're squeamish and not sure how much you want to get to know or trust the Universe, that's okay; it's a process. Whether you've experienced similar binges or boxing-ring battles, if your busyness with life has accidentally put your spirituality on the back burner, if you've been going through the motions for so long that your prayer life has plateaued into a snoozefest, if you've quarantined God to Sundays only or never quite gave a higher power a shot in the first place, here's your chance to create (or strengthen) the spiritual foundation your soul is longing for.

Every person has their own individual and unique relationship with Infinite Intelligence, and you get to decide what this connection looks like for you. Darling, please don't think that yours needs to be like mine or that it is even meant to. As a Queen, you get to design (or deepen) your own unique and supportive relationship with the Universe.

YOUR SPIRITUAL FOUNDATION

At the core of every Queen is her highly developed relationship with Source. It's the most beautiful gift a woman can give herself. As Queens, it's our driving force, our safest place, our foundation.

Looking for unconditional love, true security, complete peace, boss-lady confidence, deep belonging, total support, clear guidance, and healing powers? God's your guy. And if you're interested in eliminating the feeling that you're not good enough or not worthy, look no further.

The Universe doesn't make extra humans. That means that *everyone* matters and everyone's life is valuable. Including yours. With Spirit on your side, you'll no longer doubt your capabilities or your destiny to live the epic life. Wherever you're at on your journey, your one-of-a-kind purpose is an indestructible force within you. Though it's been suppressed, trapped in endless to-do lists, and locked up in the mediocre and limited thinking of the world, it only needs to be reconnected with the unlimited nature of Spirit to thrive.

Busy is *boring*. For modern-day women, too often we've gotten used to mindlessly tolerating passionless days at our computers, bland low-cal chicken salads, and overpacked schedules. Consequently, we fall out of practice at using our spiritual superpowers to create miracles for our epic life and defer back to society's stale, man-made rules and restrictions. You must save for retirement, they say. Get married. Secure a mortgage. Go to sleep early on a school night. Watch your waistline. Go to college and get a job. Don't touch your 401(k) (as if it's not yours). Throw in a white picket fence and a minivan named anything but what it is (Sienna or Odyssey), and somewhere along the way we've slipped back into the unconscious, scarcity-based thinking of the world and made it our gospel.

God doesn't play by society's or your great-grandfather's rules. Did Infinite Intelligence guide you to pad your savings account, or was that your financial planner's advice? Were you spiritually guided to buy the house (even though you didn't absolutely love it), or did your mother declare, "That's what responsible adults do?" Are you convinced that you can't start that dream business because you don't know enough yet? Because clearly it wasn't the Universe who made the ridiculous rule that you need ten thousand hours of experience or several PhDs to be of big service in this world.

There's a significant difference between what humans think is possible and what God knows is possible. Spirit operates 180 degrees differently from the thinking of mortals. What a relief. The Universe doesn't actually care about strategy, stats, practicality, or even probability, because its realm is unlimited possibility and daily miracles.

Spirit comes from love, and if we're not careful, humans can function almost exclusively from a fear-based mindset. Spirit believes in unlimited abundance, while people believe in lack. Spirit's way is generosity and forgiveness, whereas humans have been taught to make sure you get your fair share and put up walls of protection.

The Universe never meant for life to be filled with anxiety. You can look forward to diminished fine lines and wrinkles when taking your guidance from Source versus those who live by earthly laws. Spirit lovingly laughs at your misguided beliefs when it hears you say that you feel secure with a certain amount of money in your account, as if your bank balance is Source itself. Making other people and things God is how we miss out on living the epic life.

SPIRIT IS OUTRAGEOUS

Here's the other thing you need to know about the Universe. It's *outrageous*. I mean for real, in a Freddie Mercury kind of way. Have you watched a sunset lately? Mesmerizing. Looked into your dog's eyes? Can you even begin to count all of the different shades and colors? And what about medical miracles? Spirit just goes in and instantly has tumors vanish into thin air. Talk about amazing superpowers!

It's our turn to be outrageous, darling. When we have the audacity to show up like Queens, when we remember that Spirit lives within us, our potential is legendary. We can live our lives with the outrageousness of the icons we're all inspired by. The Malalas and the Lady Gagas, the Oprahs and the Ellens. They're the "ordinary" ones just like you and me, who *decided* to use spirituality as their superpower, go for their destiny, and believe in themselves no matter what anyone else said.

Legends ignore every whisper of "you can't," "you won't," or "that's not possible," because they are so deeply in touch with their truth that comes from spiritual connection. They constantly challenge the status quo and strive to be anything *but* normal or ordinary. They see what's currently happening in music, art, entertainment, technology, business, fashion (the list goes on) and ask themselves, "What *else* is possible?" "How can I do it *differently*?" For these visionaries, industry leaders, and innovators, who've chosen to live by universal versus traditional laws, possibility has no limit.

And believe it or not, the same goes for you. People, and very likely those you most wish would cheer you on, will try to protest your choices or tell you you're wrong. It's because the traditional mindset doesn't typically understand and is even afraid of life outside the status quo.

This was true for me several different times in my life, especially when I decided to change careers, move to California, and become a life coach *extraordinaire*. "You just spent all this time and money getting a master's degree in clinical psychology!" my colleagues and family argued emphatically. They couldn't relate to my perspective that the conventional safe route only afforded me the "opportunity" at age thirty to still be my parents' roommate. Instead, they insisted, "Are you really going to throw away your license and go join this unestablished profession?!" Because the predictable income that allowed me to barely make the minimum payment on my credit cards was something to worship and hold on to? *No, thank you!*

It took a lot of courage (and therapy) to get clear on what I was being spiritually guided to do. This new industry of coaching not only empowered me to get way better results for my clients, it also led me on the path of having a much bigger impact in the world. Plus, getting out of debt, Detroit, and the floral-wallpapered room I did my high school homework in wasn't overrated either.

When we're following spiritual guidance rather than rules set by others *and* have the audacity to be Queen, any purpose-filled career and lifestyle we desire is possible. Other people's opinions don't matter (as much) and the excuses vanish as we replace life as we know it with a commitment to using spirituality as our superpower. In that "anything is possible" space, we manifest the epic life with grace and speed.

THE LIBERATED LIFESTYLE

Jill and I met on an interview panel at a women's conference. A happily married mother of three, she was living in Montana at the time and becoming quite successful in her online consulting business. Jill talked about how great her life was, what she'd been doing in her startup, how much she loved being a mom and balancing her career and her family. Then when it came to me, I was interviewed about global impact and my lifestyle of working from anywhere, fielding questions on how I'd spent extensive periods of time in the south of France, Bali, and Australia that year while running my company.

That was when Jill piped in: "Well, Gina, you can do that because you don't have kids." Sensing that this defensive remark was only a call for help, I replied, "Jill, I can see what a great mother and businesswoman you are, how much you're prioritizing your kids and giving everything to doing what's best for your family. And, if you also desire to travel, what about using your kids as the reason, and not the excuse?"

Her eyes instantly lit up and she was speechless. She had gotten so used to going along with the status quo that she didn't think to question the conventional wisdom on how to raise a family, even though she had often done so in many other areas of her life.

After the interview, her spirit was reawakened and she called me to dive deeper into the conversation. We looked into what else was possible for her as a conscious mother, entrepreneur, and wife. At first, resistance the size of the Great Wall of China went up to defend her status quo. Underneath it all, Jill discovered a deep-seated belief that staying at home in Montana, living this good yet underwhelming life (for her) plus always being there for soccer pickups and dropping off the forgotten trombone, was what "being a good mom" looked like.

Taking a closer look at her finances and her dreams, she started to see that the only thing genuinely stopping her from designing a life on her own terms was the belief that she must ignore herself in order to put her kids first, and that living in Montana was "what's best" for them. We quickly found that this story wasn't even Jill's. It was only her inner Martyr talking, the archetype who must sacrifice everything for others (we'll talk more about her in Chapter 8).

Reminding Jill that she is a Queen, I guided her to connect with Spirit, rediscover her true values, and look into what was actually possible. Changing her mindset and getting creative financially, she discovered the power to reorganize her life on *her* terms. She not only gave herself the freedom to travel more, she also granted herself "outrageous" permission to live anywhere she wanted.

She started accessing her superpowers and asked Spirit, "How can I travel with kids and be in alignment with my husband? Where else could we live? What does being a great mother really look like for me?" She was shocked to find that her true desire was to move to Hawaii, work her business part-time, and homeschool her kids so that her family could travel anytime they were in the mood.

Her husband, once she communicated with him like a Queen, was in complete agreement, and was also liberated in the process of Jill's transformation. Through the move, he left his unfulfilling job and opened his dream café on the island! As the kids thrived in their new aloha life, Jill and her husband both leapt ahead on the path to fulfilling their Divine Assignments.

DISCOVERING YOUR DIVINE ASSIGNMENT

Your Divine Assignment is your purpose for being at any given moment. We've all been given unique and glorious assignments small and large. None is better or worse. And not one of them is boring. Being spiritually open and closely connected to God, you'll start to get clearer and clearer about what is meant for you in this current season and in this lifetime.

The Divine Assignment for Jill was to look at what it really meant to be a great mother. Our society puts us in this either/or world. When Jill stepped into her Queenhood, she took a stand for the *and*, letting herself explore what it would look like to prioritize her children *and* herself *and* her husband. Jill's entire family is happier because she voiced her truth and fulfilled her Divine Assignment. This is the way everybody wins.

Sometimes your focus will be brought to something momentous like figuring out your life's purpose, accepting your mother for who she is, undergoing a major health transformation, or forgiving an ex. Other times, you'll be given a more bite-sized though no less significant Divine Assignment to schedule a dentist appointment, treat a friend to lunch, resume your skincare routine (including the toner), empty your inbox, or give up caffeine. Whatever your assignment, it is designed to move you further on your epic journey.

The double blessing of fulfilling your Divine Assignment is that while you become your best self and experience life at its fullest, you're making the greatest difference in the lives of others in the way that *only you* can.

DEVELOP YOUR SPIRITUAL SUPERPOWERS

Desire

All you need is a *desire* to have a stronger relationship with the Universe and you'll see co-creation manifestations that add sparkle to your life. If this sounds too easy or too good to be true, it's only because you're listening to the ways of the world rather than Spirit's generous invitation. That's right. If you start by letting Source know about your interest in an intimate connection,

I promise, it'll meet you where you're at in a way that you are certain that Spirit *is* showing up in your life.

When I communicate to God my request, my prayer looks something like this:

Dear God,

I'm ready for more. More fun, more miracles, more power, more wisdom, more abundance, and more love. I know you are the Source for all of these and I'm asking you to show me how I can deepen my connection with you. Please show up more clearly in my meditations, thoughts, and intuition and guide my actions. Show me how to be more of the woman you created me to be. Show me how to be of greater service in the world. I'm asking you to flow through me in a bigger way.

Thank you for my life, thank you for this relationship, thank you for your unconditional love. And so it is.

Healing

If you lack the desire to develop a deeper spiritual connection because you "don't really believe in that stuff," you've experienced religious wounding, or you feel straight-up angry that God hasn't been there for you when you needed Him most, let's heal that now.

You can't strengthen a relationship that you're secretly holding a grudge against. The resentment is not serving you and is keeping you from receiving the benefits of a strong spiritual alignment. I understand that you may be convinced because of past circumstances and data you've collected along the way that this woo-woo thing isn't for you or that you've decided that the only person you're willing to trust is yourself.

This is not the mindset of the Queen, and remember, my darling, you are very much a Queen. What happened in the past may not seem fair. It was likely very hurtful, causing you to close your heart, because that's how you've been taught to protect yourself. The only true safety awaits on the other side of healing. The Queen within knows that everything that happens in all of our lives is there to make us the women we are. It's appropriate to feel normal levels of grief or sadness or even rage when you've experienced something hurtful or traumatic. It's just necessary that we don't self-manufacture additional pain, as victims often do.

If you're willing, let's see what else is possible on the other side of this pain. Queens know that something bigger and better is always waiting to reveal itself to us. Reality is kinder than our stories about it.

Healing begins with a simple prayer.

Dear Spirit,

I'm angry. You haven't been there for me in the way I wanted or expected. I'm hurt and it's made me feel like I can't trust you. I'm resistant to even trying to have a deeper relationship with you because I don't want to be disappointed again.

However, if you're listening, I've decided to see what else is possible for me and you. I'm asking you to show up in my life in a way that I will know it's you beyond a shadow of a doubt, and that I am loved and cared for. I'm tired of feeling bored, lost, and ignored. I'm looking for my epic life and if an exciting relationship with you is possible for me, I'm interested. Amen.

Then surrender. God will do the rest.

Customizing

How you receive Divine Guidance and develop your relationship with the Universe is of course up to you. Do you fancy a more formal relationship with God? Great. Bow your head, clasp your hands, get dressed up, and go to services in buildings with stained-glass windows. Pray and read religious books; sleep with the Bible, the Torah, or the Qur'an under your pillow. I just recommend that you don't quarantine God to one holy day of the week. Invite Spirit into every area of your life on the other six days too.

Crave a more casual connection with Spirit? Cool. Go for a walk in nature as you chat with the Universe, gather for summer solstice festivals, meditate or start your day with sun salutations. However you decide to experience the Divine, I highly suggest you *don't* use it to hide out from real life.

The answer to everything in your life is directly connected to you having and using your access to Infinite Intelligence! Don't see the solution? The Universe does. Can't forgive a past hurt? God can. Wondering where your clients are? Spirit knows. Need the willpower to *not* text your latest crush first? It comes from Source. If you truly show up for this relationship, if you let it be the most important bond in your life, if you train yourself to trust God and intuition over ego, you will experience spirituality as the miraculous superpower that it is.

If you've tried countless times to make this relationship exciting and it's still falling flat for you, chances are you're stuffing God into an overly formal or religious box. The excitement comes in when you customize the relationship. That's where you access the realm of the miraculous in a way that is meaningful to you. There's nothing dull when you're experiencing extra abundance, unshakable confidence, and undeniable "coincidences" like people calling you right after you *just* thought of them. A relationship is only tedious when all the life has been sucked out of it. Expect more, raise your standards, breathe life into this superpower, and you too will be dazzled on a regular basis.

Dear Universe,

Intellectually I know you're amazing, but in my day-to-day life I'm not experiencing the wonders people talk about. It seems like others are better at attracting miracles than I am. Please show me how to have my own unique relationship with you so that I'm allowing miracles to flow through me daily and as a result am a bigger blessing in the lives of others. Please show up in my life in ways that I don't even know to ask for. Please enter my mind so I can think big on a consistent basis and have my big thinking be used to inspire others. Please guide me on how to make my relationship with you a priority so it can thrive. And so it is.

Communicating

Keep in mind, God's availability isn't exclusive to high holy days. As with any significant, trusted personal relationship, regular, intimate communication is key. God enjoys hearing more than small talk from you. He's interested in the good, the bad, the vulnerable, the ugly; the big requests of solving world hunger and saving your marriage and the more personal requests for an imminent parking space in front of the farmer's market. The more you converse with Spirit, the more clear and less confused you'll be.

Maybe, like so many of the women I work with, you're

wondering, "How do I know if what I'm hearing is really from Source? Maybe it's my ego or fear? Or is it my intuition?" It's up to each Queen to hone her spiritual ear through daily practice. Here's how I've honed mine.

PRAYER

Praying is my way of communicating *to* God. It's how I ask for inspiration, solutions, and clarity. My prayers are simple and sincere about whatever is going on in my life. When I align my mind with the truth of unlimited possibility and my desire to make an impact, I open up to receiving insights that lead me to be my highest self.

To call Spirit into my work, I pray:

Dear God,

Please inspire my book-writing process. May the words on these pages uplift the readers and connect them with their purpose. Amen.

If I'm wavering with my fitness goals, I call in divine assistance:

Dear Spirit,

I don't feel like working out. I'm not motivated to take great care of my body. Please change my heart and mind. Please place the desire in me to want to go to the gym. Please give me food cravings for healthy, nourishing sustenance. Please unify and integrate my relationship with my body. Amen.

If I'm going through a triggering situation with a friend, I am completely honest about my feelings:

Dear God,

I'm really angry. I feel betrayed by my friend who I helped when she was down. I'm resentful for having done so much for her only to have her turn her back on me when I was in need. Forgive me for making her Source. Release this resentment and place love for her in my heart instead. Thank you for the lesson that anytime I rely on anyone more than you, I will experience disappointment. Thank you for reminding me that I can turn to you first. Amen.

MEDITATION

Receiving answers is just as important as asking for them. If prayer is how I speak *to* God, meditation is how I hear *from* God. There are hundreds if not thousands of ways to meditate. Personally, I keep my practice really simple. I sit comfortably in a quiet and undistracted place. I set an intention in search of a solution. Then I close my eyes and breathe. At first, thoughts will flutter into my awareness. Then I gently release them until I get to the place of no thoughts. I start to feel my brain waves moving, almost as if I'm about to fall asleep, though I'm very much awake. And then I let go of control and let Infinite Intelligence take over.

Every meditation experience is different. Sometimes I see visions; other times I hear words or sense a message. Especially when I meditate daily, I am lifted into a higher-level consciousness where the solution I'm seeking becomes easy and clear. Whatever the outcome, it's God's way of speaking *to* me.

JOURNALING

Lastly, I'm a big journaler. I do it daily. In fact, I've kept a journal since I was ten years old. Though it no longer has a combination lock with a unicorn and a rainbow on the front, my journal is still my sacred place where I can easily interact with God. This usually looks like a conversation on the page. I'll ask Spirit a question, write the response, and it goes back and forth like a dialogue in a movie script.

Knowing whether it's your voice or God's voice in your head comes with practice. Eventually, you'll get clarity and a feeling of knowing with certainty. Until then, I rely on *confirmation*. If I'm unsure or unclear, I continue to pray and ask for unmistakable guidance and signs that aren't mere whims but true confirmations.

The Daily Spiritual Workout

Including God as your partner throughout your day literally makes life divine. You're not meant to shoulder everything alone. Spirit is there to guide you.

As in any relationship, the more time you spend getting to know someone, the closer you become. And just like with fitness, consistency is key to keeping your spiritual muscles strong. If I'm crunched for time, my daily spiritual workout includes five minutes of reading, five minutes of writing, five minutes of meditation, and five minutes of movement. Spending even twenty minutes at the beginning of your day to consciously connect with Infinite Intelligence will nurture your superpowers, doing wonders for your life.

If you have zero issues getting yourself to the gym every day, yet feel resistance around the idea of journaling, sitting still, or stopping to pray, remember that the more you practice, the easier it gets. Plus, you can do *anything* for twenty minutes. And the more you see and feel the results of being clear on your intuition, the more you'll naturally start to rely on, enjoy, and look forward to your daily practice.

INVITATION TO USE YOUR SUPERPOWERS 24/7

Once I knew I could count on God in *every* area of my life, and not just the socially acceptable ones, I finally got to drop my escape plan of moving to Cyprus to wait tables every time life didn't work out as I desired. Having a solid relationship with Source won't mean your life is without obstacles, but as a Queen, you will come to see them as invitations to use your superpowers.

You see, access to Divine Guidance gives you clear next steps at every twist and turn. Spirit didn't design the search for answers to be as difficult as cracking the Da Vinci Code. The universal truth is "ask and it is given." In our souls, we women know this. Now it's time to ask from a deep place and on a consistent basis, so that we can claim the epic life that's meant for us.

When you're connected to God and living by spiritual laws, being outrageous will come naturally. With the audacity to be Queen, you're ready to play in the space where masterpieces are created, legends are made, and epic humanitarian efforts end suffering. When you prioritize your relationship with Spirit, your Divine Assignment will become clear.

Make living your epic life, guided by your relationship with God, your new obsession, and you'll become unavailable for any contradictory opinions of what's possible for you to enter your heart and mind. Welcome to total devotion and certainty in your potential. It's how you stop boring yourself and God.

three

THE FEMININE MYSTERY

Femininity. It's been hunted, attacked, scrutinized, silenced, hidden, underestimated, scandalized, and killed dating back from ancient times to this very day. Something that the masses across the globe work so hard to harness must be powerful, valuable, intimidating, and important. Why else would entire cultures of people around the world, initially men and later women as well, criticize femininity, imprison it, deny it, and force it into exile?

What is it? Where is it? Who is it? This is beginning to sound like a Dr. Seuss book, and sadly that's the way it looks in society as well. Most people mistake femininity for emotional fragility or donning a 1950s gingham apron. Some confuse it with the feminist movement's marches that fight for equal pay and women's rights. Still, others judge it as seductive or witchlike, threatened by what they cannot see and don't understand.

Since this invisible concept is neither taught in schools nor modeled often enough in real life, even women are undereducated about what femininity actually is. Some think it can be achieved with miniskirts and lipstick, consequently missing its profound power by a mile. Others, convinced that femininity is a weakness, have become so addicted to the masculine way of getting ahead that they avoid the topic entirely, with apparently zero interest in putting down the bottle of busyness to save their adrenals.

At the same time, there is a trend going viral with modern-day women like us who are interested in discovering and developing our femininity. We know there is a more divine, pleasurable, and smarter way to do life, and our instinct is that the feminine mysteries will show us how. But when it comes down to actually excelling in our careers, mediating challenges at home, or tapping into our potential, can we really trust that being more feminine will actually result in greater success?

Our skepticism is valid. *Femininity* is the most misunderstood, villainized, controversial, and suspicious word of our generation. And ladies, that's about to change. Grab a Burberry trench coat, and let's investigate how femininity rose to #1 on America's Most Wanted list.

THE MASCULINE AND FEMININE DANCE

Since the beginning of time, the Universe had it beautifully worked out for Mother Nature and all living things to thrive in their full glory. In this divinely designed utopia, masculine and feminine energy were created to work together in perfect harmony.

Just like nature is meant to thrive with the masculine and feminine balance, so are human beings. Regardless of gender, every person has both feminine and masculine energy within them. Fundamentally, masculine energy is about *giving* and feminine energy is about *receiving*. The integration of both is essential to all life. Each energy is designed to enhance and support the contribution of the other.

The masculine bucket is full of things like timetables and road maps. Spreadsheets and skyscrapers. It encompasses all things linear, logical, tangible, and concrete. Personified by Ed or Edith in Accounting who drives a navy Volvo, masculine energy is stable, high-performing, protective, and predictable. It's also the energy that initiates action, thinks things through, and sets up structures and systems. Empowered masculinity in the Universe's design is gorgeously strong, generous, and genius. Its purpose is to be in service to the feminine.

Take a glass of water, for example. The glass is the masculine, concrete structure that supports the flowing, feminine water. The masculine container is necessary for the feminine water to fulfill its purpose of nourishing the drinker. Without the glass, the water spills all over the place and cannot do its job.

The water, meanwhile, encompasses all things invisible, intuitive, beautiful, pleasurable, and visionary. It's the feminine energy that connects you with your dreams, creativity, and miracles. Just like your crazy aunt Ginger who's always jetting off on some amazing trip to places like Bhutan or Bangkok and comes back with rare jewels, Asian artifacts, and her much younger new beau, femininity is spontaneous, sexy, unpredictable, and unapologetic and plays by her own rules.

Empowered femininity in God's design is miraculous, mystical, and outlandish in all the right ways. The sixth sense is at her core. So is the inner ear and the third eye. Her purpose is to receive. She gives you the ability to dream up a life worth living, play way outside the box, invent creative solutions, expand your thinking, and attract your way to maximum success.

As exciting as your feminine power is, a Queen's wisdom is that you also need masculine energy. Without it, we lack the money to fund our dreams, the systems and structures to share our gifts with others, and the discipline to take consistent action on behalf of our vision. Keeping the integration of feminine and masculine is how we can have both our connection to the Divine and our ability to make big things happen in the world.

In my twenty years of doing this work, I've identified a number of characteristics that relate to the polarities of feminine and masculine, laid out in the following chart. Read the list from left to right and consider where in your life you show up more masculine or feminine.

Femininity	Masculinity
Being	Doing
Feeling	Thinking
Spontaneous	Predictable
Intuitive	Logical
Playful	Results-oriented
Beautiful	Functional
Invisible	Concrete
Circular	Linear
Dynamic	Sturdy
Vulnerable	Protective
Nurturer	Provider
Community (we)	Individuality (I)
And	Or
RECEIVING	**GIVING**

THE OBSESSION WITH MASCULINITY

The beautiful harmony between masculine and feminine is how the Universe always intended for all beings to grow, expand, and thrive. As long as both energies were present, life on earth flourished. And then fear-based humans came along and messed with perfection, dissecting these two beautiful energies within every person, categorizing masculine as male and feminine as female, and creating the ultimate imbalance that everyone on Earth and very likely galaxies far, far away are still paying for.

For over a millennium of our history, the birth of a baby boy has been cause for celebration. A son could expect the best education, the highest-thread-count clothes, and, in the right family, the throne. When a girl was born, there was mourning and shame. Women weren't considered valuable until they bore a male. Being female was the worst possible fate.

As civilization evolved with this distorted mentality, the original idyllic balance between masculine and feminine energy as well as between men and women was destroyed. Generalizing, men traded empowered masculinity for control and dominance. Women replaced empowered femininity with silence and submissiveness. Society was trained to hail to the masculine, usually in the form of men. Men made the rules. They started lording over women, and soon unequal power and "men know best" became doctrine.

At the same time, the feminine arts of intuition, creativity, delight in the unknown, and spontaneity were shoved aside for what could be seen, measured, and controlled. Communing in nature, using healing powers, and creating herbal potions became heresy, and consequently being feminine became synonymous with being a witch, girdling the wildish, feminine way.

In fear for their lives, feminine women disowned their natural abilities. The few who didn't give up their innate talents either went silent in fear or fled underground. Either way, generations of women were cut off from their true power, and thus became weak.

Femininity isn't weak and neither are women. We just haven't been allowed to thrive in the way we were designed.

The long-held tradition of bowing to men escalated to

idolization until we all wound up brainwashed that the masculine way is the right way, the way it must be done, and therefore the only way. Of course, many men buy into this way of thinking (it's what patriarchy is built on), but many women unconsciously maintain this distorted notion as well.

Meanwhile, femininity has been stilted and reduced to a pretty face, a sculpted Barbie figure, and a frivolous trophy for men to fondle, rather than a deeply valuable source of power and purpose. The feminine side of men got shut down as well. The difference is it is *our* dominant energy. The result of thousands of years of this conditioning is a culture of men and women who've been trained to dismiss and deny their own glorious nature.

The default to be overly masculine leaves women empty and their femininity crushed. Instead of wielding our own strengths, we've learned to predominantly use our masculine skills to get ahead, to be accepted, and to survive—especially in our work culture, where we've been conditioned to idolize the powerful men in charge, bow to their demands, and imitate their exact behaviors down to wearing the pinstriped pantsuit and "talking shop" because that's what got them to the top, right? And it takes some of us to the top too, but at what cost?

How often have you discounted your feelings because you were pressured to do the practical thing? How often have you felt your creativity stifled by needing to do things in a predictable, calculated way? For how long have you let your sense of curiosity, mystery, and pleasure dry up because the seemingly most important thing in life is to be responsible in the ways others define it? To the degree that successful women are secretly dissatisfied or totally burned out, the Injured Feminine Instinct has led them to the wrong strategy.

THE INJURED FEMININE INSTINCT

Modern women have arrived at the end of a long era of masculine dominance, which is how you and I both lost touch with our own femininity and our true power as women. When women don't have a sense of what real femininity is, we don't know who we naturally are or the depth of our potential, leaving us to rely on a one-dimensional view of what's possible. Society's obsession with being overly masculine has left a gaping collective wound called the *Injured Feminine Instinct*, a concept I first read about in the book *Women Who Run with the Wolves*.

To the degree that we can't receive love, attention, wisdom, and clarity at the levels we crave, we have an Injured Feminine Instinct. This is why we're not crystal clear on our desires, why we say yes when we want to say no, or why we're standing far too long in aisle 5 indecisively contemplating which brand of detergent to buy. And we wonder why we are overeating, overworking, overgiving, and overly stressed.

COMPLIANCE AND DEFIANCE

As a result of disconnecting from our true nature, we women have unconsciously turned to other, more self-destructive ways of functioning and trying to get our needs met in the world. Most often, the Injured Feminine Instinct shows up in two distinct personalities, Compliance and Defiance. When your femininity is intact, your true nature is Alliance.

We all are typically compliant in some areas and defiant in others. And we don't have to identify with all of the traits on either list to determine which is our principal MO.

Compliance	Defiance
Shame	Self-obsession
Easily embarrassed	Harsh
Inadequate	Superior
Unworthy	Entitled
Codependent	Addicted
Worrier	Domineering
Needs approval	Critical
People pleasing	Demanding
Indecisive	Inflexible
Uncomfortable receiving	Inconsiderate
Invisible	Aggressive
Underearning	Taker
Insecure	Abrasive
Depressed	Self-righteous
Overwhelmed	Know-it-all
Anxious	Tough
Overgiving	Presumptuous
Scattered	Rigid
Exhausted	Competitive

Compliance

You are compliant if, on a regular basis, you need acceptance and approval from others, believe that you're not important, think your voice doesn't matter, are terrified of what other people might (or did) say about you, fear that you're not capable, and behave like you need to get permission for just about everything. Women who have an Injured Feminine Instinct in the form of compliance often experience the world as emotionally unsafe, become easily consumed by guilt and shame, and feel a giant sense of insecurity behind every move.

Being so afraid of making a mistake leads to a perpetual state of indecision. A woman in compliance is always confessing; she's not sure what to do, doesn't know what she wants, and can't figure out the right decision to make. Wanting to be liked above all else, she's scared to speak up and frequently settles for being underpaid and overwhelmed. Putting herself last, she winds up too confused and overworked to make great decisions for herself, which leaves her unable to make moves toward living her epic life.

Defiance

Defiance typically shows up as some form of rebellion. When a woman has that emptiness of being cut off from her feminine essence and doesn't see a way to get her needs met and live her truth, that's when all forms of control, recklessness, or domineering behaviors show up in an attempt to fill the void.

As with compliance, defiant women also feel unsafe in the world—they just handle the feeling differently. Defiance can look like the know-it-all who will not admit to being wrong or the ruthless competitor who trusts no one. When a woman is so determined to never be taken advantage of that she ends up being the taker, or so afraid (not that it comes across as fear) that she's not going to get her share that her strategy becomes to grab the bull by the horns, she's in defiance. She may also be convinced she can do it better than anyone so she might as well do it all herself. Alone. She usually avoids asking for help at all costs.

In whatever form these Injured Feminine Instincts are showing up in our everyday lives, it's crucial that we become aware of them. These wounded habits are literally sucking the fierce, fabulous life out of us, and on the other side of healing them is the epic life for us all.

MY INJURED FEMININE INSTINCT

Considering the amount of spiritual and personal development work I've done, you'd think I'd have this femininity thing *down*. But I'm right here with you, sister. I too am still learning.

A few years ago I made a business move that made total practical sense. I invested a serious amount of money in my company by hiring a New York City media agency. The plan they promised seemed so logical and responsible, featuring all of the things that I "should do" to grow my audience, land my book deal, and share my message.

Fast-forward two months into the contract; working with them was already toxic. For starters, my on-camera interview training was brutal. Every video I submitted was sliced and diced with demeaning criticism. The one time I excitedly shared how I thought I had incorporated their teachings into my latest attempt, I was yelled at: "Don't *ever* tell me you nailed it; you're *years* away from even getting close to that kind of result."

Meanwhile, they connected me with a literary agent who told me for almost a year that my book proposal wasn't good enough, along with vague broad-brush notes for improvement. Every time I came back with the next edit, I was sent on the same hamster wheel headed nowhere. Nothing I did was ever good enough. I just couldn't seem to get anything right.

A voice inside me spoke up: "This is not you, Gina! Do you need to learn? Yes. And get abused along the way? Not even a little bit. You don't have to fit into this punishing box!" But sadly, in compliance, I silenced my voice, as so many women do, and tried to grin and bear it. If I had continued to doubt my instincts, I'd still be editing that proposal and you'd be reading someone else's book right now.

Overall, that experience with hiring "experts" (who in this case turned out to be total sadistic sociopaths) because I thought it was what I "had to do" to get ahead nearly destroyed my self-confidence and kept me from sharing my message. All of my aspirations were bound up in that toxic relationship. Finally that contract ended, and though it took me two years, I recovered. Talk about a detour!

One Saturday morning after the unnecessary wounds to my self-esteem had finally healed, I woke up, made my coffee, and opened my journal. I was ready to get into *alliance* in my career, and for me that meant I had to shift my energy internally.

I decided that I was no longer available to be an unsigned author without a book deal. There's a big difference between wanting something and becoming unavailable to not have it. In making that decision, I no longer listened to the words from that media agency that told me I wasn't ready or wasn't good enough. I stopped giving power to the belief that publishing a book was extremely difficult or only for the fortunate few.

Instead, I took instant action on my new decision. *This is possible for me.* Using my superpowers, I prayed, "Dear God, how can I find my book agent *now?*" I immediately remembered that a friend of mine in Brooklyn had recently landed an agent. I asked for an introduction, and sent my proposal off that day.

Later that afternoon I heard back from the agent, who said, "Your book doesn't call to me, it screams to me!" Once she pitched my proposal, within two weeks we had seven meetings with top New York City publishers, and the following week I proudly accepted the offer on my first book deal.

As it turned out, I didn't need to spend tens of thousands of dollars working with an "expert" media consultant who clearly didn't get me or treat me well. I didn't need to waste hours researching thousands of options for agents, nor did I need to spend years rewriting my proposal. I just had to connect with other women. How fabulous! How *feminine.*

As you can see, this wasn't an overnight transition. To this day, I'm still uncovering new areas in my life where I've convinced myself something needs to be way more difficult than the Universe intends. And despite popular misconceptions, it's not just in business. The latest? Weight loss.

Every spring I go on a diet. No, it's not a lifestyle change, it's a straight-up "I've gained twenty pounds and want to look hot when I get to the beaches of Europe this summer" specialized GDV weight-loss plan.

The logical, masculine ways of the world would say, "It's hard to lose weight past age forty." And my own experience reflected that. My status quo diet goes like this: Sometime in March, I embark upon my "clean eating" regimen of protein, veggies, small portions, and enough water to make using the restroom a part-time job. The first five to eight pounds of water weight easily fall off as my liver delights to find me sipping kombucha at happy hour. And then, believing the realistic advice, I trudge and sweat and deny myself all the way down the slow, hard path of shedding a half pound here, three ounces there, plateauing here, and losing an inch (if I'm lucky) there.

With a super-restrictive diet and moderate workout plan, at the speed of a caterpillar traveling through molasses, I lose my twenty pounds just in time for that Air France flight. I always feel proud of my hard work. I get myself looking much better in clothes, but as for that bikini body? Let's just say *Sports Illustrated* hasn't called yet.

I could have easily continued to tell myself I was already doing everything imaginable except daily five a.m. boot camps, and this was just as good as my body was going to get without enduring a lot more pain in the form of squat-thrusts, jumping jacks, and a starvation diet. However, I sensed something else was possible.

This year, I was determined to do things differently, *the feminine way*. So I prayed. Of course it didn't take long for the Universe to deliver. Over coffee, a friend happened to mention what a great experience she just had at The Hall Center. Acting on the Divine Guidance I received, I booked an appointment with modern-day wise one, Dr. Prudence Hall. We met in person at her Santa

Monica office, where she was *present* with me. She took the time to talk to me, ask me questions, and get to know my health desires as true healers do. She then prescribed lots of natural remedies to balance my hormones and restore optimal health.

Being in alliance with my body, rather than in compliance with the status quo thinking that carrot sticks and kettlebells are the only way to go, I can report that within weeks, the weight slipped away, healthily, faster than ever. Same time frame, a less restrictive diet, and a different belief mixed with natural potions yielded 2.5 times the results. And I still got to enjoy the occasional pasta night.

This is femininity: Major attraction power. Receiving miracles as a way of life. And big results accomplished from a pleasurable place.

Healing your Injured Feminine Instinct puts you into *alliance* with the Universe and your epic life. This is where your true power dwells. Now that you have this awareness, you too will no longer need to resort to *compliance* or *defiance* to get your needs met. Healing this wound is a process, so be gentle and loving with yourself (and other women too).

Again, read horizontally so you can see how compliance, defiance, and alliance look in day-to-day life.

Compliance	Defiance	Alliance
Shameful	Self-obsessed	Assured
Easily embarrassed	Harsh	Confident
Inadequate	Superior	Peaceful
Unworthy	Entitled	Grateful
Codependent	Addicted	Intact boundaries
Worrier	Domineering	Intentional
Needs approval	Critical	Intuitive
People pleasing	Demanding	Purpose-led

Indecisive	Inflexible	Open-minded
Uncomfortable receiving	Inconsiderate	Gracious
Invisible	Aggressive	Curious
Underearning	Taker	Worthy
Insecure	Abrasive	Certain
Depressed	Self-righteous	Optimistic
Overwhelmed	Know-it-all	Supported
Anxious	Tough	Energetic
Overgiving	Presumptuous	Generous
Scattered	Rigid	Integrated
Exhausted	Competitive	Capable

In *alliance*, we access our feminine ability to create, transform, connect, and grow, without hurting ourselves or others. We understand that solutions exist for all and that everyone matters, including us, and the unfulfilling sacrifices of compliance and defiance become completely unnecessary.

Restoring our feminine instincts, we clearly hear our intuition *and* trust it. Connected to Spirit, we become comfortable with the unknown, and when needed, we're able to breathe and live in the question rather than needing to pull the flower open just to force an outcome. No longer afraid that we're not good enough, no longer believing we must take to get our fair share, we open up to receiving once again.

Releasing the habit to comply or defy isn't an overnight transition. As Queens, we get to be gentle and loving with ourselves in this process. Just noticing a compliant or defiant pattern counts as a major victory. Anytime you do slip into old habits, making the correction is a matter of remembering the power of the feminine. For a Queen, that often looks like taking a moment to stop, slow down, and connect with yourself and Spirit. Remember the truth of unlimited possibilities and your role in a benevolent Universe that's here to assist you in fulfilling your purpose.

Women who are aware of their feminine power have a different relationship with the invisible, because they can see things not as they are but as they can be, and will be. You become the woman who doesn't believe your Divine Assignments have to be unnecessarily hard, grinding, or complicated. You get to design your own experience for how you'll accomplish your goals.

When you're in alliance with your feminine instincts and you intuitively feel guided to hire help, try a new restaurant, or sign up for salsa lessons, you do it! You also go on that blind date, talk to the hot stranger, and turn in those papers for a sabbatical. And when you slip out of your natural state in one form or the other, simply remembering the traits of femininity from the chart will put you back into alliance with the Universe, where you will receive what is naturally there to assist you in fulfilling your purpose.

A woman is a naturally dynamic, fluid, unpredictable force. Live that way. When you give yourself permission to lead your life with feminine energy, you will make decisions from a place of "I desire" versus "I should." This is when things start happening that everyone else said was impossible, without severe sacrifice, waiting forever, or being so stressed you develop a bladder infection every two months.

How to get great at receiving

An Exercise

Step 1: Ask yourself, how good are you willing to let life get?
This is one of the most powerful questions you can ask yourself. I personally do this on a regular basis. If you go deep with this

question, you'll see how *you're* the one who's been standing in the way of what you desire. This is actually great news, because you can change you!

Notice where in your life you've been blocking your good, and know that asking this question in relation to specific areas of your life will lead you to the solutions you seek. When you ask better questions, you get better answers.

Your life will get great when you get great at receiving. The feminine knows that the Universe has everything in store for you to live your best life and fulfill your purpose. Ask, and it is given.

Step 2: *Take a stand for the* **and**

Sometimes we're conflicted when it comes to receiving because we think we have to choose either/or. This is a limited and linear approach to life. The feminine takes a stand for the *and*. You can get your work done *and* take the kids to Disneyland, attend Paris fashion week with your girlfriends *and* save with your husband for the down payment on the house. In other words, the next time your server asks if you would like salad or fries with that, your unapologetic response is "Both."

Step 3: *Practice saying "Thank you" and "Yes, please"*

It's always awkward before it's elegant, but my darling, you give so much and it's time to let yourself receive. Next time someone says, "Great dress," instead of deflecting with "This old thing?!" appreciate that you do look amazing and that others have noticed, receiving their encouragement with a simple "Thank you." Or when a kind stranger holds the door for you, instead of hesitating and fumbling to reach for it yourself, graciously receive the courtesy, say "Thank you," and walk on through. And if offered assistance with lifting your bag into the overhead bin, it's more attractive to say "Yes, please."

RESTORING YOUR FEMININE POWER

A Queen uses femininity like the incredible power it is. It gives you the ability to heal and transform old hurts and past wounds as well as create your epic life. With your instincts intact, you'll hear what's really being said versus what is just being spoken. You'll become comfortable with the unknown. Spontaneity will be added to your life, and less and less will you discount the values of intuition, beauty, and connection.

Women are prioritizing the feminine arts of play, creativity, and adventure by saying "Yes, please," as evidenced by all of the travel in your Instagram feed. Did anyone *not* go to Positano last summer?

Life is way more exciting this way! And society is starting to catch on. Women are running for office with moral agendas *and winning*. They're also giving themselves permission to start geographically independent businesses, *not* become mothers, and marry the person they love regardless of how much money they make.

Your invitation today is to reconnect with the parts of you that society had once declared wrong and allow high-vibrational experiences into your life. Explore all of what it means for you to *be feminine*. Understand that every single block in your life is only happening because you didn't allow yourself to receive. Course-correct and make the choice instead to stay open to unlimited possibilities. In that moment, you can hang up your Burberry trench, pour a glass of bubbly, and consider your mysteriously lost feminine instinct restored.

RECEIVING MANTRA

To create clarity on where you've been blocking your good, recite this mantra as many times a day as is necessary to open your receiving channels.

I am a vessel for receiving _____. I am worthy of receiving _____. And I am open to receiving the honor and contribution that will allow me to _____. I know that this blessing is meant for me. Thank you for this gift; thank you for this honor. Today, I receive it graciously.

four

YOUR MEETING WITH THE QUEEN

The greatest Queen story of all time changed my life forever, and it's about to change yours. Whatever you may have deemed as tragic, torturous, and unfair along your journey, get ready to reframe the circumstances of your life and see them for what they actually are: the Universe conspiring on your behalf to set you up for a legendary life.

We're traveling back in time, to the kingdom of ancient Persia at the height of its opulence, arriving at the palace of the infamous King Xerxes. "There were couches of gold and silver on a mosaic pavement of porphyry, marble, mother-of-pearl, and other costly stones. Wine was served in goblets of gold, each one different from the other, and the royal wine was abundant, in keeping with the king's liberality. By the king's command, each guest was allowed to drink with no restrictions, for the king instructed all the wine stewards to serve each guest what they wished."

This king liked a grand party. So much so that he held this one for seven days. On the last day, while in "high spirits from wine," Xerxes commanded that his wife be brought to him so that he might display her beauty to his guests. Queen Vashti refused.

Furious, the king "burned with anger" and immediately had her banished from the kingdom.

Meanwhile, it's the fifth century BC, and simultaneously as the king of Persia is enjoying his great power, in nearby Israel a war is under way that leaves a young Jewish girl named Esther orphaned. She is then exiled to Persia, where she and all the refugees are treated like second-class citizens. Fortunately, in this new land, she is connected to her one last living relative, Mordecai, who raises her as his own.

Just as Esther is adjusting to her new life, King Xerxes issues a decree that dramatically changes the course of her existence. After banishing Queen Vashti in a fury, Xerxes is in the market for a new wife. In this ancient version of *The Bachelor*, the king's men round up all the beautiful young maidens of the land and place them in the palace harem where, for a year, they are to be primed with beauty treatments and special foods before being presented to the king to select his new queen.

Torn from her new home, Esther is taken to the palace with the others for "preparation." Following Mordecai's protective advice, she keeps silent about her Jewish identity. The moment she arrives, the palace eunuch (and in my opinion, the first life coach), Hegai, immediately notices her. It's not only Esther's beauty but her "pleasing disposition" that catches his attention. Hegai places Esther in the best part of the harem for the rest of her stay.

When it's Esther's turn to go before the king, she brings nothing with her other than what Hegai recommends (she's clearly very coachable). And by a miraculous hand of fate, Esther, the most unlikely candidate, is chosen. The king proceeds to marry her in grand royal fashion, complete with a spectacular parade and a beautiful banquet befitting the new queen of Persia.

Shortly after the matrimonial fanfare subsides, the king's best friend, Haman, deceivingly gets him to sign off on a devastating decree to kill all the Jews in the land. Amid the terror and chaos, Mordecai sends word to Esther insisting that she go to the king, put a stop to this, and save her people! Conscious of palace protocol, Esther replies that she cannot go to the king without being summoned first. Putting up with zero excuses, Mordecai declares, "If you remain silent at this time, relief and deliverance for the Jews will arise from another place, but you and your father's family will perish. And who knows but that you have come to your royal position for such a time as this?"

Awakening to the great truth in his words, Esther accepts the call on her life, bravely replying, "I will go to the king, even though it is against the law. And if I perish, I perish."

Approaching this life-threatening feat the feminine way, Esther first seeks spiritual guidance by praying and fasting. At the end of three days, she discovers her answer on how to proceed. She dresses in her royal robes and goes to stand before the king.

The king is known to be a violent man quick to execute those who question his authority. Esther is aware that she will be either killed or granted the favor. When the king sees Esther, he asks, "What is it, Queen Esther? What is your request? Even up to half the kingdom, it will be given you."

Following the Divine Guidance she received, Esther responds with a powerful sense of feminine mystery, "If it pleases the king, let the king, together with Haman, come today to a banquet I have prepared for him." Intrigued by her invitation, the king happily agrees.

At the banquet, after being elegantly wined and dined (you gotta know your man), the king asks again, "Now what is your petition? It will be given you. And what is your request? Even up to half the kingdom, it will be granted." Keeping the allure alive, she says, "Let the king and Haman come tomorrow to the banquet I will prepare for them. Then I will answer the king's question."

After a second lavish feast, the king asks his question again. Finally, Esther answers him profoundly with direct Queenly communication, "If I have found favor with you, Your Majesty, and if it pleases you, grant me my life—this is my petition. And spare my people—this is my request. For I and my people have been sold to be destroyed, killed, and annihilated."

"Who is he? Where is he—the man who has dared to do such a thing?" the king exclaims in shock.

Esther reveals the responsible party is the man sitting next to the king: his best friend, Haman.

The king is *furious* and has Haman immediately put to death.

According to Persian law, even the king himself cannot overturn the codified decree and stop the attack from happening. However, Xerxes *is* able to amend the decree so that when the army is sent out, the Jews can fight back, and they victoriously prevail over the Persian soldiers.

Only because Esther had the courage to fulfill her purpose, her people were saved. And for me, she became the heroine of all time, modeling for ordinary women everywhere that we all have a calling and it's up to us to answer it.

THE ROYAL ROAD TO QUEENHOOD

Every woman has a story. Getting intimate with Esther's will help you make sense of your own. Just as everything that happened to Esther was preparing her for greatness, the same is true in your life. Do you realize how much work went into getting this Jewish orphan girl into the position of queen of Persia?! The king had to oust his queen, a war had to take place, and Esther had to be orphaned and exiled, all so that she could be in the right place at the right time to fulfill her calling. What could have easily felt like the end of the world in each moment was actually the Universe working on Esther's behalf.

Much has been orchestrated behind the scenes on behalf of your destiny as well. You too have been called for your own "for such a time as this" moment. However, it's difficult, if not impossible, to be Queen and live an epic life when we don't understand the true meaning of our challenges, haven't made peace with our traumatic past circumstances, or are naïve to the way life really works. Once you see how every single life event that you've experienced happened *for you*, not *to you*, you'll understand more deeply that you too have been prepared for an equally important purpose.

Feeling Orphaned

The royal road is not an ordinary one, and Esther's journey to becoming queen starts when she loses her father and mother. Most women can relate to being orphaned on some level, whether they were given up for adoption, emotionally orphaned, or both. We all know what adoption looks like, though being emotionally orphaned is a lesser-known concept, so let's explore.

If your parents were there for you physically but not emotionally, you've been orphaned. This can be confusing and difficult to detect, since emotions are invisible. Perhaps your mother showed up in physical form, helping you get dressed for school, making sure you had lunch, and putting you to bed at night. Yet because of her own Injured Feminine Instinct, she had other unhealthy priorities that weren't really about mothering you. If she suffered from compliance, she may have been too afraid of your father to speak up for you and your siblings. Or, if she had no sense of her own worth and worked three jobs for crumbs, she couldn't have brought her full self to her own life, let alone to motherhood. It could also be that she had a legitimate mental health issue and never got it handled, abandoning herself as well as you.

Doing the pendulum swing into defiance, your mother could have been a narcissist, an alcoholic, or a workaholic, or maybe she had a new husband every three months. All of these scenarios would have made her emotionally unavailable, inconsistent, and untrustworthy, thus leaving you orphaned.

Same for your dad. If he was lacking that masculine provider, protector energy, then you have experienced being without a father in a symbolic sense. Compliance and defiance are default modes for men too, taking them out of their own empowered masculinity. If your father was in compliance, he might have been afraid to set boundaries with your mother or didn't protect you from her. Maybe he did whatever his boss told him to do and spent his career playing small, regretting that he never went for his big dreams.

On the other hand, he could have been the defiant risk taker who grabbed at thrills to the point of destruction, putting you and your family through a roller coaster of lavish highs and anxious lows. Or perhaps he was the unpredictable addict who would blow up at you for getting one B-minus on your report card or losing the soccer game, and the more you cried, the louder he yelled. Either way, if you were without that protective, masculine role model, you've experienced being emotionally orphaned.

When the original wounding goes unhealed, emotional orphaning spills over into adult life. If the little girl in you didn't feel loved and nurtured, that can show up as attracting romantic partnerships that re-create the experience of being neglected and ignored. Or if you grew up feeling unsafe emotionally or physically, you might attract a toxic work environment that still has you scared to make a mistake with your team or terrified to get in trouble with your punitive boss or clients.

The key to healing any form of orphaning is to master the art of "mothering" and "fathering" yourself. Unlike when you were young and needed parenting to come from the adults in your life, today you can powerfully be there for yourself, nurture yourself, and protect and provide for yourself. Didn't feel seen or heard? Change the pattern by taking the time to see and hear your needs, fears, and desires. You can write them in your journal or talk with God and with those you trust. Didn't experience being nurtured? Draw a bath and add some beautifully scented essential oils to it, making self-care a priority. Didn't feel protected and safe? Learn to use Queenly communication to set healthy boundaries. Had the experience of not being provided for? Enjoy developing the part of you that has what it takes to make more than enough money.

When I became aware of the areas in my life where I felt orphaned, and consistently nurtured and provided for myself, it was a major step of energetically transforming weakened-little-girl energy into Queenly power. Without these opportunities I would not be the woman I am today, and for that I am grateful.

Once you consciously decide that you can meet your needs and manifest your desires, the way will be shown. Remember to pray and ask for guidance. Miraculous support is always available. You'll see new and exciting ways to take care of yourself, and you'll also attract the people and resources necessary to do so. Life is so much more fun this way!

Thriving after Exile

Exile is another challenge many women experience literally or symbolically on the road to Queenhood. So many of our global sisters are experiencing this, with their governments and econo- mies in such disarray that they literally can't live in the country they know as home.

Other women experience exile symbolically and know all

too well what it means to be banished from a place where they thought they belonged. For some, this displacement comes from family; for others it could come from a marriage, workplace, social circle, or religious group.

Whichever group you may have been outcast from, the experience is relatively the same. You're on the inside one minute, and then all of a sudden, you do something, say something, or think something that doesn't go along with the status quo, and your invitation to Thanksgiving (or the quarterly board meeting, or the bachelorette party—whatever way you're used to being included) is rescinded, never to be seen again. We may be able to laugh about it now, but I know that when it happened to me, I felt a severing at my knees like my roots had been cut.

Exile is one of the popular methods for controlling big-thinking women and keeping them down. It is a powerful manipulation tactic. We can still feel the fear of excommunication in our cells because for thousands of years, when a woman was banished from the tribe, she died. She was eaten by an animal or either froze or starved to death. This is how powerful women were literally killed off.

Holding on to that cellular-level fear of not belonging, we subconsciously stop ourselves from standing out, being too fabulous, looking too beautiful, making "too much money," or behaving in any way that would challenge the status quo. This is why we find ourselves falling in line to this day. It's why we're so terrified of what other people are going to disapprovingly say about us. We're so afraid of those consequences that we'd rather not go for our big dreams, or if we do, we pursue them in hiding. We're too anxious to shine because we risk being the outcast.

When we are exiled literally or symbolically, just as in Esther's story, it doesn't happen by choice. It's something that is done *to us*. Getting fired, being told "I've met someone else," and having your adult children stop including you in the lives of your grand-children are all forms of rejection that leave women feeling left out, left behind, and unappreciated. *Rejection breeds obsession.* The more we're cast out, the more we want in. We self-manufacture so much pain seeking love, approval, and acceptance from others who don't get us, rather than receiving it from ourselves or from those who already accept and celebrate us exactly as we are.

Handling Exile Like a Queen

Queens realize that a seemingly closed door is actually spiritual guidance to move in a new direction. Got fired? Chances are *you* didn't like the job anyway but weren't willing to resign, so the Universe in its loving way made a move on your behalf to escort you to a new career where you'll thrive. Those divorce papers? A Queen can admit when she hasn't been happy in the relationship for a long time, and now she's free to attract someone who's a per-fectly aligned match.

Change is necessary in keeping life fresh. It's humans who become overly attached to circumstances staying the same. Spirit is alive and ever evolving, and if our soul is available for growth, we can anticipate change on a regular basis. And beyond antici-pating change, when it does appear, our role as Queens is to wel-come it, embrace it, and open up to how our lives will be blessed in much bigger ways as a result of trusting Spirit's direction.

The key here is to first remember that whatever the exile is, it's not human rejection, it is Spirit's redirection. When this is your starting place, you will have faith that your good is coming to you. We live in a gloriously abundant world. With almost eight billion people on the planet, yes, your soul mate exists. And with endless possibilities in the global marketplace, there's a perfect career for you. We think we're big idea people and therefore have thought about all of the possible options, but if our beliefs leave us limited, sad, depressed, or in any form of suffering, I can assure you, something else is possible. Spirit always has a plan.

Your Power to Discern

Esther didn't fall victim to the inner monologue of the Injured Feminine Instinct. She didn't blurt out, "I'll never be picked to be queen. He'll never think I'm beautiful enough." That's how we modern-day women take ourselves out of the game all the time. "I'm just not that talented. No one cares what I have to say. Other women are so much better than me." A Queen knows that all this negative self-talk holds zero truth.

Having excellent judgment about when to speak up and when to let a situation play out is a cornerstone quality of a Queen. I see so many women self-destruct by not developing this attribute. I've witnessed women in loving relationships or incredible jobs who are unwilling to speak up about small matters and let their dissatisfaction escalate into an unnecessary explosion and completely destroy any chance of repair. In most cases, simply discerning for herself that it was important to share her perspective in the first place would have gotten her exactly what she desired.

Although Esther did, in the end, reveal her truth in order to save her people, the time she spent keeping her Jewish identity to herself was *discerning*. The wisdom here is that not all pieces of information must be shared with everyone, all the time. As Queens, we get to keep our own physical and emotional safety in mind when we choose what to disclose and to whom.

Attractive Energy

A positive attitude aids in your discernment powers. The scriptures say Esther had a "pleasing disposition." That attractive energy got her noticed by the right people, which opened her up to receiving the title of queen of Persia. It's not just about having a great attitude when everything is going the way you want, it's developing the emotional maturity to also maintain optimism when challenging circumstances present themselves. Believing that a fantastic outcome is always available opens you up to new ideas, solutions, and abundance. Every thought has a vibration to it, and if you are thinking high-vibrational thoughts, especially during a difficult time, you will magnetize a high-vibrational solution to your dilemma.

Modern-Day Mentors

Being mentored was an essential element in Esther successfully fulfilling her calling. Though she might have looked abandoned and alone, the Universe set it up for her to always have guidance from both Mordecai and Hegai, and she wisely followed their advice.

When humans lived in tribes that included four generations in tight-knit proximity, astute input was built into the way of life. Historically women received counsel from the elders, both male and female, on rites of passage, spirituality, relationships, cooking, parenting, the arts, survival, and so on.

Modern-day women, raised in Western culture, are much more isolated, making professional guidance necessary for successfully navigating to their full potential. All people at the height of success—professional athletes, Olympians, A-list actors, multiplatinum rock stars, business moguls, and heads of state—are known to work with coaches, mentors, advisors, and experts. And a Queen is no exception.

So why is having a mentor not more pervasive in our culture? Mentoring is about receiving support. So to the degree that a woman doesn't have this set up for herself, the Injured Feminine Instinct has gotten in the way. Many compliant women don't hire a mentor because they don't want to "impose" by asking for help or haven't given themselves permission to invest in themselves. Defiant women can be averse to receiving support because they think it makes them look weak or they stubbornly believe they alone have all the answers and can "handle it." A Queen knows that expert guidance is essential for maximum success.

Think about your own life. In what area would you benefit from receiving personalized support? Fortunately the subject range is limitless, from personal to professional realms. Looking to start dating again, effectively get out of a toxic relationship, or improve your marriage? Thousands of qualified relationship coaches and therapists are available to take on new clients. Looking to deepen your intuition and connection with the Divine? An abundance of spiritual mentors are waiting to serve you. Have an idea for a side hustle but don't know where to start? Hire a business coach. Ready to slim down and increase your energy? Countless health coaches and naturopaths who've healed their own bodies are ready to help you achieve your wellness goals. Struggling with your toddler or teenager? An experienced parenting coach or counselor can help you restore your sanity and your morning routine.

Whatever area of your life would benefit from mentorship, find someone who has already done what you desire or as close to it as possible. There are all kinds of services from free to high-level programs to choose from. Find the starting place that's right for you and schedule an appointment *today*. I've participated in every range of support from no-cost trainings to significant investments, and I would not be where I'm at personally or professionally without all of the incredibly wise and talented people I'm proud to say have mentored me.

"FOR SUCH A TIME AS THIS"—WHAT IS YOUR ROYAL ROLE?

Only from the position of Queen can you fulfill your purpose. Queenhood gives every woman the power, resources, influence, and confidence to play a bigger part in the world. For me, the moment Esther truly became Queen wasn't on her wedding day. It was when she accepted her Divine Assignment, got out of her own fear and limited thinking, and became available to show up for her role and her people.

So it's your turn to ask yourself, what is *your* "for such a time as this" moment and who are your people? It doesn't have to be as intense as a life-or-death situation, but your epic life depends on you getting clear on your role and saying yes to your calling.

We all have a purpose for being here on this planet right now. Accepting yours is the moment you become Queen. You have no idea how many lives will be positively impacted because you decided to play big. If you're not sure exactly what your Divine Assignment is, pray for it to be revealed to you. And keep reading. By developing your spiritual connection and getting to know yourself more deeply through the exercises in this book, you'll become unavailable to be unclear on exactly what your epic life is.

Using Prayer as a First Resort

Now, I don't know about you, but if my life and the lives of all my people were on the brink of extermination, fearfully I'd likely take matters into my own hands, frantically march into the king's chambers, and demand, "Listen, this isn't fair and you need to change this now!" That's what women do when we're disconnected from our femininity. Right? We default into masculine energy and attempt to control a situation, often trying to out-king a king.

Responding with feminine wisdom, Esther remembered to rely on her relationship with God, where true power resides. She first turned to prayer to ask for the solution, because the solution always exists.

Ask and it is given. When you use prayer and meditation as a first resort, you receive clear next steps for what to do. If you're saying to yourself, "I've done this and it didn't work," don't give up. Developing your intuition and ability to hear from Spirit is like developing a muscle. Strength grows in increments, and it's a process. Over time and with consistency, you'll be able to receive clear messages by inviting Spirit to flow through you. You'll no longer have to carry the weight of challenges on your own, or question your ability to solve them. Infinite Intelligence will always guide you to your zone of genius.

Communicating Like a Queen

Queenly communication is a big subject, and we'll be exploring it in myriad ways throughout this book. The lesson from Esther's story is to clearly articulate your message, at the right time and with the right strategy, without apology. Remember that when it came time to state her request to the king, Esther rose to the occasion without disclaimers or self-dismissals.

Too many modern-day women start sentences with, "This is probably a stupid question," "Sorry to bother you, but...," or "I hope you don't mind...," immediately weakening their position. Please remove "I'm sorry" from your vocabulary. It doesn't serve you or get your message across. If you have true amends to make, feel free to say, "I apologize." It's a much stronger statement.

So often women are afraid to expose who they really are and share what matters to them with the world. So we've watered down our voices by speaking in circles or distracting from our point with long-winded stories.

A Queen is not afraid to be visible and speak her truth. She confidently participates in conversations that matter to her. She's not looking for public approval. Because she has a sense of self and an intact intuition, she's able to clearly get her point across. People hear what she says because *she's heard herself first.*

Part of being a great communicator is being a great listener. As a Queen you listen to Spirit, yourself, and others. In doing so, you'll be able to use your words to create, heal, empower, bless, and inspire yourself and others. Language is powerful, and by choosing words consciously, a Queen uplifts her internal self-talk and uses her voice in service to her calling.

These lessons from Esther's story are timeless. Never disqualify yourself. Go into prayer instead of panic when life brings you a challenge. Communicate confidently and people will greatly assist you with reverence. This is how a Queen responds to life's crises and carries herself with grace through any obstacle. You too have access to this powerful, feminine voice within. And it's time for you to meet her.

The Secret Lives of Archetypes

While studying to get my master's degree, I wondered how ordinary women like us, with zero prospects of sitting on any royal thrones, might fully experience Queenhood with all of its impact and glamour in our own lives. An *Aha!* moment occurred when I studied the work of famed psychiatrist Carl Jung, a pen pal of Freud's, who believed that almost all human behavior can be understood through the lens of archetypes.

Residing in our "collective unconscious," brought to life in myths and fables, archetypes are larger-than-life characters that shape our innermost thoughts and beliefs, our actions and reactions, driving human drama across all time. Everyone has an internal operating system that interprets the world by categorizing people, places, things, and experiences into archetypes.

Jung believed that all people were born with the same subconscious model of what a "hero," a "mentor," and a "quest" are, and that's why people who don't even speak the same language are inspired by the same stories.

Pop culture's evolution of archetypes became even more relatable when Joseph Campbell introduced the *hero's journey* in his book *The Hero with a Thousand Faces*. We watched this in action in *Star Wars*, where we met Luke Skywalker, Darth Vader, and Yoda, who represent the hero, the darkness, and the wisdom within. We also saw the *heroine's journey* in *The Wizard of Oz*, where Dorothy and her friends represent our inner desires and power as well as our insecurities and fears. When I realized that these extraordinary characters not only live inside us but are the forces that contribute to either strengthening or destroying our lives, I became obsessed with how to use archetypes masterfully in living the epic life.

MEET YOUR INNER ARCHETYPES

Of all the symbolic figures in the human psyche, it was the Queen archetype that truly mesmerized me. She is femininity in its most empowered form. And yet she is not *all* feminine, which I loved. She's not a goddess. She's not a priestess. She is a masterful blend of the masculine and the feminine. As Esther's story illustrates, sometimes she's in her masculine energy, initiating, leading, communicating directly and taking action on behalf of her purpose. Other times, she's very feminine, nurturing her spiritual connection, receiving beauty treatments, or entertaining in her finest royal robes.

The Queen gets the totality of life and human nature. And as you'll see throughout this book, every time you reach to your inner Queen for guidance, you'll be amazed at the power and clarity that resides in you. Conversely, we all have (usually unconscious) inner archetypes that, if we don't get a handle on them, will take us down. I'll be illuminating the way these dark shadows can show up to sabotage our success and quality of life and exactly how to get back into your Queenhood stat.

THE PERILS OF BEING A PRINCESS

Let's start by exploring what differentiates the Queen mentality from that of a *Princess*. Princesses hope to be saved by their prince. Princesses need everything in their life to be perfect or else they react unpleasantly. Princesses are naïve and entitled and expect the world to be handed to them on a silver platter. A Queen, on the other hand, is wise and understands that regardless of how it seems, everything is happening *for* her, not *to* her, in preparation to live her purpose. She's aware of her power and capabilities and knows that at all times she is not alone, because she is co-creating with the Universe.

Here are some more essential distinctions between the Queen and Princess archetypes:

Princess	Queen
Wants to be liked	Self-assured
Emotionally lost	Purpose-led
Naïve	Wise
Avoidant	Confidently confronts life
Lives in fantasy	Creates her own reality
Expects life to be perfect	Knows there's a reason for everything

Waits to be saved	Takes personal responsibility
Afraid of challenges	Obsessed with creating solutions
Self-dismissive	Communicates directly
Complains and blames	Gives others the benefit of the doubt
Feels entitled	Benevolent

THE AGE OF QUEENS IS NOW

When I realized the power of stepping into this archetype, to say that I became obsessed with the whole Queen thing is an understatement. Through activities like hosting Queen Esther retreats and teaching courses on topics like becoming Queen of your finances and relationships, I was moved to share this life-changing story and its powerful message with women around the world.

There has never been a more important time on our planet to be a Queen. This is your moment to show the world who you are and what you're capable of. This is your time to connect with your God and confidently get clear on *your* unique purpose. You no longer have to squander away the years hiding out in the corners, and you don't have to apologize for who you are and what your destiny is. Making your highest contribution, with a greater sense of power and complete purpose—it's what you came here for. For such a time as this, *you* are being called.

Accepting Your Call to Be Queen

AN EXERCISE

It's your turn to start to get clarity and deepen your understanding of what your purpose is. Contemplate this: What does being a Queen look like to you? Take out your journal and write down your vision. You can't do this wrong (only a Princess is scared of not getting it right). Think about what the Universe has been preparing you for that you've been procrastinating about.

"For such a time as this," have you been nudged to launch a passion project, foster a child, go back to school, write a book, volunteer on a campaign, or start a family, and yet perhaps you've been a Princess about it, telling yourself you don't have the time, you don't know enough, or you're not ready?

Where a Princess avoids her calling in fear, a Queen declares, "I'm clearing three hours a day to work on my book proposal, confident that my manuscript will make a difference in the lives of others." As we learned from Esther, a Queen never makes excuses, dismisses her ability, says it's not possible for her, or puts things off for the future that are meant to receive attention today. She asks for spiritual guidance, makes a decision, and then takes action. Start now with reflecting on what your calling is and affirming that with God, anything is possible, and make a move on behalf of your dreams today.

PART II

Your Royal Initiation

five

STEPPING OUT OF THE SHADOWS

Epic life? Feminine instincts? Unlimited possibility? Queen-hood? How are we supposed to create a fabulous life and prioritize pleasure when our perpetual state of overwhelm makes our greatest possible win getting the four food groups on the table tonight? How is it feasible to be unapologetically outrageous when we're so stressed financially that the thought of logging into our online banking is enough to send our nervous system into code red? How can we be certain of our calling when the commitment of buying a domestic plane ticket feels as high-stakes and permanent as getting a tattoo and adopting a child from Papua New Guinea all at once? If the epic life feels out of reach, it's because we've exiled the Queen from her throne. In her absence, our inner seven-year-old has taken the reins, has fled the castle on horseback, and is now recklessly trotting down the detour of life.

We're about to compassionately clear up why most women are *not* living as Queen and how you can turn it around ASAP. Worry not: (a) *you're not alone* and (b) *it's not your fault*. It's the same reason you feel you "don't have what it takes," think you aren't worthy of love, or walk around wondering, "Who am I to get the promotion, hire a housekeeper, drive a Porsche, or speak up about world matters?"

Straight up: Somewhere up to age seven, *we were all brainwashed.* That may sound scary, but fortunately for a Queen the situation is entirely reversible, and that's the exciting part. We get to receive this frightening-sounding news as the opportunity it truly is. Designing your mindset is one of the most fun and empowering skill sets a woman can develop. You'll discover your ability to control your thoughts and thus shape the outcome of your life versus the other way around. If your brain is producing less-than-ideal results for you, that's because it's been programmed with falsehoods and has been running on elementary school autopilot ever since.

Letting other people's false beliefs, commonly known as *conditioning,* take a foothold on your life ends now. This chapter will get you in alignment with what actually matters to you so that you can take back the reins, return to the palace, and sit your adult self on the throne for good.

WHAT IS CONDITIONING?

Your brain is a powerful manifesting machine. The popular philosophy "Thoughts become things," coined by the New Thought author Prentice Mulford back in the 1800s, describes how everything we see and experience in the world originates in our minds. Yes, our thoughts create our reality. And our minds are highly invested in giving us what they *think* we desire, based on what we've been conditioned to believe.

My gorgeous, intelligent friend Katie, for example, seemed to have the worst luck with men. She was always falling for emotionally unavailable guys or those who didn't "have it together," and therefore she was chronically single. When she finally made it through a hot and steamy three months with Rob, a funny,

successful lawyer with a stylish apartment, she was in total disbelief. Over dinner she confessed to me, "I can't believe he wants us
to be exclusive! He is better than I could have possibly imagined.
Marriage material, for sure."

Katie's residence on cloud nine was short lived. What began
as gleeful astonishment soon devolved into mistrust. Rob's initial
warmth cooled in subtle ways that Katie was afraid to bring up,
lest she be called crazy. And yet there was no hiding her neurotic
insecurity. Deep down, she didn't believe she was worthy of such
a great catch. Growing up with a father who was in and out of
her life, her conditioning was that men couldn't be trusted to be
there for her in the long run. And since she didn't really believe
lasting romance was possible for her, she started to behave like
the unworthy woman she was so afraid of being: picking constant
fights, needing nonstop affirmation from Rob, and neglecting
her own life in the process. She was so focused on the fear that
Rob would never love her enough that after six months she got
exactly that, when he called saying he wanted to take some space.

In psychology, *conditioning* is the programming that's been
embedded in the deepest reservoir of your mind, your subconscious. Whatever thoughts are in your subconscious programming, whether positive or negative, your brain will try to achieve
them for you. Until we become conscious of the thoughts we've
been allowing to live rent free in our minds, we're not fully able
to direct the outcomes in our lives.

To be fair, conditioning isn't always about low-vibrational
beliefs and limited thinking. We can thank those who raised us
for our positive worldviews too. Let's say your mom had a knack
for finding a great deal on a house in the best part of town and
therefore you now have excellent housing karma, always securing
the ideal residence. Growing up with a fun dad who believed that
life is short so it's important to celebrate those you love in a big

way could explain how you've happily become the party planner *extraordinaire*. And your heart is naturally warmed to remember how your parents conditioned you to give generously to those in need so that to this day, you always make sure there's enough money in your budget for the monthly donation of your choosing.

Whatever awesome conditioning you have that's in alignment with your values, own it and strengthen it. The remainder of this chapter will help you see the areas that are holding you back and keeping you small so that you can replace your negative conditioning with thoughts and beliefs that will serve your big purpose.

CONDITIONED TO PLAY SMALL

With conditioning, what we've taken at face value to be true are beliefs such as these: You can only earn a certain amount of money. All the good men are taken. Losing the weight will take forever. Buying a house is the responsible choice, and nothing is more important than being responsible. Good help is hard to find. Yacht week will never be an option. Though it sounds nice, you can't become your own boss and replace your corporate salary. Groan. Your soul (not your thoughts) always knew this wasn't true.

As long as we believe other people's truth versus our own, we'll be living some version of the unlived life. Whatever particular stories are scripting your reality, we're all conditioned to think that's just the way life is. The "safe" jobs that keep us from our dream careers, the three same outfits in our closet we're confined to since we put on those pounds because they're the only ones that fit, the TMJ after phone calls from our mother-in-law that we wish we didn't have to pick up—it all boils down to the core belief that we're not worthy of something better.

It's not that solutions aren't available for all of our desires. It's that we've been programmed to believe we're not meant to have *that* level of health, happiness, and success. Our conditioning has us expecting less than what the Universe designed. Our thoughts are constantly running like a machine, creating actions and habits to produce exactly what we believe and tell ourselves. We've taken in the data of our life experiences, what our parents taught us, and how society and culture told us to be, and we've used that data to define our truth. And even worse, our future.

Until we get into our feminine power and become aware enough to uproot these preprogrammed beliefs, no amount of wanting or hard work can dispel the influence they have to create needless and endless suffering. Even real-life evidence of our ability to succeed won't prove them wrong. At least not for any meaningful length of time. Plenty of women do willpower their way to a certain level of success, and yet conditioning is sneaky enough to creep in and sabotage our progress somewhere if it is left unquestioned. I've seen many of my smartest, most accomplished friends and clients buckle under the weight of their conditioned stories, letting other people's limited thinking hold them back from their full career and love potential, even after showing themselves how capable they are.

THE SABOTEUR STRIKES

As a young executive unfulfilled in corporate life, Michelle was driven and spiritually inspired to start her own company. She was willing to work hard, so at first she became the "weekend entrepreneur" and straddled both responsibilities for a few years. Exhausted from the juggling act, she decided to get support and mentorship to finally go full-time with her dream business. She enrolled in one of my coaching programs to receive the business training, personal development, and spiritual guidance to reprogram her mindset out of smallness and lack. With her new beliefs based on possibility rather than what she learned as a little girl, she courageously handed in her resignation, freed herself from the golden handcuffs, and felt secure enough to go full-time with her entrepreneurial vision.

We all know how starting something new goes. Whether it's pursuing your singing career, baking a soufflé, or signing up for barre class after a three-year fitness hiatus, results can be up and down at first. Likewise, while Michelle was still working on reprogramming her mind, her sporadic income mirrored her wobbling beliefs. I coached her through the mindset of her fear-based conditioning and we developed a solid marketing plan to bring in the clients and cash she desired. I challenged her to follow the coaching, be laser-focused, and commit to getting the results she's capable of.

Like the powerhouse she is, Michelle went in with full feminine fierceness, reciting her mantras and prioritizing her daily rituals. Following up her morning routine with highly structured and intentional work days, in thirty days she made $20,000, her highest-earning month yet.

Amazing, right?! Now you would think this montage closes with Michelle in a flowing caftan, on a yacht in the Mediterranean somewhere, on a conference call with Oprah and Richard Branson. I mean, if you can make $20,000 in a month, out of nowhere, you can do anything, right?

And yet the following month, instead of increasing or even at least repeating her proven-possible income, Michelle went AWOL from her business and her mentorship commitments with me. She stopped showing up on our group coaching calls and ignored my team's reengagement emails.

Maybe she just needed a breather before going back into her business? I wish. When she finally resurfaced on a call, I asked her how her rock star status was going. That was when she broke the news to me that business had slowed down to a standstill, she had gone into debt, and consequently she was closing up shop, updating her LinkedIn profile, and crawling back to corporate life.

Next, Michelle confessed that after her quick financial win, she had chosen to take twelve days off to go on a cruise and a shopping spree to the point of spending *all* of her cash influx. No wonder she couldn't keep her new baby business afloat! Last time we spoke, I had supported her desires and affirmed that her vacation and up-leveled wardrobe were meant for her, as soon as she got her business to the level of supporting that lifestyle, and I had also explained to her that as a new entrepreneur, she needed to reinvest a big portion of revenue in her business to get it stable. Admittedly, Michelle agreed, she didn't follow the coaching.

At this point, a lot of women will ask, "What if Michelle was spiritually guided to pursue this 'impractical' vision and it was actually meant to lead to her success?" It's true that Spirit will sometimes guide you to prioritize pleasure or take what appears to be a risk, and yet that wasn't the case here. Spirit will never give you the direction to sabotage your success or fall back into a binge of self-destructive habits. It's safe to say that for Michelle to leave her baby business while spending all her cash was not Divine guidance, though her inner Princess was tempted to believe so. As a Queen, having an intact intuition and clear powers of discernment is how you tell the difference between true spiritual leadings and fear-based impulses.

Although self-sabotaging sprees are not exactly uncommon, I'm always curious what the specific conditioning is when such a smart woman does this to herself. So I asked Michelle *why*, after experiencing her own power and potential as a Queen with full authorship over her own financial success, she would run away from living her ultimate dream and go on to throw her business down the garbage disposal?

She replied, "I've been so irresponsible. I just don't think I'm good at this. I can't sustain the passion and commitment."

"Even after you had a twenty-thousand-dollar month and proved you can bring in way more money on your own than you were making in your corporate job?" I asked, knowing there was a deeper block here.

"Well…that twenty-thousand-dollar month was just a blip," Michelle said, trying to convince me, "like manna from heaven. I got lucky and I didn't believe it would happen again."

As I continued coaching her, we unraveled the difference between Michelle's thoughts and her beliefs. Intellectually, Michelle is super-smart, and she *knows* she can sustain a profitable business doing what she loves. However, simultaneously her *beliefs* were telling her the opposite was true. When you think you're talented yet your goal is not happening, that's a sure sign that your conditioning is running the show.

Deep down, Michelle believed that she wasn't capable of being anything more than a one-hit wonder. When she told herself that she always "gets bored easily and quits," her brain would make that her reality, sabotaging her potential. What might have sounded like overconfidence on the surface was actually unconscious fear. She desired a successful business on the level of thought, but never actually believed it was possible. Thus she was so afraid that she couldn't have her career and lifestyle desires that in defiance, she anxiously binged on living out her entire Princess fantasy at once.

From there, we discovered that as a little girl, Michelle got this whole fear-based story from her parents. "My dad had big dreams, but even bigger fears," she told me. "He would take us to open houses of luxury homes, get the whole family excited about moving, and then back out at the last minute because he was too scared to invest. I also watched my mother try out so many different professions. She would become obsessed with something new, totally go for it, and then quit at the last hurdle. I think of both of them as people who don't see things through and now, I'm conforming to that."

Giving up was Michelle's conditioning. What was modeled for her became her identity. She learned that the good things in life were too difficult, too uncertain, or too much work for "someone like her." Unconsciously she was so committed to her self-image of not following through on her dreams that her conditioning quickly seduced her away from her spiritual, purpose-led path and back into the clutches of the corporate paycheck.

You see, Michelle hadn't stepped into the archetype of Queen when it came to running her business. Instead, she had a different character running the show, the *Saboteur.*

As you may recall from Chapter 4, archetypes are the inner personas that are secretly running our lives. We default to certain archetypes because they were modeled to us as how one does life. In our formative experiences, whether good or bad, we learned that playing these roles is the way for us to survive, thrive, and establish our value. Falling into line with these old plot lines is how we either comply to maintain a sense of belonging in our families or set ourselves apart in defiance. That's what happened to Michelle. Sadly, right when Michelle was about to fly through the glass ceiling of her parents' story, the Saboteur showed up and clipped her wings.

And Michelle is not the only one letting her disempowered conditioning steal the show. We're all smart women who have experienced being blindsided by the Saboteur in the areas of our lives that we care about the most. Her sneak attack typically happens when we're on the verge of growth and unconsciously afraid of change. Fully invested in keeping us small, the Saboteur may paralyze us with doubt over our ability to achieve what we desire most. Often her scheme involves making us hide from friends and mentors so they can't hold us accountable. While nobody else and certainly not our inner Queen is looking, the Saboteur convinces us to do the opposite of what we know will get us to our ultimate goal. Seduced by the Saboteur's sophisticated logic, we don't notice their meddling until the damage is done.

For Queens like us, this all too common self-destruction ends now. Identifying where you've been self-sabotaging and playing small, backing out at the last minute, and being led on detour after detour will cast blazing daylight on the Saboteur's subtle antics. This is your moment to reclaim the truth that you're in charge and recondition your beliefs so that the big, bad *S* is permanently evicted from your life.

TAKING BACK THE REINS

I honor you for your bravery in taking a deep look into your life and being honest about what your own limiting conditioned beliefs are and how they may be fueling your inner Saboteur. Remember, it's not your fault that you've come to be like this. You've just followed what was modeled for you. Listening to disempowered archetypes is how you've known to be safe.

Take it from a woman whose former Saboteur kept her broke, in debt, and single for more than a decade: it can be scary to challenge what we've taken on as gospel for so long and rewrite the rules. It can feel groundless to question what for your entire life have been your core, foundational beliefs. Yet ultimately it's liberating. Identifying exactly where the Saboteur shows up will lead you to your truth. The days of you listening to everyone else's stories are over.

An End to the Sabotage

AN EXERCISE

It's time to turn on the spotlight to your own Saboteur conditioning so that your Queen can take center stage again. What limited beliefs have been keeping you hidden in the wings? Have you been saying that you're not worthy of matrimonial bliss or superstar success, and certainly not both at the same time? Have you been listening to the voice that says your dreams are unrealistic, and that you don't have what it takes to launch a YouTube channel, secure a round of funding for your startup, or hire part-time help so you can enjoy your son's fifth birthday party instead of cleaning up after the piñata?

This exercise will help you pinpoint how you've been self-sabotaging and why, so that you can release the limiting beliefs that have been holding you back. Take out your journal and let's bid the Saboteur a permanent sayonara!

Step 1: Ask yourself where you are craving something better in your life

Think of one area of your life that's important to you, where you keep hoping a situation will improve yet nothing changes. It can be anything, big or small. Are you still doing mindless tasks you've mastered at work even though you know you're capable of taking on more exciting projects? Do you keep complaining about your noisy neighbors while dismissing your desire for a house in the country? Have you kept saying you're going to spice up your marriage but can't remember the last time you went to dinner without both of you being on your phones the whole time, so that it actually felt like a date?

To walk you through the exercise, let's use the example that you've set a health goal to shed some extra pounds and look fit in that new swimsuit by the time you and your posse hit Phuket for your friend's fortieth.

Step 2: Identify where your actions are misaligned with your words

A Queen understands that wanting something, and even knowing you can have it, isn't enough to manifest it, especially when limiting beliefs say otherwise. You may think you're "trying everything" to reach your weight-loss goal for your Thai getaway, but let's be honest. Yes, you've reactivated your gym membership. You've also committed to drinking gallons of water a day, working out first thing every morning, and subsisting on kale salads. Done, done, and done. And then, day three rolls around. It's eight p.m. It's been a long, hard day and you find yourself thinking about pasta and chardonnay. You give in to the craving, pour yourself a glass of Chablis, boil the water, and, once the cavatelli is perfectly al dente and generously buttered, sprinkle the parmesan cheese on top.

The next morning when your alarm goes off, you immediately hit snooze. You're still feeling full, and sluggish. The last place you care to go is to Pilates fusion class at the gym. You roll over and tell yourself you'll go tomorrow. And this up-and-down, "I'm in, I'm out" pattern becomes the status quo for weeks. Meanwhile, the number on the scale isn't budging. The Saboteur has stopped you in your tracks.

Whether you've chosen health, career, your marriage, or decorating your guest room, write down the exact ways in which your actions are not in alignment with your words, taking you further away from your goals. Identify how you've been self-sabotaging so that we can release the power of your conditioning.

Step 3: Confront the Saboteur

It's much harder to manage what you can't see, so let's pull back the curtain and reveal the Saboteur's identity. Visualizing what this archetype looks like for you will help you see its sneak attacks coming. Flip to a fresh page in your journal. Close your eyes and ask the Saboteur to show you what it looks like. Sometimes it's a person, sometimes it's an image, or it could be words or objects. Draw what you see. It takes courage to confront what may feel like a very negative energy, and it's understandable if you want to avoid it. This drawing is your chance to see who the Saboteur is and get it out of your body, and you know it's much scarier to leave it there in the shadows.

Next, tap into why the Saboteur has shown up by asking what message(s) it has for you. Every archetype is always working on behalf of a secondary gain, an unconscious benefit that may undermine your conscious goal and yet helps you feel "safe" from a feared experience. For our Phuket-bound dieter, you could say, "Why do you keep showing up to sabotage my weight loss?" The

Saboteur will answer in words, phrases, or images. It could reply with a message like, "If you keep the weight on, you can put off having your photo taken and setting up your online dating profile, and you won't have to face your fear of romantic rejection," clearly demonstrating that the secondary gain you're getting for keeping the weight on and self-sabotaging is about your need to feel protected in your love life.

Or the Saboteur might actually get you to believe that "No matter what I do, I will never have a great body," or "Losing weight is too much work and it will take too long." And the reason you have this belief is that you watched your big sister, who you idolized, try every diet and fitness fad in existence without ever releasing the pounds, and now you're re-creating her reality that was modeled to you. The secondary gain of following in her footsteps is fitting in with your family by not being seen as more fabulous than her.

Underlying every act of self-sabotage is a limiting belief (or thirty). Take a look at what yours are. Do you believe you can't do what you love and make great money? Do you think the only way for you to have more free time is to downsize your business? Are you afraid that if you look too good, you'll intimidate your friends, alienating yourself? Do you tell yourself your glory days are behind you? Have you given up on the idea that you and your significant other might actually have fun together in this lifetime? Or have you been convinced that you'll never attract a person who you genuinely have chemistry with?

Once you've received your message from the Saboteur, you can dismiss its power by responding back: "Thank you for revealing to me why you've been running the show. I no longer need your assistance with my body, health, and fitness; I no longer want your advice about love; and I will no longer fall prey to my big sister's limitations. You have no power with me anymore. Leave now. I've decided to get my advice elsewhere."

Step 4: Summon your inner Queen

The easiest way to call in your Queen is through meditation. Sit down in a quiet, undistracted place, close your eyes, and breathe deeply. Simply ask her to reveal herself to you.

Hello, Queen,

I need your help. I desire to make better choices in the area of weight loss, and I know that you have the answers. I now know that I have been using my body insecurity to stay safe in my singlehood and avoid the fear of putting myself out there. However, it has not kept me safe; it has kept me alone. I'm asking for your guidance on how to make positive and healthy choices when it comes to dating, so that I no longer need to carry around the extra pounds. Please show me where to begin. Please give me the courage to approach relationships with the belief that I can be loved and cherished by someone I'm madly in love with.

Also, when it comes to food and exercise, please remind me that I can make the choices that are right for me and follow through on what will set me up for success the pleasurable way, without deprivation and with big results.

By summoning your inner Queen, you will tap into an adult level of emotional maturity and a freed mindset. She will tell you what the solution is and what you can do immediately to implement step 5 and transcend your conditioning.

Step 5: Set yourself up for success

Just as where there is light there cannot be darkness, self-sabotage can't exist when your Queen is in charge. If she sees you tempted to get off track, she reminds you of your goal. Is this weight loss really important? Wanting doesn't count. A Queen gets real about what her priority is and makes a decision one way or another.

Sometimes women self-sabotage because they've mixed up their own desire with what they see other people doing. For example, I've seen new female business owners set aggressive financial goals with their startups because they've seen the big results entrepreneurial superstars have achieved, comparing the beginning of their journey to someone else's middle. But then they keep falling short and beating themselves up for not putting in the time, until they realize that they have no real issue being financially supported by their significant other, and working long hours to move fast toward six figures is not their need or true priority as a Queen.

On the other hand, if a Queen determines that hitting her financial goals is top priority, she will do what it takes to be true to her word. If getting in shape and looking great in swimwear this summer is her must, she will activate her willpower and enjoy her workouts and macrobiotic meals. She'll ensure her success by following a no-excuses policy and provide herself with the support and accountability she deserves.

Getting assistance doesn't mean you're weak, and Queens aren't cheap with themselves. The feminine approach in any situation of ongoing self-sabotage is to empower yourself to receive help and get it quickly. It's having the wisdom to understand that if you could have done it alone, you would have done it by now. Support for getting fit might look like making an appointment with a personal trainer, a jogging buddy, a health coach, or scheduling a meal delivery service. For your specific desire or goal, you may choose to work with a therapist to get to know thyself, sign up for Toastmasters to prepare for your lecture at Lincoln Center, hire a business coach to start your billion-dollar brand, sign up for voice lessons so you can land your record deal, or enroll in a yoga teacher training program so you can lead wellness retreats in Bali. Do it. *Whatever it takes.*

Write down what your decision is and how you're going to be held accountable. Affirm that your desire is possible for you. "I am capable of following through on my fitness goals and commit to calling my bestie to be my running buddy *today.*" A Queen knows to take action in the present and set herself up for success, so don't delay. Your epic life, and beach body, are waiting!

Six

THE DISEASE TO PLEASE

Finally, you've secured the coveted reservation at the new culinary hot spot raved about by all your foodie friends. You're in for a splurge, but you've earned it and you're treating yourself tonight. You decide to go for the Wagyu filet topped with white truffles. As you excitedly cut into the perfect melt-in-your-mouth Japanese delicacy, your heart drops. You see that your "medium-rare" steak is actually medium (and then some). You've just admitted your extreme disappointment to your friend when the waiter swoops by to ask, "How is everything?" Reflexively you tighten into a smile, and quick as lightning you straight-up lie: "Great, thanks!" because you don't want to sound too high-maintenance or inconvenience the chef.

You've likely felt this same impulse to sugarcoat your truth at least once at the salon. Like that time you asked for beachy waves and Taylor Swift bangs only to find Chewbacca staring back at you in the mirror. "It's perfect!" you awkwardly fib to your stylist, because you'd rather leave as soon as possible so you can go home and fix it yourself rather than hurt his feelings.

And you've probably been on a long flight where despite your best efforts to hydrate, you've wound up so parched that you would gladly trade your Social Security number for a glass of water. You're relieved to see the flight attendant approaching until you assess that she's quite busy and not too happy that 17B hit the "call attendant" button *again*. So you lower your hand because you wouldn't want to be an imposition and upset her.

Why this ridiculous fear among women that if we speak up we won't be liked, approved of, or accepted? Even when our truth is simply "I'm thirsty"? I know my husband certainly wouldn't hesitate to flag down the flight attendant no matter how tight her French twist was. Why do we find ourselves so afraid of inconveniencing someone with our desires and yet have no problem inconveniencing ourselves and sacrificing our needs?

You already know why. It's your Injured Feminine Instinct that is uncomfortable receiving, but this time, it's showing up in the form of *the disease to please*. What started in childhood as you wanting and needing to please your parents, your teachers, your dentist, and that cool girl Tiffany who ran the playground eventually turned into a disease to please just about everyone else. Spouses, children, pets, demanding bosses, self-righteous sisters-in-law, high-maintenance friends, needy plants, and the IRS.

MY SURPRISE DIAGNOSIS

As a young twenty-something with a master's degree in clinical psychology, I didn't self-identify as a people pleaser *at all*. Having been in therapy since the seventh grade and done plenty of personal development and inner-child work, I didn't see myself as insecure and certainly not codependent.

Codependency is the clinical term used to describe an addiction to getting your emotional and self-esteem needs from other people or things. Most commonly, this addiction gets latched onto just one person, thus the notorious *codependent relationship.* However, codependency can also be found in a reliance on drugs, alcohol, social media likes, or other external sources of validation.

I had studied the ways codependency appears in a person's life. Still, in my mind, it was a condition for weak or broken people and couldn't possibly apply to this seemingly confident, big-thinking, naturally extroverted (not to mention psychotherapist) woman... right?

Ahem. Let's just say that my bubble of oblivious beliefs burst as soon as I started my own business, aka the best personal development seminar on the planet (I hear motherhood ranks pretty highly too). I was so excited and ready to launch my first website when the mirror appeared, reflecting my deep-rooted need for public approval.

The truth I found looking back at me? I was terrified to get visible online. For weeks I obsessed over how other people would view my new business-owner status. "What will they say about me? Is my branding okay? Will my message even resonate with people? Who do I think I am to help people with their lives when my own is such a work in progress? If they see my rates, will everyone think I'm just in it for the money?"

Instead of confidently pursuing my dream and trusting Spirit (who led me into this new industry in the first place), I spent several more months of my precious life hunched over my computer at my dining room table in my tiny Santa Monica apartment, future-tripping about the *what ifs.* Instead of putting myself in the position to change lives and help people, I remained broke, in debt, friendless, and totally miserable because I wasn't fulfilling my calling, using my gifts, serving others, or living my big life.

To be dependent on others' approval is to be self-obsessed. And here I was, totally controlled by getting my worth from other people! I saw it in conversations with those I looked up to and wanted to befriend. Whether they didn't like what I said or merely disagreed with me, their response would instantaneously sting me with such shame that I would feel as if I were unworthy of even being alive.

Then there were those family members whose opinions I made more important than my own or even God's. Desperately seeking their blessing, I placed them on pedestals and made them all-knowing, almighty, and always right. I had been calculating my every move just to please them. And when, heaven forbid, I crossed the line of what I knew they deemed acceptable, I threw myself into panic and purgatory.

This wasn't selfless behavior at all. It was totally ego-driven. Unconsciously, I was trying to manipulate everyone into liking me. I believed at my core that the only way for me to be safe in the world was to be *Little Miss Perfect*. She is the archetype that so desperately needs everyone else to like her that she lives in a constant state of terror. Her greatest fear is making a mistake that might upset someone. Being hard on herself is an understatement; this archetype will make you obsess over every tiny detail before you can ever, if even, speak up, share your work, or reveal your truth. The danger of criticism and disapproval is just too much.

For years, Little Miss Perfect fooled me into thinking that if I could be good enough to live up to everyone else's ideals, my right to exist would be incontestable. The pressure was on to speak, act, and behave perfectly according to others, as if I were an enlightened Jedi master as opposed to an ordinary human in her thirties. It's how an email from a client expressing even the slightest dissatisfaction was enough to send me groveling for eternal forgiveness in addition to offering free sessions. And every time I upset someone or wasn't able to live up to their unreasonable expectations, the fallout was typically compromising and completely devastating.

LIVING OUT MY WORST NIGHTMARE

Then came Little Miss Perfect's most dramatic meltdown yet, along with the ultimate healing to my codependency. It happened just a few years after my website was (finally) live online. At this point, my business was picking up nicely. Despite my new success, not only did I still have to wrestle with this disease to please within myself, I also got to see Little Miss Perfect's biggest fears play out in person and across the Internet.

Toward the beginning of my entrepreneurial journey, I met a woman at a networking group in Los Angeles. She quickly became a fangirl and wanted me to teach her how to grow her business. She jumped at the chance to join my yearlong course, signed the contract, and paid the first installment on the payment plan. She was a complete gem of a participant, always asking great questions and highly engaged in the community, and she regularly emailed my team with enthusiastic updates about how grateful and thrilled she was to be getting such big results in her own business as an outcome of what she was learning in the program. According to her, I was walking on water.

So imagine my surprise when just three months in, I received an email stating, "I want to quit. I no longer want a coaching business, I want to start something new."

Having fallen out of love with her whole startup idea, she insisted on being let out of her clearly stated, lawyer-approved, no-refunds, no-cancellations contract. This is like signing a lease on a BMW and three months later saying, "Actually, I'm no longer in the mood for a BMW; I'd like to cancel my contract because I'm now interested in a Land Rover."

On my end, having a contract in place was a conscious decision to stand for the quality of my work and have my clients be

100 percent committed to their success, plus it's solid business sense. I make logistical and staffing commitments based on the number of people in my programs. If I let one person out, then I have to do the same for anyone who asks. Why have a contract if it doesn't do its job?

I was transparent about my reasoning and maintained my boundary. I wish I could say she responded with "I totally understand, thanks for explaining your policy." The short version (you're welcome) of the true story is that she went completely ballistic. She left rants in every feed she could find on the Internet and complained about me to every single person who would indulge her cyberbullying campaign. My name and reputation were smeared. I had friends and acquaintances calling me every other day, saying, "People are talking about you in every corner of L.A."

Rewind! We're talking about Gina DeVee...the self-proclaimed Little Miss Perfect. Someone who desperately needed people to like, approve of, and accept her. This was not a personal preference, people! This was a matter of life and death!

Evading the public humiliation, I fled underground for weeks. With the fridge stocked and the shades down, I puttered about in my pajamas, pendulum swinging between demonizing myself as the worst human being on the planet and fantasizing about making a voodoo doll of this irrational ex-client. One moment, I wasn't worthy of being alive; the next, she was demoted to devil status. Either way, at any given moment one of us was being tarred and feathered.

After enough of this dizzying anger, anxiety, and depression, I prayed. I remembered that Spirit is benevolent. Regardless of how catastrophic my circumstances, in my heart I know everything is happening *for* me, not *to* me. I asked, "Dear God, please show me my part in creating this pain. Please reveal to me what I must see to transform this."

And just like that, I saw that *I was making this so-not-ideal client into God.* I was consumed with wanting her approval even though she lacked the integrity to follow through on our contract. I could understand if I was this upset about a conflict with a long-term best friend, but this level of fixation over the kind of person who doesn't honor their commitments seemed insane to me. I let her go in love and surrendered the entire situation.

> Dear Spirit,
>   Thank you for reminding me that anytime I make another human my Source and look to their approval over your guidance, I'll be disappointed. I give this person and this circumstance back to you. I release any hold that the opinions of others had over me and return to my connection with you. And so it is.

Freedom! I no longer saw this client's defamation attack as a reflection of me or my worth. I saw that her opinion of me did not make me bad or wrong. *I realized that when I don't make it my business what other people think of me, I'm at peace.*

As I reconnected to Spirit, I was freed from my disease to please. Yes, growth is a lifelong process and there are always deeper layers of codependency to work through. But it's nowhere near the level of dysfunction that it was. At the end of this saga, I was stronger as I became inspired to refocus on serving the clients who valued my work and were committed to their dreams more than their drama.

People can spot crazy. Women who were in it to win it and serious about guaranteeing their own success viewed this smear campaign for the excuse-based revenge plot that it was. And they appreciated that I had enough faith in my own policies to withstand the unfair pressure. My response showed them I was a mentor they could count on for honest feedback and total accountability: a leader who would take a stand for their greatness and support them to never give up.

And of course, *these* were the women I was passionate about working with. So rather than continue to try to please whomever I could get to work with me, my inner Queen gave me some great advice. She had me create a Client Requirement Checklist and refine my messaging accordingly, so that I was empowered to attract the ideal clients that I desired. My programs officially became a complainer- and quitter-free zone. Unapologetically standing strong in my conviction, I attracted a much larger audience and a flock of dream clients, and the focus for us all returned to transforming lives.

This is how a Queen powerfully responds to disapproval, condemnation, and gossip where Little Miss Perfect would have crumbled in defeat. The sad reality is there isn't a successful woman out there who *hasn't* lived through her share of negative chatter. It doesn't matter how right you are, how clear your communication is, how authentic your energy is, or how positive a contribution you're making; many people who are committed to their woundedness are not going to see it that way. So when a character assassination attempt happens to you, know that you're not alone. It's up to high-vibe women like us to stick together and support each other in remaining true to our vision. And it's up to each of us individually to make sure that the only source of validation, approval, and security we draw from is God.

LETTING LITTLE MISS PERFECT GO

This Greek-tragedy-level drama revealed to me that it was time to give Little Miss Perfect her final curtain call. She needed to exit stage left so that I could become Queen. Now it's your turn.

Think about how Little Miss Perfect is running the show in your life. Is she spending thirty minutes editing a two-sentence email to your boss, obsessed over whether she'll approve your request or agree with your point of view? Is she analyzing everything you said at the ladies' dinner again and again, making sure none of it was offensive, stupid, or too much? Is she up all night baking five different kinds of muffins for the baby shower in consideration of everyone's hypothetical dairy-free, gluten-free, and sugar-free needs? If you're attending a wedding, does she beat herself up for being the only one in a bright, colorful dress when everyone else is wearing neutrals? If you're focusing on growing your platform, is she ruining your day wondering why you didn't get better engagement on that post, and whether it was too vulnerable or not vulnerable enough? And if you're at the industry seminar, is she stopping you from raising your hand to ask that burning question? For Little Miss Perfect, the enormous fear of possibly looking uneducated, inarticulate, and in any way imperfect in front of an entire room outweighs the benefits of contributing to the conversation and receiving valuable insights any day.

Time to give yourself a break. We women are so hard on ourselves! If you've set yourself up to live as Little Miss Perfect, you're invited to step down from your pedestal. I'm here to welcome you back to the flawed and fabulous human race. No one is perfect. Including you. Including me. The *only* exception is J-Lo.

I understand that you're afraid of what you think others are going to say about you. But guess what, my darling? They've probably already said it. And likely for a long time. Those family members and back-home friends who don't think you can achieve your dream have agreed that you are crazy and irresponsible or are never going to make it. So what you're afraid of has actually happened. What a relief! You've already survived what you feared the most.

PERMISSION TO BE HUMAN

The cure for this toxic, paralyzing disease to please starts with getting your security from your spiritual connection instead of the peanut gallery. Time to give yourself permission to be the real you. You're going to be more successful, attract fabulous friends, and have a lot more fun with those who genuinely appreciate you and share your values.

Once you become aware of your conditioned codependency, next is making yourself available for transformation. When anxiety or fear comes up, immediately ask Source to show you what's true. In my situation with the disgruntled contract canceler, I learned that because I had an unconscious fear of getting in trouble, I attracted clients who gave me the experience of being wrong and at fault. As with all situations and challenges, the people in your life are a mirror of your mindset. If you believe that other people have the power to say you are wrong, then you will attract clients, bosses, romantic partners, and friends who repeatedly put you in the position of being in trouble. Voilà, this is your brain giving you what it thinks you want once again! It's exactly what I mean by "you get what you focus on."

Reality is always kinder than your story about it. You always have access to Infinite Intelligence, which means every idea you need is available to you as you raise your consciousness to the vibration of the new thought.

When I asked Spirit to heal this perception, the affirmation I received to dispel Little Miss Perfect was this:

I am loved. I make a difference in people's lives. There are an abundance of people who need and want what I have to offer. I am only available to work with people who appreciate me, take personal responsibility, and are open for growth.

Values for Unapologetic Queens

It's time to get rid of Little Miss Perfect and her life-sucking disease to please. You are ready to release that conditioning and live with a Queen's mindset. Here are a few statements that you may want to print out and post on your wall that have empowered me to live life on my terms:

What others say about you is not your business

Queens aren't interested in third-party conversations about them. Anything anyone says is ultimately a reflection of themselves. Happy, confident, high-vibe people focus on solutions and possibilities; unstable, insecure, low-vibe people focus on problems and limitations. We're more interested in what the former have to say.

Apologize when you get it wrong; otherwise, don't

When a conflict arises, evaluate the circumstances. If you find you have missed the mark or contributed to the conflict, take personal responsibility. Get great at apologizing and moving on quickly. If the issue has nothing to do with you or your actions, don't say "I'm sorry" and thereby take on guilt for what isn't yours. You wouldn't pick up someone else's jewelry and wear it, and their wounds and fears won't look good on you either.

Surrender the other person to Spirit

You are not responsible for saving anyone. Their journey is ultimately not up to you. If they are unavailable to meet you on common ground to transform the situation or move forward with you, let them go in love. God's got this.

Go live your life!

While having boundless compassion for others, Queens are above all focused on living out their purpose. That's how you're going to have the most positive impact versus fixating on one person's negative worldview.

LATER, HATERS

Our epic lives are waiting on the other side of the disease to please. Once we break the chains of codependency and ship Little Miss Perfect off on a one-way train, no longer does the fear of what others think (or say) have any power to stop us from living our truth.

Sure, we all run into crabby critics along the way. There isn't a successful woman who hasn't. As Queens, we need to master what every accomplished person has: the power to find the blessing in haters, not make others' judgments our truth, and never let an Internet troll ruin our day again. This path will get you comfortable with confidently voicing your opinion without worrying about being an inconvenience, getting judged, or hurting someone's feelings.

Once you stop focusing on your detractors, you'll appreciate the beauty that most of the people on this planet are not complainers, whiners, criticizers, and, in short, bullies. Everything is healable. Especially the disease to please.

Today I'm not afraid to let the busy waiter know if my steak isn't medium-rare, and I don't assume my stylist will get his feelings hurt if I ask for more curls. Flight attendants and I have open communication throughout the entire flight and if someone needs to launch a smear campaign, I don't take it on. In choosing to be Queen, consider your disease to please cured. Your freedom to shine starts here.

seven

THE COMPARISON TRAP

"*She* got on the *Today* show, *again*?!" Grrrrrrr. "They hired a *full-time* nanny?" Whaaaat. "Does she own anything that's *not* a crop top? We're all well aware of her twelve-pack abs." "She closed *another* six-figure deal this quarter?" *Ugh!* "He flew her to Lake Como just for the weekend?!"

We all know there's nothing supportive or uplifting about comparing our lives, our bodies, or our relationships to other people's. Whether you're putting yourself down or making judgments about someone else, no good can come from that. And yet we all do it every single day.

You couldn't possibly spend more than three seconds on social media and not immediately activate comparisonitis at the highest level. Whether you're looking at her midriff, her makeup, or how many likes and comments her post got, an innocent scroll can quickly devolve into vicious territory, or else the defeated realm of "It'll never happen for me" or "I wish my life were like hers," *and that's just social media.*

Ladies. What are we going to do about falling into life's limitless comparison traps? Aren't you tired of having your energy drained by all the envy, attention, and endless time spent obsessing over those women who are "further ahead," or judging the ones who are nipping at your heels?

Queens have no time to be mean. When you compare, you're being either mean to her, mean to yourself, or mean to your Maker. And all three rob you of your power.

This is your royal wake-up call to focus exclusively on you and your epic life. Being Queen gives us the ability to never get stuck in the comparison trap again. Or if we do end up there, we know how to release ourselves from the insanity instantly.

QUEENS DON'T COMPARE

A Queen doesn't feel the need to keep herself small to make others feel bigger. She doesn't dim her light over drinks with a girlfriend because it'd be too awkward to reveal all the romantic details of the private cabin with the fireplace *and* hot tub she enjoyed during her Valentine's Day getaway to Vermont when her friend's big date was at Chipotle.

Nor does she put others down to pump herself up. Like when you're lurking on the profile of another woman in your industry, judging that she's nowhere near as talented as you. And yet, as you continue to prowl her page, you're left wondering how she got to be so much more successful than you, letting your creativity and joy float away in a storm cloud of superiority and judgments.

Comparing happens in countless combinations. And we all know which strain hits hardest. Envy. When *she* lives in the dream house and we dwell in the shoebox. When *she's* in Santorini and we're in Scranton. This leads us to the familiar downward spiral of fear that dumps our spirits into the "I can't have that...*ever*" doldrums.

It's here that we encounter our deepest fear-based conditioning. We've been trained to believe there's not enough to go around, or somehow that other women are luckier or more highly looked upon by the heavens, leaving us to think grandness is not meant for us. Forgetting our own epic life potential and connection to Infinite Intelligence, we tell ourselves, "I'll never hit it that big." "I'm too old." "I guess she's just more talented than me." "Not everyone has the Midas touch."

As we discussed in Chapter 2, Spirit didn't make all these ridiculous rules. These are earthly laws infesting our subconscious, making us falsely imagine we live in a world where the supplies of love, money, opportunity, and joy are limited. We see someone else achieve what we desire, and we think we've lost, forever to be left behind. Suddenly the world is closed to us yet again. Life feels heavy and unending, with no hope for change in sight. It's enough to have us give up and numb out with too many pints of Ben & Jerry's Chunky Monkey, let our inbox pile up as high as our laundry, and waste our precious days rewatching *Breaking Bad* for the third time. Tired of being bummed out and exhausted? Me too.

A Queen, of course, remembers the truth of abundance before busting out the tub of ice cream. She is far too in tune with her spiritual Source to let such a scarcity-based mindset take hold of her. That's how she doesn't let the jealous ping of comparison cage her in a low-vibe funk. You may wallow for a moment; however, *she* has far more important things to do than sign in to Netflix and revisit Walt's drug-lord downward spiral in season 3.

THE DEFEATIST

Oh my, how the angels must scratch their halos wondering why we doubt our power, forget that miracles are available, and wind up letting the *Defeatist* run our lives.

This archetype sees us envying others and immediately

proclaims failure. It's here to sign our permission slip to stay home from the school of life today (or this month). The Defeatist knows we can't take action and manifest our dreams when our heart's in the gutter and our soul's gone into hibernation.

I know what it's like to be skipping along, high on life, and then one comparison-based thought is all it takes to unconsciously invite the Defeatist to completely engulf you. It's like getting a shot of poison and instantaneously being convinced that your epic life can't and won't happen, because for some reason the Spirit Guides have blessed the person you've compared yourself with more than you. You start believing you're meant for just "good," not great, and that basically everything about your life is less than ideal.

I've sat in these dark clouds, just staring at the wall and twirling my split ends. As if a death sentence for my dream had been issued, and no matter what I did, the result I craved would never come to be. Then my ego would grab the mic, turn up the volume, and announce how embarrassing it would be when everyone found out I couldn't reach my goals. Over the loudspeaker of my mind, it would broadcast what a loser I am because this other woman had done what I wanted and evidently had more talent, more support, and more insider information than I did. Or perhaps her destiny was just grander than mine, the narrating voice would conclude.

It feels real, doesn't it? Those swivel-chair moments when the gloom just drains the life out of us. We keep going through the motions, tending to our basic needs and responsibilities. Just taking a shower becomes a daily triumph. But that spark of infinite possibility? Gone.

Where does the Defeatist show up for you? What areas of your life are most vulnerable to her party crashing? As your awareness increases, you'll see her coming before the cake is destroyed and the guests are deciding to go home early. Whether you're comparing your love life, your home, your health, or your career, resist the temptation to put on the Defeatist's custom-made play-list of self-flagellation.

These familiar old blues aren't just a vibe-killer, they also affirm your perceived (and conditioned) view of reality—comforting on some level, and light-years away from the truth of what's possible. You see, the Defeatist's agenda is to keep you in this bleak dimension, where nothing new and exciting can greet you. Once you're stuck in the clutches of the comparison trap, this archetype will hold you there for as long as possible.

DEFEATING THE DEFEATIST

The solution always exists, and the Defeatist is just blocking you from seeing it. Take Chrissy, for example.

From an outside perspective, Chrissy had no reason to feel anything but fabulous. She had it all: the sexy fiancé; the successful career leading workshops and retreats for creatives; the perfectly toned, organically fed yoga body; the quintessential San Francisco community that makes living there a total love fest. She was a big thinker with a positive outlook who was always seeking spiritual expansion and never missed a Burning Man experience.

Underneath her big smile, something was clearly off. I saw an emotionally vulnerable post she made on social media, sharing personal information that exuded a sense of defeat. This was *not* the Chrissy I knew, so I reached out and asked her to call me. As soon as the phone rang that Tuesday evening, I asked her, "What's going on?" She started with the usual pleasantries. Feeling a ping in my intuition, I interrupted the small talk and asked her again, "What's *really going on*?" Simultaneously my emotionally in-tune dog Lily jumped up on me and started licking me like she wanted to crawl through the phone.

"Chrissy...there's a clear message from the animal kingdom coming to you. Lily wants you to tell me the truth. What's happening?"

"I'm lost, Gina," she admitted, breaking down in tears. "I've never been this lost before. My depression has gotten so bad that we postponed our wedding. I'm no longer leading retreats and I'm struggling financially. I just don't know what to do."

I could tell this was the Defeatist, not Chrissy, talking. Deep down, her Queen always had access to the answers.

Tenderly I asked, "Chrissy, what triggered these feelings?"

"Well, two years ago my ex-boyfriend started dating an incredible performer. She's doing everything I want to do. It's like I'm obsessed with her now. Stalking her online and losing my life force every time I do it."

"Well, what are you obsessed with about her?"

Without missing a beat, Chrissy quickly replied, "She's *fully* expressed!"

"What does that mean to you?" I asked.

"She's doing this one-woman show and basically doing everything *I* want to do!"

It's amazing how we don't see ourselves clearly. Chrissy is a young, beautiful, hilarious, extroverted woman. Her star power is comically obvious.

"Chrissy, you're a performer. You're not obsessed with her, you're obsessed with self-expression. You're enrolled in a stand-up class. You obviously need to do *your own* one-woman show."

The silence was deafening. (Even Lily's tail stood still.)

"She's doing everything that's meant for you," I continued, "and she just appeared in your life to show you how."

"*Yes!*" she screamed, with a beautiful sense of childlike excitement.

Being Queen makes life so much simpler than we've been taught. Freedom is a thought away. When you make a decision from the place of Queen and follow it up with quick action, you get quick results.

"Chrissy, here's your assignment. Tomorrow, go look for venues *and book one*. Outline your script. Spread the word and it's done."

Just like that, this woman was on *fire*! The next morning, she leapt out of bed and sprung into action, texting me that very afternoon: "Gina! I found the perfect venue for my one-woman show and booked it for next month!" Eeeeeeek! With more passion and energy than she'd had in years, she dove into the writing and quickly struck creative gold. She didn't need to process *another* emotion in therapy or settle for posting *another* boring Facebook invite promoting *another* workshop she wasn't excited about ever again. She was ready *now* to move in a fresh and new direction with her career, her lifestyle, and her life purpose.

FROM COMPARISON TO QUANTUM LEAP

Isn't it ironic how the comparison we thought was our kryptonite is actually meant to reveal what's meant for us? It can be challenging to see this on our own. (Almost impossible if the Defeatist is around.) Chrissy had nearly forgotten who she really was.

Every Queen deserves a mentor, and the benefits of following expert advice include results like Chrissy's. Once she experienced the power of being seen and supported, her *Aha!* moment hit and her Queen showed up and immediately took action to claim the opportunity that was right in front of her all along.

As for Chrissy's stand-up special? Tickets were sold out in one week and the venue was packed! In her full entertainer power, she had 110 people laughing and crying throughout her entire performance! On that stage, Chrissy shared deeply personal stories that few would dare to reveal, parents in the audience and all. She shared insights and wisdom learned from trauma, made light of her own human struggles, and crafted a set that was as moving as it was hilarious. You could definitely say that Chrissy was "fully expressed." You could also say that she pioneered a new genre of transformational stand-up comedy.

One week after the event Chrissy sent me this text message:

"Another celebration! I sold out the next show! And guess who bought the last two tickets? My ex and his fiancée, the woman who inspired me to create this show in the first place. Oh, the full circle of healing." True story. (I know, *only* in San Francisco.) She continued, "I'm totally back in the flow and money is coming in easily now. And I'm up-leveling this time, by selling live stream tickets too!"

Chrissy took her moment of envy as a clue in the direction of her dreams and skyrocketed straight out of the comparison trap. She didn't lose any momentum by hesitating in self-doubt. Now that she was aware, she didn't linger on her obsession, second-guess her capability, or wonder if this was really meant for her. Instead, she chose to be laser-focused on her path and nobody else's.

Chrissy's epic life is now officially back on. In getting out of what she was "supposed to do," she and her man discovered that while they are deeply in love and committed, the big wedding *wasn't* their truth. Packing up their house, choosing to work from anywhere, and enjoying an exciting globe-trotting lifestyle *was*. Amid this romantic adventure of a lifetime, Chrissy is currently in all her creative glory, joyously writing her next one-woman show, with an even bigger theater booked for the next performance, which we all know will be sold out. Once the Queen turns the key to unlock the comparison trap, it's *final*.

Escaping the Trap

AN EXERCISE

Step 1: Remember the epic life

Comparison paralyzes women when it ought to propel us. If you remember that the epic life is, without a shadow of a doubt, meant for you too, you'll never get stuck in this trap again. A Queen knows that she is more than capable of manifesting anything she desires and that her potential is limitless. That's how comparison stops being an invitation to have the Defeatist over for tea, gossip, and commiserating over doomsday scenarios that never come to pass. Stay focused on your purpose, and you'll no longer be so easily convinced that what you desire isn't possible for you.

And if you do happen to forget your crown and let yourself be triggered by someone else's great news, financial windfall, bold career change, or fabulous apartment reveal (I get it, it happens!), the first question to ask yourself is, where did you get the assumption that it's *not* possible for you too? Did your Defeatist show up and trick you into withholding permission to go for it? What does your Queen have to say in response? Remember that seeing what you desire in someone else is a sign that you're meant to experience your own version of the same thing. And for a good reason.

Step 2: Call in Queenly support

The first way that you can bring in support for your dream is by inviting spiritual forces in to assist. As stated in *A Course in Miracles*, "Miracles occur naturally as expressions of love." For your dream to manifest, you'll likely need a miracle, a quickening, or a spiritual awakening. All of these are available when you're connected to the Divine and open to receiving guidance. I highly recommend that you don't wait for the Defeatist to show up or use prayer as a last resort. Start now by asking Spirit what's meant for you and believing that what you desire is on its way.

The next way that you can go about getting support to keep you out of the comparison trap and en route to what you desire is by bringing on a mentor. As I've mentioned before, mentors are essential in helping you grow throughout your life. Not only can they help you achieve what you never thought was possible, hold you to high standards, and keep you accountable every step of the way, they are also great at helping you see your truth that you've become blind to. And as I did with Chrissy, a great mentor holds a bigger vision of you than you can for yourself. That, my Queens, is priceless.

Step 3: Send a cosmic thank-you note

This is one of my best gifts yet. It works *every time*. You're not always going to be able to eliminate the temptation to compare; however, here's how you deal with it, quickly. Allow yourself to notice other people and their success. But do not minimize yourself in the process. Give yourself the freedom to explore what you're inspired by in them. Never again tell yourself, "Well, I can't because [insert reason or obstacle or excuse]," or "Well, she can because she's younger, is more educated, has a trust fund, doesn't have small children, got really lucky, or married a wealthy man!"

When you see someone with the "get a room" relationship, the distractingly hot body, skin as smooth as a baby's ass, the happy-at-the-holidays-in-matching-pajamas picture-perfect family, or the "how is that even her job" glamorous career, you send that person a thank-you note. That's right! Whether it's mental, verbal, or getting out the monogrammed stationery. Write:

Dear _____,

Congratulations on _____! I've been noticing how successful you've become with _____. I want you to know that I'm truly inspired and deeply grateful that you have modeled for me what is possible. I've been craving _____ and after seeing it happen for you, I know it can happen for me as well. Thank you for showing me the way.

I remember the first time I was so jealous of a woman who had a major collaboration with a number of famous names in my industry. She was a smaller fish than me (but who's comparing?), and the fact that she was interacting with the big fish had me take the bait that sent me into instant envy. You would have thought I had stepped on a jellyfish. Oh, the sting! It was painful.

I had to own it; I wanted to play a bigger game and be known by those high-vibe people! Apparently so did she, but she was the only one who took action on her desires. It had *never* dawned on me to reach out to them, assuming that I wasn't in their league. So I took my own medicine, sat down, and wrote her the thank-you note I just shared with you. It was empowering. She responded with encouragement and I took initiatives I wouldn't have previously.

A STAR AMONG STARS

A Queen knows that when you celebrate another woman while owning your own power, it's called being a star among stars. Growing up, we've been taught that if someone's getting more attention, there's less for us. We've been trained to think there can only be one supernova shining in the room...well, ladies, Queens don't dim their light, ever. And certainly not among other Queens. We're rewriting the rules, the feminine way. God created us all to shine, to be celebrated, and to celebrate each other.

So get out your linen stationery and feather pen. Who's the inspiration behind your next thank-you note? Writing this down will get you one step closer to living your epic life.

NEVER ENVY ANOTHER WOMAN AGAIN

When you are Queen, you become so clear on your calling that you never envy another woman again.

You now have the opportunity to use comparison to your advantage. Here's your new instant reflex to seeing someone else with what you desire: "Amazing! I'm next." No longer will the Defeatist have the power to convince you otherwise. Welcome back into the realm of opportunity and who you really are. A Queen. A woman who's so lit up about her purpose and contributing to the world in the way only she can that no one else compares.

eight

BENDING SPACE AND TIME

When I lived in Michigan, I had a lengthy daily commute to work. It took a good hour to drive across town. Every morning, about five minutes before I'd arrive at the office, to my weary delight, I'd see this little girl. She was somewhere around five or six years old. Dressed in her purple sequined ball gown and tall, glittery pointed hat, wand in hand, she would breeze down the block as if she were the creator of the Universe and all was under her command, on her yellow scooter.

She had mystical powers *and she knew it.* She loved her life, dressed the part, and took responsibility for the outcome of her day seriously. She was pretty, yes, but it was more about the essence of how she carried herself that was compelling.

Confident and on a mission. A *big* mission. Nothing could stop her or slow her down. She had the capability to valiantly fulfill her quest.

She embodied what the German philosopher Martin Heidegger called *Dasein*.

Heidegger describes this phenomenal way of existing as "Being-in-the-world." With *Dasein*, a person transcends the trite and numerous temporal concerns that lead to an inauthentic life and becomes occupied instead with fulfilling one's real potentiality. For Heidegger, the all-determining focal point of Being-in-the-world was going tragically unnoticed in the daily realities of human existence. "Knowing" was a kind of Being, and *Dasein* only discovers itself when it comprehends reality.

Loosely translated, for those of us without nineteen PhDs and a knack for twentieth-century existential philosophy: the low-vibe mentality that has allowed us to fill our days with mundane tasks has zapped our magical thinking. Instead of accessing our miraculous powers to turn straw into gold and water into wine, we've unconsciously invited mediocrity and her evil stepsisters "I can't," "I'll do it next year," and "I'm sure (aka hope) our relationship will get better" to dominate *our* way of being in the world.

The Queenly art of transcending our circumstances and manifesting our most fabulous lives is what I call *bending space and time*. We access this power by having the deep knowledge that solutions beyond what we can see are always available, and that we are meant to fulfill our purpose in a tremendous way *now*. The Universe never intended for us to waste decades at the mercy of random fate, waiting for a member of the judges' panel to hit the golden buzzer on our lives. As Queens, the crown is already ours.

THE CHOICELESS CHOICE

Thinking we're powerless over space and time is how too many smart, capable, well-intentioned women wind up stuck in the settle. We feel perpetually boxed in by our backgrounds, our bodies, our zip codes, and our endless responsibilities. Tethered to our past choices and our scrawny paychecks, we're blinded to the infinite alternatives available to us in every given moment. We are left coping with what we think is the choiceless choice.

In hindsight, I can look back at my own life and see all the ways I let my own wand get dusty. In forgetting that I had mystical powers, I too thought I had no other options: overworking myself in low-paying jobs, assuming that calling the student loan office to ask Mildred to defer my payments every three months was normal, deeming international travel too much of a luxury and something to only hope for in the future.

Sadly, I let my inner Martyr take the lead, becoming so willing to trade dollars for hours that it limited my freedom, so overly responsible that it stifled my youth, so dutiful to my family that it limited my social life, and such an overachieving student of religion that it limited my sex life. All of these choices have left me with years of lost experiences I'll never get back, the ultimate regret.

In short, forgetting the magical powers that the little girl in all of us knows we have, I settled. I settled by not thinking for myself, living by other people's rules, and failing to be more curious as to what *else* was possible for me. All the while, I never completely gave up on my dreams. And yet, since I didn't know how to bend space and time, I tolerated my status quo with hope addiction that "one day" my epic life would arrive.

WAITING-FOR-THE-RIGHT-TIME SYNDROME

Have you ever endured an unfulfilling relationship, clinging to the fantasy that it would get better "one day" because somehow you were *sure* your partner would change? Or have you tolerated a struggling acting career, a body that looks like your kid's lumpy-bumpy cake, the belief that life is difficult, or that you're "fine" being single? If any of these sound familiar, I'm sorry, because that means that you too dropped your wand and forgot you could bend space and time.

For millions of bighearted women across America, *hope addiction* is the balm that numbs the pain of feeling stuck, stopping us from taking the action to manifest our epic lives. We stay in underwhelming jobs and unfaithful marriages. We drive sensible cars and live in average neighborhoods. We find ourselves at the same company in the same position for years even though we've worked really hard the entire time.

Typically, we know we can do better, it's just not the "right time." We're waiting for that illustrious "one day" where we'll have a cushy savings account and empty space in our calendars the size of Texas.

Months of stalling turn into years of unlived life. Day after day, we keep procrastinating, telling ourselves that as soon as we send the youngest off to college, pay off the mortgage, and land the next client, as well as have every item checked off our to-do list, then, at last, we'll finally have the time to create the pitch deck for our startup idea, learn French *in* France, or renovate our olive-green '70s kitchen to the all-white marble version on our vision board.

Can somebody puh-leaaase tell me who came up with this concept of "the right time" and left us all fantasizing that it's on its way? The truth is, it will never feel like the "perfect moment" to quit your job, file for divorce, start your family, and the list goes on! And if you've been stuck in hope addiction, rather than being a Queen who activates her superpowers to bend space and time, it's not your fault. You've been played. By a very convincing archetype with a flair for menacing.

THE MARTYR MAKES AN ENTRANCE

The *Martyr* is the age-old archetype who keeps well-meaning women exhausting themselves on a treadmill of imagined duty, missing out on the epic life. Her infamous catchphrase is "Well, I can't do that [insert glorious, epic experience, or even a nap, here] because I have to get this work done, pay all the bills, be responsible, and take care of everyone else." Her usual story is that if she doesn't do it, no one else will. And so she quiets cravings for more with appetizing whispers of hope, keeping us hooked on the fantasy that our future life will be different. She convinces us we'll get there one day, though in truth she's too conditioned to sacrifice and miss out to ever hit the "let's create real change" button. You just have to understand, it's up to her to save the day, including picking up the neighbors' mail while they're off enjoying white truffle season in Italy.

You may be surprised to find the Martyr running around in your thoughts. I know that I certainly wouldn't have resonated with the term back in my twenties. Who would have guessed that beneath my optimistic outlook on life, the Martyr was the one blinding me with duty, submissiveness, and small thinking.

Women. We've gotten so responsible, serious, and masculine, especially with our careers. We've put more faith and trust in paychecks than in prayer and possibilities. In losing touch with our spiritual superpowers and being pushed out of alliance, we've submitted to what the Martyr says we must do in order to have value in this world.

Deep down, a Martyr-possessed woman has been conditioned to believe that the world around her will fall apart if she doesn't make sacrifices for her family, her clients, her coworkers, or her career. Being the selfless savior is how this archetype lends significance and logic to the insanity of hope addiction. She's the culprit for such phenomena as under-eye bags worn like badges of honor, earned after staying up all night to prepare the presentation alone because no one else on the team knows the client like the Martyr does. With false promises of future glory, the Martyr excuses any situation a woman has settled for. You can find her pointing the finger at the important responsibilities in a woman's life and blaming them for her illnesses, gray hair, disappointments, crushed dreams, nonexistent social life, and protein-bar dinners. The result is that every choice in her life feels like "damned if I do, damned if I don't." When the Martyr is in charge, we just never win. (Cue the violins.)

THE MARTYR TAKES MANHATTAN

The sad result of this self-denying archetype roaming free in the female consciousness is leagues of talented women putting up with life-draining work environments for way longer than is necessary. Just like any plateaued relationship you stay in for too long, jobs where you're surrounded by toxic people or doing the same exact thing year after year become stale, monotonous, and boring, because if you're not growing, you're dying.

And yet the Martyr convinces us that we have no other options. "Good work is hard to come by." "The golden handcuffs aren't that bad." "I have to be the one to do this, I have no choice." We're so confident that doing the "practical" thing is righteous that we won't let ourselves even look into what else is really possible. And so the Martyr calms our nerves with delusions that one day we'll leave, become our own boss, be discovered, or come into an unexpected *Beverly Hillbillies*–level inheritance.

Beth, a strikingly stylish top executive who worked in Midtown making six significant figures, attended one of my Queen retreats in New York City to explore what more was possible for her future. And there's no softening how she described her corporate position. She absolutely hated it. On a plane nine times a month, away from her husband, staying in beige airport hotels, and surrounded by people who care about nothing other than "how it's always been done," Beth didn't exactly feel like she was living out her life purpose.

She was the rare ray of sunshine in her gray, institutionalized company. A born leader with an amazing talent for recruitment and team building, Beth knew how to bring out the best in top professionals. And deep down, she knew she had so much more to give if she could only do work on her terms.

In the spiritual, feminine vortex of the retreat, we discovered a bit more about Beth's vision. She dreamed of being her own boss and using her gifts to train executives in a way that would be inspiring to her and have an impact on benefit-driven companies that were actively changing the world.

And yet her inner Martyr had her soul fully booked for duty until the infamous "one day" when it's the "right time." Waiting for the proper moment to safely "go for it" and planning for security, the Martyr had made her dangerously comfortable with having her one life experience simmer on the back burner indefinitely. And part of her was even in hope addiction that her job would get better even though intellectually, she knew that the culture in her company would never be one where she could fully come alive.

A Queen is, of course, unavailable to endure such chronic low-level consciousness. And thankfully, Beth got the memo. Notably inspired by the high vibration at the retreat, she was prompted to finally set a deadline for turning in her resignation. She shared her daring plan with the group: "In three to five years, I'm going to leave my job and start my own executive training and recruitment business."

Though this crowd was too compassionate for outright eye rolling, none of us believed this. There is nothing real about a plan to quit your job in three to five years, so why waste your time and money to attend a retreat to talk about something that will *never* happen?

Knowing how quickly Beth could replace her corporate salary

if she were to start now and take the right actions, I was curious as to why she was so stuck in hope addiction. "Why not sooner?"

"Financially, it's not a good time for us right now." Her inner Martyr quickly justified her decision. *Liar.* You see, we get real and share personal life details at my retreats. In Beth's case, she had already revealed that she had *significant* savings.

With this fear-based archetype clinging to a corporate mentality, Beth was genuinely convinced that it would take another three to five years for her family to become financially stable. And almost like a punishment, she was willing to spend that time in corporate custody.

It never dawned on her that she could actually make more money in less time, while also being a more fulfilled wife, and have the flexibility to start her family if she were to venture out on her own. No one had ever told her she had magic powers.

THE MARTYR TAKES ON THE MARRIAGE

Angela's relationship was a classic case of hope-addicted settling. In what started as a fairy-tale love story, this powerful doctor married her medical school sweetheart. By the time we met, these two physicians had been together for almost twenty years and had three beautiful children under age ten.

As far as all the other moms could see, Angela had it all. Little did anyone know, she was going through the motions with a massive hole in her heart. Though her husband, Justin, was a solid provider, a devoted father, and even a great person, he wasn't a great romantic partner. Like so many women, Angela kept hoping that after he attended couples therapy, read the latest "restoring your relationship" book, and was a frequent caller to Dr. Laura's radio show on Mondays, he would change. She was sure that the marriage would get better and somehow become more fulfilling.

Forgetting where she left her wand, she settled for the kind of predictable cohabitation agreement in which though they loved each other, they were no longer *in* love. Consequently, throughout the years, Justin lost himself and started seeking attention and affection from other women.

He felt terrible about what he secretly and then not-so-secretly was doing to Angela and their family. His all-consuming guilt over the cheating led to binge drinking, depression, and complete emotional shutdown. Meanwhile, Angela, with her big heart and willingness to look the other way, remained in hope addiction that her marriage would get better. Besides, at the mere thought of separation, the Martyr told her that she couldn't possibly do that to the kids.

When it came to the biggest relationship of her life, listening to the Martyr meant putting everyone else first, leaving Angela last. For over a decade, as her pain, desires, and preferences were left unattended, her soul grew heavier. She tolerated a marriage that left her empty, a husband she couldn't trust, and the lie that she was doing the "right thing" to keep her family together, while her own happiness and self-esteem went down the matrimonial drain. With the Martyr blocking her view of the possibilities, she didn't consider that she might actually be a better, more present mother for her kids by prioritizing her well-being. She didn't see that as a Queen, she had an opportunity to model for them how to compassionately navigate change and to give them permission to live a fulfilled life in a healthy relationship.

The saddest part is that, like so many women, she felt she was stuck with the choice she had made twenty years earlier. And because the Martyr also convinced Angela she had to do everything herself, she didn't see how she would have time to raise the kids alone while working full-time at the hospital. "Maybe when they go to college," she'd think, "*then* I'll be free."

THE MARTYR TAKES THE WHEEL

The Martyr isn't just committed to sacrificing your career dreams or romantic relationship. She can have a lot to say about your personal choices too. Let me introduce you to my gorgeous, smart, hard-working client Marissa. Marissa left her corporate design job and its six-figure salary to start her own interior decorating business.

For a single mom, this was a risky leap. It was solely up to Marissa to provide a great education and lifestyle for her teenage son, the high school basketball star, and she met that responsibility with boundless love and care, as most women do. Thus far, her choice of job, address in Colorado, and personal schedule were all orchestrated around what she felt was best for him, with little consideration of her own desires.

Stepping into Queenhood, Marissa found the power to silence the Martyr, turn in her resignation, and sign a lease on the perfect little design studio in town. She made herself visible, online and in the real world, and told everyone in her network about her offerings. Within ninety days, she was already attracting high-end paying clients and turning a profit!

Around the five-month mark, Marissa raised her hand on a coaching call to go over her goals and intentions for the month. She told me her financial target and I asked, "What is the purpose of this money?"

With lightning speed, she declared, "A new car."

"Why a new car?" I asked.

"The minivan I'm driving has 180,000 miles on it and is the same age as my fourteen-year-old son."

"Well, it's time! As a Queen, you're due or past due." (I also reminded her of a few safety regulations, as it didn't sound wise to be driving her clunker through the icy Colorado winter.) Finding that Marissa had more than enough money in her savings account to trade in her van and lease a new car, I gave her an assignment to go car shopping that upcoming weekend.

Her breakthrough came with squeals of joy. "I can't believe this, Gina! I always said I had to make more money first before I could get a new car. It's amazing to finally give myself permission to make this upgrade now!"

"Yes, Marissa! You're ready for this. Call me Monday and tell me what you've picked out or purchased!"

When a week went by and I didn't get the call, I had a feeling that subzero winter basketball drop-offs were still happening with the worn-out vehicle. So I reached out and asked, "Hey, Marissa! So what are you driving around these days?"

"I just couldn't do it," she confessed. "I hate that I'm driving this old clunker. I hate that *this* is how I take my son to basketball practice. And I hate that both of my ex-husbands bought Teslas this year! But I just couldn't part with the money in my savings account."

As a single mom, Marissa felt she needed to have the money in the bank more than she needed to honor her desire. She was attached to old money rules that say "Don't lease, you must pay in full," and wasn't comfortable with her savings account dipping a bit lower than her preference. Just as she was about to reach her next level, the Martyr stepped in and said, "Be responsible, wait until you have enough money in the bank to pay for the car in full in cash," putting out the delicate flame of her desire. She didn't see that as long as the Martyr was in control, "enough money" would always be a vague fantasy number, forever going up and making it impossible to ever wear her pointy hat or zip around on her magic yellow scooter.

THE DANGER OF BEING OVERLY RESPONSIBLE

It can be so easy for the Martyr to run the show and keep us connected to security rather than our spirituality. Beth, the chic

New York City executive with the star power to launch her own company, was putting her security into a steady paycheck with the belief that she had to endure her soul-sucking job for the sake of her family. Angela, the brilliant doctor tolerating affairs and addiction in her relationship with the father of her kids, was putting her security into the traditional idea of marriage and being a "good mother." And Marissa, the single mom driving the ancient minivan down icy streets, was putting her security into her savings account, which the Martyr insisted was only for emergencies (as if this wasn't one).

All three of these women are smart, spiritual, hardworking women, and yet none of them really consulted God about their ability to bend space and time to actually make their desires happen. Understandably, the Martyr has brainwashed us into thinking that such responsible, reasonable choices are what we *need* to do to stay safe. We are well-meaning women led astray.

FROM SECRETARY TO CEO

What we never forget as Queens is our power to bend space and time. Almost any prescription for how long something will take or how many flaming hoops you'll have to jump through is just a self-drawn limit around your thinking. Spirit sees beyond the walls we've put up. This is the infinite realm we're talking about!

The feminine art of bending space and time starts with you and your spiritual connection. When a woman steps into her Queenhood and accesses her magical powers, reality changes *fast*.

Ask Brynna. She had the coffee at the naturopathic integrative clinic in downtown Portland preprogrammed to brew every morning at 7:40 a.m. Like clockwork at 7:45, she would waltz through the front door, ready and eager for another highly productive day as the front office receptionist. Scheduling appointments, overseeing all operations, and managing the entire staff, Brynna, with her cup of joe in hand, was basically running the operation for its visionary physician.

For a year now, the doctor had been mourning his late wife, and, understandably, had been distracted from the executive needs of the clinic's team and finances. Thanks to Brynna's dedication, love, leadership, passionate belief in the doctor's life-changing work, and caffeine high, the operation was in a groove and business was slowly picking up again. Seizing every opportunity to grow and be a liaison for healing, Brynna became an amazing representative of the clinic's healing cutting-edge treatments and often sold high-ticket procedure packages over the phone. And even with her perfectionistic standards and preference for having "everything done now and done correctly," the entire team adored and respected her. The doctor thought the world of her. It was a rare case of "my job is awesome" vibes!

And yet Brynna was ready for a change. She had been settling for her given position and secretly had much bigger dreams, so she too signed up for one of my transformational retreats. Her goal for the weekend of working with me was to map out a plan to become CEO of the clinic in three years. When Brynna proposed this timeline, I knew she too had lost her wand and misplaced her ball gown, as she was not seeing her magnificence. I could tell, she *already was the CEO.*

I looked at her and said, "Brynna, three years or three days. It's your choice. You can claim this CEO role now."

The look on her face was pure bewilderment. My suggestion immediately triggered her feelings of "Do I have what it takes?" She stopped acknowledging her true talent and came up with a slew of reasons why it wasn't going to work. "I'm not good with numbers!" she insisted. "I don't know *exactly* what the position would entail. And I don't want to step on anyone's toes!"

I helped her see what she knew deep down. "You do have an idea of what this job involves. You can get trained on what you don't know. And you'll be taking all of this work off the doctor's plate. He'll be thrilled so he can focus on his true passion, healing people!"

Queen Brynna opened up to a new perspective. A higher vibration. She saw herself differently. She saw that in fact, she *was* already CEO.

After flying home to Portland three days later, she asked her boss if they could have a conversation soon, to which he replied, "Sure, let's have it now!" Surprised, and not having said as many preparatory "Can I have a promotion" mantras as she'd hoped, she stumbled through her request like a first attempt at the tango. Still, she landed all the important twirls. And he said *yes!*

Unlike the Martyr, the Queen will seize any opportunity to bend space and time. When she does, the Universe will meet her there. Accessing the realm of the miraculous, she transforms excuses into reasons to take inspired action. When a victory you thought would take three years happens in three days, that's *bending space and time.* Asking "How is my desire (or the path toward it) possible now?" "I am available for my up-level in this moment. What can I do immediately?" Take note, this is your script for defying the gravitational pull of hope-addicted settling.

GET BIGGER THAN YOUR CIRCUMSTANCES

Women always have a choice. We can settle, or we can bend space and time. We can be the Martyr or the Queen. We can play small, or we can work miracles. When did we decide it's "responsible" to wait months or even years to ask for something we really desire (or even need)? At this point, doesn't it seem far more irresponsible to procrastinate on your calling?

The days of women thinking so little of themselves, staying quiet, and looking the other way are over. So is the era of thinking we must do everything ourselves or be everyone else's savior. Bending space and time often includes getting support. Whether you need to get takeout for your family one night a week so you can study for your graduate degree or hire a personal assistant or nanny so that you can actually get your pilot written or your blog going, you deserve support so that you can focus on doing what only you can do.

If it's humanly possible for one of us, it's humanly possible for all of us. And none of the women you met in this chapter are still taxing their soul with a dissatisfying status quo.

PICKING UP THE WAND

For security-driven executive Beth, bending space and time was a matter of collapsing her growth curve by getting the support of mentorship and connecting with a community of other feminine and spiritual women who were also committed to their own big audacious goals. Seeing the coaching I did with Brynna on day 2 of the retreat, Beth found her lost wand, brushed the dust off, and opened up to what *was* possible for her and shortened her three-to-five-year plan for quitting her corporate job to one year. Exit plan officially in place!

I'm also delighted to share that Dr. Angela has stepped out of playing the Martyr to her marriage. Choosing to pick up her wand and be the best possible mother by prioritizing her well-being, she made her kids the reason, not the excuse, to be Queen. Bending space and time was as simple as deciding she needn't wait till they graduated from high school to be happy. Whereas she would otherwise still be miserably married, Angela is now amicably divorced and happily co-parenting her children from her brand-new home that she absolutely loves.

And as for Minivan Marissa, the smart, successful woman driving the safety-hazard clunker as it dilapidated before her eyes? She reconsidered the level of settling she had been allowing in all areas of her life. Not only did she put on her pointed hat and ball gown and trade her Colorado address for a new one in Southern California, but after outfitting the garage in her new home with charger ports, she finally swapped the *Sanford and Son* minivan for the Tesla of *her* dreams.

Where Can You Bend Space and Time?

AN EXERCISE

Whatever dreary scenarios you've settled for, it's neither too late nor too soon to bend space and time and experience what you truly desire.

Once you get clear on where you've compromised because you didn't know better, or gave up because you didn't have the possibilities modeled for you or were straight-up afraid to decide to change things, fret not, my darling; we'll make up for lost time together.

This exercise can be a journal activity or a meditation. Where are you ruining your life because you're being the Martyr? This can be tough to admit, but I know you can do it because I've done it. Once you identify one stuck place in your life where you've settled, bring it to the forefront of your mind. Invite your inner Queen to access your big thinking and start asking questions that will lead to you bending space and time.

Who can help you with this area? Where can you bring in support? Where have you been giving much more time and energy than is actually required of you?

Remember, a Queen doesn't settle, self-abandon, or continuously sacrifice her true desires. The impact you're destined to have won't happen without high standards! Transforming and manifesting now requires that you take action immediately. Make a commitment that proves to the Universe how available you are for the up-level. Hire that mentor. Email that colleague. Put an end to any relationship that is holding your epic life hostage. And once you're seen to be decided, committed, and set up for success, your inner Queen will come out with her glittering pointed cap and purple sequined ball gown and wave her wand. Space and time won't stand a chance.

PART III

Qualities of a Queen

nine

THE ANSWER TO EVERYTHING

At my high school, tenth graders were forced to take geometry. And there I was, staring at Mr. Hodgeson with his protractor. I assume you too were tortured with the Pythagorean theorem, and I'm betting neither one of us has used it since. If only high school taught useful lessons like all eye creams are not created equal, dry shampoo will save your life, and this is how the brain *actually works*.

In the world I grew up in, the wisdom that "thoughts are things," that you get what you focus on and what you believe becomes your reality, wasn't at all in the conversation. As for most people, my view of life was that events happen to us, and then we react.

For example, when I thought and believed that being a psychotherapist, seeing clients in person, and trading dollars for hours was my *only* option, that was my reality. And it stayed that way up until I reprogrammed my mind to believe that I *could* turn my yearly income into my monthly income, be geographically independent, spend my summers in Europe, and mentor clients from anywhere in the world. Once I realized the power I had to manifest my desires, first by changing my thoughts and then by following up with the right actions, I was hooked on brain training.

HOW THE BRAIN WORKS

By design, the human brain is a goal-achieving machine, constantly working to attach meaning to every piece of information that it takes in—including the thoughts of our mind. When our thoughts (mind) are sent to our goal-achieving machine (brain), the two work in tandem to create our reality.

Up until recently, people believed that the adult brain was hardwired and set in its ways. As our understanding of quantum physics and our picture of the brain became more sophisticated, scientists found that we have *neurological webbing* that can, in fact, be changed. They call this factor *neuroplasticity*. Not to get too textbook on you, but the idea is that the brain is moldable, just like soft plastic. And it changes over the course of your lifetime as you take in data in the form of thoughts, emotions, behaviors, and experiences.

Your brain already contains existing webbing, like cobwebs linking the thoughts and feelings you most frequently rely on. Fresh ideas take you beyond the dusty old webs you've gotten used to. A lightbulb goes off, triggering a tiny spider to make *new* mental connections at lightning speed. And boom! You can then strengthen those pathways through conscious repetition, "rewiring" the webbing in your brain so it can help you create more of what you desire and less of what you don't.

Let's say, for example, that you have a belief that "I'm always late." You're used to squeezing in three too many things at the last minute, boggling the logistics and showing up to every meeting in a stressful flurry. You don't want any more of this situation or the unnecessary drama it creates, so you start telling yourself, "As a Queen, I always give myself more than enough time to arrive at my appointments." And soon enough, your brain is making great decisions to plan your transportation in advance, wake up earlier, and skip the impulse to suddenly change your hairstyle before walking out the door.

What I know for sure from working with thousands of women to adopt new belief systems is that neuroplasticity is your opportunity to overcome any conditioning and help manifest your biggest dreams. Isn't that exciting?! And the best part? *It's easy.*

It starts with introducing new, conscious thoughts (consult your Queen for these) that, through repetition, will become your new beliefs and then your new reality. Whether you've currently got the neurological webbing of the Princess, the Martyr, the Saboteur, or a mix of all of the above, it's time for you to rewire your brain with the mind of a Queen.

The Princess	Life should be easy and I shouldn't have to put in much effort.
The Martyr	I have to do everything myself, because no one can do it as well as me.
The Saboteur	My dream is too good to be true, so I'll quit before I'm rejected.
The Queen	My life has a purpose, I have access to all the resources necessary to fulfill my calling, and I always manifest my desires.

THE THREE SCHOOLS OF LIFE

As we're updating our mindsets, the Universe is always giving us chances to learn the lessons that we need most. In my work with women young and old, from dozens of cultures and countries, I've noticed how stuck we get in wired beliefs that chronically challenge us in one of three main areas. I've labeled these recurring, wounded areas the *School of Money*, the *School of Love*, and the *School of Health*. Although we all experience lessons in all three subjects, most women find that one of these is responsible for repeatedly bringing them to their knees.

The school you're in is typically your weakest area, and through rewiring your brain, it can and will become your strongest. Not sure which classroom you belong in? Ask your Queen within. She's here to guide you into healing and awareness on the subject you feel most inspired or defeated by. Just as our individual journeys aren't meant to be compared, these three schools are each distinct, as is the experience of every woman in them. The stories I'm about to share are simply individual illustrations of how a Queen trains her brain to receive all challenges as beneficial to her highest good. As you'll see in these examples, though I've certainly had and still have much to learn about relationships and health, I continue to find myself in the School of Money.

THE SCHOOL OF MONEY

Is it just me, or does everyone seem to think money problems are lower on the totem pole than health or relationship issues? Asking for help or a prayer over a diagnosis or to save your marriage seems acceptable, but asking someone to pray for you because you need help to pay your mortgage on time? Rather unheard of. For health and relationships there's support. Money? You're on your own. My belief is that every lesson is a spiritual one, worthy of transformation. So if you too are in the School of Money, push your shoulders back and know that healing is about to take place.

When I was a business rookie, the task of keeping up with all of my bills and expenses on a fluctuating income regularly sent me into financial paralysis. During the early years of growing my company, the process of retraining my brain saved me. The ups and downs of entrepreneurship are a hotbed of two a.m. fear spirals deep and dark enough to send any woman in the School of Money back to class.

I remember waking up, *again*, one Monday in the middle of the night. Payroll was due on Friday and I didn't have the full amount of money to pay everyone on my team. The impending doom was almost too much. An anxious pit in my stomach I could handle, but this was an all-consuming force that gripped me by the solar plexus and hung me from the ceiling rafters.

It wasn't the first time I had felt the dread of expenses looming. More than a mere annoyance, if I didn't do something fast, suffering my worst nightmare of letting my employees down was an imminent reality. What could be more awful than having to tell my team I'd need more time to pay them? What a deplorable human being I would be, letting them down when they're counting on their paycheck for their own bills. I felt like a total failure. How could I teach women to build businesses while being in this pathetic position?

Then I got angry. At God, for not providing the cash to support me so I could compensate these amazing people. At the prospects who didn't sign up that week so there could be money in the bank. At the clients who owed me money or had weaseled out of their contracts. At the banks that wouldn't extend my line of credit. At the innocent lady in line in front of me at the grocery store for assuming we all have nothing better to do than watch her fumble with her wallet, pulling out her change one dime at a time.

Once I was done blaming everyone else, I was left with no one to condemn but myself. So angry for being here *again*. "I'm obviously not good enough! If I were, I wouldn't be in this mess." I worked myself into a pulp of barely deserving to exist. It was probably during one of these stressful two a.m. moments that my escape plan of moving to Cyprus to wait tables was first invented.

After at least three hours of this downward shame spiral, as birds were chirping and the sun began to rise, I remembered that *the solution always exists*. I prayed, asked God for a miracle, and was guided to call in my Queen. She whispered, "Write this in your journal, 'I'm thrilled this is happening because...'"

What is she *thinking*?! This is the worst possible position I could be in as a business owner. There's *nothing* to be thrilled about.

Having zero other options in that moment, I followed her advice. I opened my journal and wrote, "I'm thrilled this is happening because..." To my disbelief and shock, I literally felt my brain rearrange. It was like the *Titanic* turning around in my head.

I'm Thrilled This Is Happening Because

"I'm thrilled that I might not be able to make payroll, ummm... well...maybe, because...I can see where I've had such dismal expectations for myself with money that on some level, I was 'available' for my bank account to get this low. Ugh. Hard to admit but true." Let's try it again: "I'm thrilled this is happening because...uhhhhh, I've been ignoring my profit-and-loss statement and waiting too long to assess my cash flow. Time to grow up!"

This wasn't fairy dust, but it was life-changing. If you're available for it, seeing the truth really will set you free. In that moment, I became conscious of the Princess who had been in charge. The Princess has many facets to her, and specifically I was being the Avoidant Princess. A Queen knows where her money is on a daily basis, and apparently I did not!

It may not sound like thrilling news to discover your brain is programmed to behave like an Avoidant Princess, but if you're available to take radical responsibility, you can use the opportunity to reprogram your mind to take you from the brink of less than enough to manifesting payroll and then some.

This School of Money gal was loving the empowering lessons

that kept flowing. "I'm thrilled I might not be able to make payroll because I'm now crystal clear about my cash-flow ups and downs, and I know that I must create a new marketing funnel that generates reliable, consistent income. I'm also going to look at what positions are on my team, analyze where I'm overspending, and figure out how I can be smarter with my resources. All of which will set me up to *never* be in this position again.

"And I'm thrilled this is happening because, since I remember that I have the ability to bend space and time, I actually do have enough days to turn this around and make the money to pay my team by Friday. I forgot that a miracle can happen, and as a Queen, I always have the power to ask the Universe for assistance."

The next day I woke up miracle-minded and was inspired to offer a flash sale on one of my online courses. I took quick action and sent an email to my list that this downloadable course would be 50 percent off for one day only. Thankfully, with my Queen thinking, I was able to transform the relationship with that list of prospects I was previously mad at. They jumped at the time-sensitive opportunity *in droves*, and payroll was made in full and on time.

Graduating from the School of Money is ultimately a double blessing. Not only was I broke without consistent cash, I wasn't serving as many people as I could. Without a higher level of dependable income, I couldn't take on as many team members to help attract more women and support all of their transformations.

Guaranteeing multiple salaries is a major responsibility for a freshman entrepreneur. For most of us, managing payroll comes with a learning curve. These two a.m. tests are there to show us how important it is to focus on consistent cash flow so we can support our community and our cause. And I would have flunked the final exam without my brain training.

Every woman deserves to be supported financially, whether

we're taking responsibility for others or starting with ourselves. And whether you see yourself in the School of Money or you're simply taking an elective course, stay tuned for your own money story transformation coming up in Chapter 14, because Queens have all the necessary resources to fulfill their life purpose and enjoy financial relaxation.

THE SCHOOL OF LOVE

Although I've also had my own drama with love and the local loser rock stars of Detroit (I'll divulge all the not-so-juicy details in Chapter 18), I thankfully found wise mentors and learned how to train my brain so I could graduate out of the School of Love.

My millennial-rock-star team member Kylie, however, didn't yet know what was possible for a Queen when it came to love. Like so many amazing women, she had been conditioned to expect only so much from her romantic relationships and could have easily spent a lifetime settling for less in the romance department, as far too many worthy women of all ages do.

Wicked smart, super-hot, uber-positive, and totally "in love"... or so she thought. At the tender age of twenty-four, Kylie had been dating her "soul mate" Blake for nearly three years. As we got to know each other more personally after hours, she would talk about "him," the walking Armani ad, down to the great style and the trim physique, chiseled in all the right places. As the years went on, my husband, Glenn (who now runs my company with me), and I noticed that Kylie seemed to be making all the effort in the relationship.

Everything seemed to revolve around what Blake wanted and what was convenient for him. The worst part was watching this young shining star of a woman believe "That's just how it goes after dating someone for three years, right?" She would overlook his self-centeredness, telling herself, "This is my man, he's young, he'll grow out of this one day and become a King." Little did she know, she had lots of Queen training to come.

With their three-year anniversary (which also fell on Valentine's Day) approaching, Blake mentioned to Kylie that he got her something *really* special. Something thoughtful and from the heart that she'd absolutely love and wouldn't be able to top. Amid a serious panic, Kylie jumped in her Jeep and was off to Nordstrom's where she accumulated a pile of his favorite shoes, cologne, and some dress shirts, putting together a bag full of ten things that would accompany ten sweet notes about why she loved him.

Having made a significant dent in her bank account, she was anxiously placing her final pink sticky note reading "You run through my mind all day" on top of the box of shoes, so excited for the "special gift" that awaited her. Promise ring, maybe?! They had talked about finding a place together that summer, so maybe he'd picked out something for their future home?

The *Naïve Princess* had completely taken Kylie over. This archetype tends to ignore the obvious warning signs that wise Queens spot instantly, and for purposes of self- or relationship preservation, she convinces you of an alternate happy narrative to escape what's really happening. The Naïve Princess, much like a child, sees the silver lining in every cloud, however in a very rose-colored-glasses kind of way.

Speaking of roses, Valentine's Day arrived and Kylie was getting ready for what she anticipated would be a special night. Blake showed up at her place early and sat her down in the living room, immediately begging Kylie to open his gift. She nervously received the package, hands shaking. As she went to open it, he started filming her. She thought this *had* to be good.

Inside, she found a miniature desk calendar. Stay seated, it gets worse. Each month featured a picture of his Armani-esque ass, nakedly on display on different beaches he'd visited while study-ing abroad in Europe. Yep, she received an ass calendar, from this emotional amoeba, for their three-year anniversary celebration. No card, chocolates, or (much needed) wine in sight.

Quivering, holding back the tears because her inner Little Miss Perfect didn't want to upset *him* or ruin the night, she did her best to put on a happy face and proceed to their happy-hour date.

The next day Kylie came in to work, seemingly upbeat as ever. Curious about the anniversary celebration I had heard so much about, I asked, "How was your evening? What was your big sur-prise?!" Kylie hesitantly replied, "It was fine. He made me a cal-endar." Revealing the contents, she tried to laugh it off, but I knew better. I could sense the aftershock of being worked up into grand expectations and then having her spirits crushed.

"Are you okay?" I responded, immediately concerned. She brushed it off, wanting to move on and forget it happened. From there on out, Blake's self-obsession escalated to Kanye West levels, and even though they had discussed finding a place together for over a year, two weeks before they were due to move in, he bailed on their cohabitation plan. Then, as the four-year mark approached, Blake secured his own bachelor pad in SoCal and "out of nowhere" dumped Kylie. With no reason other than that he had to "find himself."

Kylie was devastated because her Naïve Princess was still thinking "ass-calendar man" would grow up and treat her better one day. Glenn and I knew she deserved so much more, and that a way better significant other was available. Unfortunately the Naïve Princess was keeping Kylie in the School of Love, oblivious to what a thriving relationship looked like, instead of retraining her brain to receive the kind of romance she was meant for.

"He wasn't a King, Kylie," I advised her. "Trust me, this is the best gift he could possibly give you." We all know the sting that comes with being the one who is broken up with; practically nothing can make you feel better because, remember, *rejection breeds obsession*. Kylie, not feeling it just yet, held her tears back and listened as I continued, "There's a true King out there waiting for you. One who will show you what a healthy, loving relationship really looks like, and how a real Valentine's Day is meant to make you feel. And not to mention...a man who will love you more than he loves himself."

Always one to land on her feet, Kylie took my advice and dove into retraining her brain to believe that new love was possible. She got clear about the type of relationship she now desired and deserved, and repeated mantras affirming that her King was out there for her.

Three months of retraining her brain by visualizing, journaling, reading, and reciting affirmations, Kylie had created a deep belief that her King existed. She went home to attend a high school friend's wedding and right there on the dance floor was King Nathan. Since then, this super-hot, emotionally intelligent, complete gentleman of a man has sent her endless "just because" flowers and cards. He calls her every day and texts her on the first of every month wishing her "Happy Month-a-versary" and now, ten joyous months later, they are happily living together in their new apartment. And Blake? The latest we've heard is that he's auditioning for reality stardom on *Love Island*. Good luck, dude.

THE SCHOOL OF HEALTH

A lot of us grew up thinking that our body was its own separate entity, barely within our control, that came down with illness randomly or because of the weather. Lesson one in the School of Health is that in fact, like a great romance and financial empowerment, it usually starts in the mind.

For the woman who finds herself in the School of Health, one metaphysical explanation can be that she isn't speaking up for herself in important ways. So her body ends up speaking for her. For example, suppose your boss wants you to go and represent the company at an industry conference in Milwaukee; not feeling good enough to be the spokesperson, you're dreading it. Being compliant, you just say okay, go home, and order a new neck pillow for the red-eye flight. Not digesting this decision well, stuffing your stress and emotions in, you develop an ulcer. Your body spoke for you, creating debilitating pain so now you don't have to get on the plane, and you also don't get to enjoy your life or anything other than bland food for the next six months while you recover.

On the defiance side, we can enter the School of Health by overworking and wind up out of tune with our bodies. Rosanne is a perfect example of an incredibly smart, highly educated, and strong woman who was surprised to find herself in the School of Health. Her lessons focused on her desire to have a baby. Rosanne was thirty-six years old when she and her husband actively started trying to conceive. At this time, she was a powerful attorney in Northern California prosecuting sex crimes. She was completely in her masculine energy 24/7, a workaholic and, in her own words, a *Gladiator*.

This archetype is all about the grind. Plowing through, working hard, and doing the heavy lifting is how they achieve superhero status. This is how Rosanne got through law school and how she prosecuted ten trials in thirteen months, three of which were contesting life sentences.

The Gladiator is how she did life, and it's also how she tried to conceive a baby. And I'm sure it's no surprise to you that trying to get pregnant while operating exclusively in masculine energy doesn't work.

Determined and ambitious as ever, Rosanne kept trying and trying. After the natural way didn't seem to bear fruit, she did the maximum allowable rounds of IVF treatments. Each one failed. And every time a doctor told her it wasn't possible for her to conceive, she'd go find a new one, only to hear the same thing.

But that wasn't going to stop Gladiator Rosanne. For years, she refused to give up on her pregnancy goals. And, at age forty-one, she was wise enough to realize that something, or everything, in her life needed to change. And fast.

Rosanne wondered what else was possible for her as she explored leaving her job as an attorney. She went online and found Divine Living and our programs. "At first I was pretty resistant to all this feminine energy stuff," Rosanne told me. "And the whole 'mindset training' thing seemed very woo-woo. But I felt there was something in it for me, took the leap, and enrolled. That's when I started learning about my neurological webbing. It was scary at first, taking a look inside was something my upbringing wired into me to never do. I learned that I'm a creator, and that 'thoughts are things.' And I started to ask myself, what thoughts do I have about not getting pregnant?" That's when the truth was revealed.

Rosanne, in all her external confidence, was in disbelief to find that deep down inside, she felt unworthy of having a baby. Her own mother had always dismissed her big ambitions, warning her that "you can't have more." And since she already had the loving husband, the beautiful home, and the successful career, her belief was "Who am I to have it all?" By keeping her barren, her body was fulfilling the prophecy of her conditioning.

Then Rosanne came to one of my seminars in Paris. I guided the women through the exact exercise that saved me on that excruciating night when I was short on payroll. Rosanne, still unsure of this whole spiritual thing, went along with it and wrote down, "I'm thrilled I haven't gotten pregnant after six years of trying because..." Can you imagine?!

For one of the toughest fill-in-the-blanks I've seen to date, Rosanne's inner Queen had the answer. There was a feminine receptivity that needed to take place. What spilled onto the page was "I'm thrilled I haven't become pregnant yet so that my child wasn't raised by a Gladiator mother."

"*What?!* This is amazing!" she thought. "I'm thrilled I now have the opportunity to reconnect to my femininity before becoming a parent. I'm thrilled I get to step into my true self and conceive from a feminine place."

Now that Rosanne was forty-two years old, every doctor gave her a single-digit chance of getting pregnant. And yet, immediately after returning home from Paris, Queen Rosanne used the mindset techniques to rewire the belief that she did, in fact, deserve to have it all, and that pregnancy was possible for her.

You could say Rosanne got great at receiving! She conceived naturally. And we are all thrilled to say that at age forty-three, Rosanne gave birth to a healthy baby boy.

Here's what Rosanne did to become available for the miracle of motherhood. Every day, she visualized herself being pregnant and having a healthy baby. She also programmed her mind with mantras such as "I am a mother. I can have it all. I'm so happy and grateful to be pregnant." To support her transformation, she nurtured her feminine energy with all of her favorite forms of spiritual practice, self-care, pleasure, and play. She followed her Divine Guidance to move on from her prosecuting career in the courtroom and began designing her own business. Meanwhile she made it non-negotiable to have fun and spend time in the high-vibrational sisterhood of our community, where she culti-vated real friendships. No isolation for her! When training our brains to manifest, Queens know the importance of being in the presence of others who think as big as we do.

Not only did this miracle bless Rosanne and her family, but babies around the world have been born thanks to what she learned on her journey. Rosanne now runs a super-cool company where she works with women to open *their* minds and bodies to become mothers, so they too can receive the gift of life.

HOW TO TRAIN YOUR BRAIN

Ready to get your diploma from the School of Money, Love, or Health? Developing new neurological webbing is how you create your desired reality and manifest your epic life. As a Queen, you're only available to live your highest truth, and it's time for your brain to get the memo.

The ancient practice of reciting mantras is one of the most powerful tools in training your brain to think like a Queen. If you've read enough personal development books to know all about the importance of positive thinking and auto-suggestion, you may be tempted to feel bored and gloss over what I'm sharing here. Resist, because "I already know this stuff" is the sneakiest killer of continuous growth.

Yes, most people have heard of mantras, and have even flirted with them (despite the tempting eye roll) because they found themselves on the edge of total despair and were willing to try anything. The misunderstanding is that mantras are not meant to be a quick-fix remedy to get through challenging times; they're meant to create deep reprogramming that dramatically influences your life experience. And few people carry their commitment to reciting mantras through to the point of long-lasting transformation.

Through daily repetition, a mantra affirms your highest truth until it becomes your new default mode. What you used to associate with pain, lack, and negativity is no longer emotionally draining. I want you to experience this life-changing power so you can manifest your epic life.

In the beginning, a mantra may seem like a lie. Say it and feel it often enough, and you'll start to believe that it is your truth, and next thing you know it becomes your reality. I recovered from my payroll drama with mantras like "I absolutely love that I pay my team twice a month," "I'm always able to make all of my expenses on time and with ease," and "Payroll is a beautiful reminder of all of the support that I have from these amazing team members who are helping me make a difference in the lives of our clients." I said these statements over and over again. I told myself it felt amazing, powerful, peaceful, natural, and abundant! I visualized always having more than enough money in the bank to pay everyone with ease and *felt* it deeply. My energy around the responsibility became clean, and the funds flowed through unblocked.

All of this became the new normal in my business, as well as every other area of my life I've applied brain training to, and quickly. Studies say it takes twenty-one days to habituate new neurological pathways, and don't be surprised if it takes longer than that for your new belief system to get really strong for you and produce results. Brain training and clearing your energy is like strengthening a muscle. You get to decide how quickly these beliefs will be your new normal.

When your dream represents a massive transformation, like losing a hundred pounds or getting out of one hundred thousand dollars of debt, it takes intense up-front training to truly reprogram your mindset. Once you've lost the weight and paid off the loan, maintenance demands less of your time but is of no less importance. It's too easy to slip out of high vibration if you're not surrounded by positive people, reading nourishing books, staying connected to your desires, and affirming your truth daily. Thinking like a Queen is an ongoing commitment, and one that makes life epic.

GRADUATING FROM THE SCHOOLS

Now you know how to call in your Queen and reverse any form of the two a.m. fear spiral sucking you into the false belief that life as you know it is over. On the other side of "I'm thrilled this is happening because…" you'll find a game-changing piece of wisdom to aid you on your journey.

You'll see how you can wake up to new lessons and make different decisions. Not every lesson is "fun." We certainly haven't consciously signed up for most of the classes and don't typically see the pop quizzes coming. But if you rewire your brain to receive any challenge with a sense of joy, adventure, and gratitude, your new natural response will be "Awesome! I can do this!" instead of freaking out and taking a six-month detour via financial paralysis, a broken heart, or a stress-induced ulcer.

Never again will you assume you're being punished or that you're bad, unworthy, or not good enough when something doesn't go your way. Whereas all your previous neurological webbing instructs that what you're experiencing equals doomsday, this simple act of filling in the blank after "I'm thrilled this is happening because…" reconnects you with Spirit and lifts you up into your highest potential.

When you train yourself to believe that everything is happening *for* you, not *to* you, you'll start to think more about what gifts the Universe is bringing you. You'll see how to bend time and space, assign a different meaning to what used to be perceived as an unfortunate circumstance, and step into a higher possibility of what's meant for you.

You'll find where your vision was limited but God's was not. Where you thought you were weak, you will become strong. And where it seemed there was no way out, you'll break through to a fabulous realm of unlimited possibilities. With a Queen's mindset, there's not a problem that can't be answered. There's never a dead end. There's always a higher level of opportunity. And you don't need a Pythagorean anything to get there. Welcome to the answer to everything, darling.

ten

COMMUNICATING LIKE A QUEEN

You know that time when you shot your mouth off (I know, just pick one) and it ruined that friendship? Or when you stayed silent (aka "being polite") and later realized that boldly speaking up would have stopped the apartment you had your heart set on from being swept out from underneath you by the applicant with the Chihuahua? Or what about all of those times you hesitantly said yes when you so badly wanted to say no to babysitting your sister's kid, listening to your serial entrepreneur friend talk about idea #347, or going on vacation with your mother-in-law?

How did we get to be grown women and not know how to communicate effectively or have the courage to speak honestly? We've been taught to apologize for our needs, not how to ask for them—something most women have been told *isn't* okay for us to do in the first place. It's no surprise that so few of us know how to use language powerfully.

What has mostly been modeled for us is compliant or defiant communication where we cower in invisibility, become verbally accommodating, or assert our bitchy demands. Domineering speech can ruin your life as much as silence and avoidance can quietly crush your soul. Trust me, I would know. Communication has been one of the most frustrating, blindsiding, challenging, and humbling areas of my growth. Until our Injured Feminine Instinct is healed, unconscious conditioning will monopolize our communication style and thus our lives.

I have successfully healed my compliant people-pleasing tone, survived the pendulum swing of defiant and shaming communication, and gotten into alliance with my voice. Once I learned the lessons I'm sharing with you in this chapter, including the life-changing art of letting my "yes be yes" and "no be no" while speaking the truth in love, communication has become one of the most healing, transformative, freeing, and rewarding skills at my Queen's command, and it's about to become yours too.

THE GHOST: THE INVISIBLE COMMUNICATOR

It was Saturday night. My friend Zoe had an invite to a big party at a prominent artist's loft in downtown L.A. Her mover-and-shaker community would be there in full swing, plus plenty of new fascinating friends to meet.

She was excited to bring her boyfriend, Zack, a charming extrovert who's always fun at parties. They had been together for six months and so far, the relationship had been effortless. It was going to be a fabulous night of introducing him to her aspirational world.

One slight complication. Before they left for the party, Zack and Zoe had ordered in Thai for dinner, and more food had shown up than the couple was expecting. Innocently thinking "sharing is caring," Zack decided to text a few of his hipster buddies to come over to his place before the loft party to partake in this glorious feast.

This seemed reasonable to Zoe. After all, she wouldn't want all those pad see ew noodles to go to waste, and she found his long-time pals Brody and Mark entertaining enough in small doses.

However, she was secretly harboring worries that if they came for dinner she might have to bring them to the party. Showing up with a whole squad of bros wasn't her first choice, especially when she knew they would embarrassingly leech onto Zack all night, seriously limiting the star couple's social potential. Despite her growing concerns, under no circumstances was Zoe going to tell Zack that inviting his friends over was a bad idea. She was possessed by the Ghost.

Afraid to speak her truth, religiously compliant to other people's preferences, the *Ghost* archetype vanishes our voices until we go completely invisible. With a belief that we're unimportant compared to everyone else, she tells us our own desires are wrong, sending us into full shutdown status. The Ghost feels that we have no say in the matter, so why speak up? Or she's so fixated on not wanting to hurt someone else's feelings that she jeopardizes our own happiness.

Zoe was relieved when Brody, always a bit of a "Donnie Downer," said he didn't want to go to the party. Completely unaware of her Ghosted feelings, Zack persuaded him, "Dude, you have to come! It's going to be awesome!" Zoe choked down her irritation, nervously playing with her chopsticks as again and again, Brody groaned and moaned about having to go to the invite-only insider party, and sweet Zack, totally unfazed and loyal to his childhood friend, kept insisting that he tag along.

Packed into the back seat of the Uber between Brody and Zack, with Mark playing DJ in the front, Zoe's mood plummeted as she endured Brody's nonstop complaints over the obnoxious music. "I don't know about this. I shouldn't have come. This is going to be stupid. I'll probably leave right when I get there." She wanted to snap, "Okay, then why don't we pull over right here and let you out?" But the Ghost continued to bite her tongue.

Trying to convince herself that she was fine with Brody's brooding, Zoe was hope-addicted that it would all work out. Afraid of looking like a Bitch, she told herself to just be nice. Still, nothing stopped her dread from turning into a swirl of anxious thoughts. Was she rudely including too many people unbeknownst to the host? She felt bad about introducing low-vibe energy to the party, and thus started to beat herself up in silence, telling no one how she felt and vanishing from the conversation.

Arriving at the party full of eclectic, stylish people, with a live band and full open bar, Brody settled down while Zoe couldn't shake her mood. Or him. She no longer had the energy or excitement to mix and mingle. She was on edge and awkward with the few people she did end up in conversation with, and when the bros wanted to leave at eleven p.m., just as the party was getting going, she was all too happy to call it quits.

Stewing all the way home, arriving to the smell of pad see ew still in the air, Zoe completely came undone with all of the classic emotional bells and whistles. Crying, snot dribbling, distraught belly flop on the couch; it was a total damsel-in-distress collapse. Poor Zack, thinking he and everyone else just had a great night, stood there in shock. Yet he quickly rose to the occasion of providing emotional support during this first meltdown of their relationship.

"What's going on?" he asked Zoe. She finally confessed the truth of what was bothering her, along with scathing commentary about what a drag Brody was. And at that moment, she realized that she too had become a total drag in succumbing to the Ghost and not communicating her true desires. Zack agreed that Brody had been difficult, though he had no idea it was making her so upset, and was disappointed that his woman hadn't clearly stated her truth. Accessing the Queen within, Zoe realized that a simple "Babe, I really want it to just be you and me at this party tonight" could have stopped her unnecessary inner trainwreck in its tracks.

Can you relate? Have you wound up stewing in silent disappointment while your beloved (or best friend, boss, etc.) obliviously carries on, only to wind up haunted by the damage the Ghost has done?

As a Queen, you deserve to confidently communicate your point of view. It's not even about being right or wrong. It's about letting your yes be yes and your no be no. Your voice is there to express what's true for you. This is not about being inconsiderate, it is about you speaking up to be in the highest service to everyone involved. Remember, Brody didn't even want to go to this party! Zoe's truth would have been compatible with his desires and enhanced her own enjoyment, and Zack would have been much more satisfied knowing he made his woman happy.

The Ghost shows up when we've been conditioned to put ourselves last, think of others first to our detriment, just be nice and go with the flow. Heaven forbid we be the Bitch who wasn't including everyone in everything. We get so worried about hurting other people's feelings, but we're okay with getting our own feelings trampled on. That's why it often takes complete reprogramming for this style of direct communication to feel natural to any woman familiar with the Ghost.

Empowering ourselves and others to express our truth, we find freedom in Queenly communication. On the other side of it, if you don't get the invite, you don't have to make it mean that somebody doesn't like you. It may be that they just want to go to the party with their boyfriend *alone*.

Being visible with your desires without blaming or accusing is the best way to get your needs met. My friend Chelsea recently put Queenly communication into practice and it worked. Newly wed to the man of her dreams, Chelsea was basking in marital bliss. But there was one area where she was Ghosting her own desires. Her wonderful husband, like so many partners in their provider-protector energy, thought it was impractical to spend extra money on clothes and hair appointments. Thus when it came to her looking and feeling sexy, Chelsea was unfulfilled.

She decided to be visible and own her desire for a Queenly beauty treatment. So she sat with her husband, channeled her inner Queen, and from a feminine perspective shared with him how she felt.

"Darling, I love you and I'm so grateful that you treat me like a Queen. But I'm a woman. Sometimes I need more than you telling me that I'm beautiful and sexy. I have to feel it too. For me, that means wearing well-made clothes I love and getting occasional blowouts at the salon."

This is what alliance in communication looks like. Chelsea's husband instantly understood. He realized that just like his personal non-negotiable of working out at the CrossFit gym every morning, her feminine practices weren't frivolous and irrational, they were an essential part of what made her feel great about herself, taken care of, and confident. Glossy beach waves may sound trivial, but for Chelsea, they're not. They're an example of what it looks like for her to be in her Queenly power where she might classically defer to masculine practical values.

Boom! Fresh from the salon, Chelsea messaged me thrilled about the new blowout membership she just purchased. With Queenly communication, she transcended Ghost status.

THE SWEET TALKER

I remember a few years after becoming a psychotherapist, I went to a wellness resort that offered numerous spa treatments and personal development classes. One of them was a unique equestrian experience intended to elevate awareness of the mind, body, and spirit.

I had never really been around horses, so when the rugged cowboy-looking facilitator took my group of therapists into the arena where they kept those big, beautiful stallions and mares, though I was attracted to one named Misty, I was intimidated.

Our first activity was to go over to a horse and pick up its front foot. The Marlboro Man facilitator went first, confidently picking up the massive hoof like it was a feather. A few others went ahead of me, succeeding and making it look like a piece of cake. Once my turn came around, I timidly walked up to the horse and started petting her. I told her how pretty she was and that my name was Gina. I figured I had to get to know her first, *right*?

"I'm just going to pick up your foot really quick, is that all right?" I whispered to her.

I slowly crouched down, wrapped my hands around her silky calf, and puuuuuullled with all my might, and…nothing! Not a budge. That damn hoof felt like a thousand pounds.

Everyone else seemed to do it right except me. I was so embarrassed. It didn't even matter that no one from my group was judging me. I was the one who wanted to do it perfectly. I felt my stomach tighten and my face flush. I sheepishly looked at the instructor. I wasn't looking forward to the public feedback I was about to receive. But I was there for personal development, so I took a deep breath and then said, "Give it to me."

He quickly responded, "Gina, do you always bullshit people before you ask for what you want?"

Oh. My. Gawd. I wanted to die right then and there. The sad part is, according to my programming, I *was* doing everything right. I was being nice, considerate of others, and politely acting how I was "supposed to."

The cowboy continued, "You can be direct in your communication. You don't have to butter people up before you get to your point. Go back in there and try it again."

"I can't believe this effing horse is blowing my cover," I thought. That horse became my mirror. Misty saw right past my BS small talk and weak, asking-for-permission energy. She knew that I wasn't there for the "you're so pretty" fluffing.

In that moment, my *Sweet Talker* archetype revealed herself to me. I saw how much I needed everyone to approve of me. The cowboy trainer. The other therapists. Even the damn horse!

Taking the lesson, I adjusted my energy and invited my inner Queen to step up. I closed my eyes and silently said to myself, "Queen Gina, how would you have me lift the foot?" I felt my energy shift and my chin rise. I strutted right up to that stubborn horse and, without saying a word, lifted up that foot like it was a cream puff.

Ironically, when we release the Sweet Talker, that's when people (and animals) respect us more. For many of us women, this insecure archetype defines our communication style on a daily basis. The Sweet Talker is the one who dismisses herself with rampant disclaimers, trying to manage any possible blow of crushing rejection. Lacking self-belief and being chronically self-critical, she's the one who speaks indirectly and in circles, opening up sentences with, "Would you mind if I...?" or "Sorry to bother you...?" or "I love your blouse!"

Whether you're seeking approval from your coworkers, husband, friends, father-in-law, or children, speaking confidently and directly is the antidote for the Sweet Talker.

Here's how a Queen confidently communicates her desires without needing the vast majority of the popular vote. Think about when you're at a restaurant and the server asks what would you like for dinner. If you used to say, "Can I have the Dover sole?," you will now place your order like this: "I would like the Dover sole, please." And you will feel much less "high maintenance" when instead of hemming and hawing, "Um, I'm thinking about the wedge salad...would it be possible for me to get it chopped...and maybe can you have it tossed too?," you simply state, "I'd like the wedge salad, chopped and tossed, please." (Consider yourself free from an evening of sawing through iceberg lettuce. You're welcome.)

You can release the permission-seeking, sweet-talkin' energy in your career too. So many women put their worst foot forward at work, introducing their thoughts with, "You may not like this idea, but...?" or "This may sound dumb, but what do you think about...?" As a Queen, you can stand in your brilliance and say, "I have a great idea I'd like to share with you."

And as for your beloved who loves making a plan and sticking to it, know that a Queen has the right to change her mind. If on Monday you get an OpenTable email confirmation for your Thursday night sushi reservation, and when Thursday rolls around you're just not feeling like you're in a wasabi mood, you don't have to be afraid to share your truth directly, while also considering your date, just like this: "Hey, did you have your heart set on sushi tonight? I appreciate you making reservations for us; however, if you'd be open to changing plans, I'm really in the mood to stay in and order Chinese instead."

Practice being direct, and your Sweet Talking confrontation style will be released. The less you couch your words in fearful fluff and flattery, the more your message will be received and accepted.

If the thought of direct communication activates your IBS, keep working on releasing your disease to please. Revisit the chapter and its exercise. Remember that your worth and security comes only from Source. Stick with your spiritual connection and daily communication with God, and you will start feeling safe sharing your truth with the world like a Queen.

THE BITCH

When a woman's words come out harsh, vengeful, bitter, ill-meaning, and overall shaming, it's because the *Bitch* has stolen the mic. We all know this archetype well whether we've been on the giving or receiving end.

Some women become confused about this style, defending it as being direct, speaking one's mind, and just being honest, which many people think is the only way to get heard (they're wrong). Others simply just don't realize the cruel vibes they're giving off. We've all heard "It's not what you say, it's how you say it," and yes, the main difference between being the Bitch and speaking your mind is the energy and intention behind your communication.

One year, I was excited to host a fun Easter brunch. A certain unnamed family member, her husband, and their three beautiful children were on the exclusive invite list. I prepared the delectable delights in true Divine Living style, a feast for the eyes and by no means simple. As a Le Cordon Bleu–trained chef, I went to town creating three different kinds of quiches, arranging flowers into custom centerpieces, setting up the bellini bar, and picking up the freshly made baguettes. I gave my all to making this experience memorable.

I had strategically arranged everything to be ready at noon on the dot, and asked everyone to arrive between 11:30 and 11:45 a.m.

So 11:55 rolls around and the timers for my several hot dishes start dinging, ringing, and singing like a symphony. The food was ready, the table was set, but my guests were MIA.

At this stage in my life, I was still on a journey to get out of my compliant communication style (specifically the Ghost) and did not want to upset anyone. Convincing myself that "They have young children, Gina. I'm sure they are on their way. Give them some time," Glenn and I continued to wait around, stare at the clock, and resist great temptation trying not to dig into the perfect quiches as their savory aroma wafted through the house.

Once 12:25 p.m. rolled around, I was pissed. Pissed because they were late, pissed because no one even had the courtesy to call me with an update, pissed because I hadn't reached out and said something. Just pissed. I finally convinced my inner Ghost to vanish so I could speak up. I took some deep breaths, picked up the phone, and called my relative.

"Hey there! Just checking in...is everything okay? The food is getting cold!"

She responded, "Yes, Gina, we're just now getting in the car. See you soon."

In an attempt to be Queen, be seen, and communicate directly, I replied, "I understand that you have small children, but in the future, if you know you're going to be late, I'd appreciate a call to let me know so that I can plan for it."

Aggressively, she hissed, "Gina, the only thing making us late is the person keeping me on the phone," and hung up.

I was stunned. No apology. No reasoning. Just ruthlessness! *What a bitch.* I wanted so badly at that point to stand up for myself, uninvite her, and tell her, "Just don't come." But my Ghost took over and silenced me again. She desperately wanted me to "be nice" and avoid "stirring up drama" as the Bitch might have done had she leapt to my defense.

Entitled and remorseless, they arrived thirty minutes later. They visited, they ate, they left. Afterward, I had this awful feeling that I had been walked all over and somehow *I* was wrong?! "That bitch!" I thought.

DEALING WITH THE BITCH

To an extent, we can all identify with the Bitch. And she can show up when we least expect it in our communication style. Whether in our love life, with our families, children, clients, coworkers, or the clerk at the grocery store talking to her friend instead of bagging your items quickly when you're already ten minutes late to pick up your kid, sometimes it comes as a natural instinct to let the Bitch come out and do our bidding.

And trust me, I've let the Bitch take over my own communication styles many times too. In the past, I very well may have gone off on this special family member and told her she was wrong in a Bitchy chain reaction. And I've certainly snapped after Ghosting an issue for too long. Whether the Bitch is taking it out on your partner, the server who took too long to bring the chips and salsa, the telemarketer who won't stop calling your cell phone, or the Wi-Fi that's not loading fast enough, she is sneaky and can take you over the second your guard is down, causing you to forget that with Queenly communication, a solution to take care of everyone always exists.

This reflex isn't our fault, it's what was modeled to us. We were taught that the world is a "right or wrong" place, especially for women. We learned that people only cooperate when punishing consequences are involved. And we saw that not only was the Bitch accepted in this world, but with the right hair and wardrobe, she could even run the whole show.

Think of movies with the infamous "bitch." They depict her with the harsh communication, abrasive comments, and bluntly shaming tendencies, and yet they still make her look so cool, right? There's Miranda in *The Devil Wears Prada*, Regina George in *Mean Girls*, Helen in *Bridesmaids*. These are women who have all the power, get what they want, and look good while they're at it. No wonder this is so confusing for us women.

None of this is a justification, only an explanation. The Bitch shows up because we don't know how else to get our needs met, and fortunately, nobody is better at getting everyone's needs met than the Queen.

Putting ourselves in my family member's shoes, we feel for her. She was totally overwhelmed as a relatively new mother with three small children, feeling bad about herself that she wasn't "more together" as a parent. To top it off, she had gotten very little sleep that night because the newborn kept her up.

Embarrassed that she was running so late, she was being the Avoidant Princess who so badly wanted to escape the fact that she was behind that she couldn't even acknowledge it. Then when I called her to find out where she was, she went from being the Avoidant Princess to being the Bitch.

If her Queen had been confronted in this scenario, she would confidently take full personal responsibility and, without crucifying herself, apologize. Her response could have looked something like this: "Gina, I apologize for not calling you sooner. Every time I thought we were ready to get in the car, one more thing would happen that delayed us and time slipped away. I really appreciate you hosting this brunch, we're all looking forward to it! We'll be there in thirty minutes. Next time, I'll let you know sooner so that you can plan too!"

BYE-BYE, BITCH

Far too many Bitchy moments emerge only because we haven't taken the time to set up ourselves and others for success. I know that for me, being distracted from my work during crunch time is one of the biggest triggers that gets my inner Bitch instantly snapping. And being that I work from home with my supportive man who's also running the company, helping to lead my team, and still going about his life at the house, there are plenty of opportunities for his actions to trigger me on a daily basis.

Whether he's sitting in his infamous squeaky chair while I'm recording a video, bustling in with groceries and the dog while I'm coaching a client, or attempting to ask me a thousand questions while I'm writing, if I'm at all stressed or on a tight deadline, I can easily go into Bitch mode: "Stop interrupting! You're distracting me!" or "Glenn, seriously, zip it!" or the worst, "Glenn, go away!"

As a Queen, I have to take personal responsibility where the Bitch would rather blame others. If I've set up my workspace in a common area that he also needs access to, I can't exactly expect to work all day in complete silence. It's up to me to safeguard my environment and create a distraction-free zone, by either putting on headphones, going into my office and closing the door, or getting a coworking-space membership.

When I do genuinely desire a common area to myself, then it's on me to communicate my request ahead of time and ask for agreement, in consideration of Glenn. "Sweetheart, I've got to take a video conference call with clients today in the living room from nine to eleven a.m.; are you able to be elsewhere so I'm not distracted?"

And in the case where we confirmed and he barged in anyway? The Bitch is still not needed to defend me. The Queen says, "Hey, babylove, we discussed that I was going to have this space distraction-free during this time, and then you came in with your Whole Foods bags, started unloading, and really interrupted my flow. Why?" Be curious when you confront. The apology, the totally reasonable response, and the solution to make it work better next time is always available.

This is how a Queen makes confrontation a total win-win for everyone. That's alliance in its glory.

SPEAKING THE TRUTH IN LOVE

Like every other element of Queenhood, our communication is always in pursuit of the double blessing. Having the courage to speak our truth no matter what others think of us doesn't mean we don't consider other people.

The Ghost, the Sweet Talker, and the Bitch are the ones who grew up in a fear-based culture where someone always wins and someone always loses. Queens know better. Compassion for ourselves and others flows naturally when we remember that with God, a solution for all is always available. We see our own needs and desires, and we know how to make them visible without having to show our teeth.

Communication affects every relationship in our lives, not only with people but with God, ourselves, and, for so many of us these days, our audiences. Most of us go about our interactions, and especially our interior thoughts, without really considering the words we are saying, or not saying, and the powerful meanings they carry. Choosing language in alliance with what we seek to create in the world is one of the most powerful tools at our disposal.

The more you function from the core belief that everyone has a perspective and everyone matters (including you), explore powerful solutions from a place of love, and move yourself energetically into alliance with Spirit, yourself, and others, the less you'll slip into defiance and compliance. In remembering your place in a benevolent Universe, you'll feel safe enough to find your authentic voice. In that deep level of spiritual security, Queenly communication with others becomes second nature.

Wherever you're at in your journey of mastering communication in any area of your life, be gentle with yourself. Like any new skill, speaking up for yourself and others can be learned and must be practiced. Commit to being conscious and communicating like a Queen, and you will find the voice that is most kind, honest, authentic, and unapologetically you. Developing this skill happens one prayer, journal entry, dinner order, email to your coworker, and conversation with your beloved at a time.

Imagine never again feeling afraid to speak up, set a boundary, or state your point of view. Envision being so aligned with every word that you speak that your energy behind it is totally real, authentic, and clean. With a big part to play in this world, you are meant to be seen and your voice is meant to be heard. The age of invisible women is over.

HOW TO COMMUNICATE LIKE A QUEEN

- Make sure your voice is heard first by you, then by others.
- Let your yes be yes and your no be no.
- Always strive for the win–win and remember that a solution exists.
- When the tendency arises to go into Ghost, Sweet Talker, or Bitch mode, ask for guidance to instead be the Queen.

Dear God,

In this situation, please show me how I can communicate your message. I know there's a better option available than allowing myself to become invisible or to shame another. Please show me how I can speak up, ask for what

I desire, and achieve my intention without diminishing myself or the receiver. Please help me transform from my current fearful state to instead being excited to speak up with power and grace, feeling confident once again that my voice matters, to speak the truth in love, and to be completely available to navigate difficult terrains that may arise. In this moment, I pray that you please help me be the Queen that I am. Amen.

eleven

THE END TO CRAZYMAKING

Excuse me while I brush the ashes of my self-combustible thoughts off my body. I've had a rough couple of days. I got triggered and my emotions erupted on me in a big way. I'm just now collecting myself as I crawl back from a level of patheticness I'd rather forget I plummeted to.

I didn't see this coming. Especially not with this team member. She's loyal, dedicated, smart, hardworking, and fun to be around, and she always goes the extra mile. In short, she's all-around fabulous.

We had recently arrived in Sydney with our highest-level group of clients. Though we've traveled together on many work trips over the years, some of the dynamics at this event were different. Granted, she performed all of her tasks, including handling the behind-the-scenes logistics, working with our hotel liaison to make sure everything was ready for when our guests arrived, and posting pictures of our clients on social media, at the incredibly high level she always does. However, this time, my *perception* was that she repeatedly blurred the lines with our clients. In my company, we have a policy of being "friendly, but not friends" with our participants, and on more than a handful of occasions on this particular trip I saw her, in my opinion, getting too chummy with the attendees.

My antenna went up in irritation. After not addressing the issue the first or second time, I did the classic thing so many women do. I became possessed by the Ghost and didn't speak up about my preference regarding her client interaction because I didn't want *her* to feel uncomfortable. Queen mistake number one. Isn't it crazy what we women do? We torture *ourselves* as if a solution for everyone to get their needs met doesn't exist, because we can't bear upsetting someone else.

Then, as easily happens with triggers when they are not immediately resolved, I let my thoughts escalate into *Paranoid Gangster* territory. You see, a Queen will never steer you wrong. A Queen is untriggerable. However, the Paranoid Gangster lives for the drama of the trigger. This archetype shows up at our deepest emotional vulnerability, assumes we're under serious threat, and ultimately leaves us groveling for our crowns.

Seeing this assistant continue to schmooze with my clients triggered me to turn her from superstar to supervillain. Underneath my forced smile, I saw my aggravated thoughts heat up into anger.

Self-aware and annoyed with myself, I thought, "Really, Gina? *This* is how you're responding?" Then I decided that everything I was thinking was completely wrong, believing I was being the Bitch, too rigid and overreacting. Feeling horrible about my inner monologue, I self-abandoned, negated my own experience, and silently stuffed my emotions away. Little did I know, my thoughts were just getting started to rev up into a cyclone of trigger-fury.

My mighty mind started flipping through all the past negative experiences I had with former team members who developed close relationships with my clients and then ended up leaving, often sneakily taking some of them. Having worked so hard and invested so much time and expertise to both train team members and attract ideal clients, this always felt like the ultimate business betrayal, and it was always an expensive hit too.

"Whatever," I told myself. "Just get over it, Gina." After all, the trip Down Under would only last a few more days, and then I could fly home and leave this bothersome matter behind. Easier said than done. Because I hadn't resolved the situation, I returned to the States with the Paranoid Gangster still lurking around quietly in the dark corners of my mind.

What you resist persists. Since we live in an abundantly kind and loving Universe, and because I failed the first eighty-nine opportunities to be a Queen in this situation, I was provided with *another* chance to go around this confrontation mountain, aka grow up.

Now home and scrolling through social media with the Paranoid Gangster living rent-free in my thoughts, I saw this same assistant posting selfies she had taken on the trip to Oz *with* my high-level clients. Ugh.

I pushed my feelings aside once more until the final blow. She submitted the latest mock-up of our company's upcoming newsletter to my inbox for approval, featuring herself with a picture that was linked to her *personal* social media profile! In *my company newsletter*!

I blew a gasket. Seeing red was an understatement. Someone sound the buzzers for immediate emergency evacuation because I was now triggered in a Kim Jong-un kind of way. Rage. Anger. Resentment. And once again, my past betrayals swirled to the surface. "Who does she think she is?!" Adrenal explosions were going off left, right, and center. My nervous system was on full-kilter spastic mode, and any grip I ever had on my Queenhood was gone.

Now, to give myself a morsel of credit, that's not entirely true. In the past, I would have instantly gone full Sicilian mobster, picked up the phone, and started slicing, judging, and doing irreparable damage that would lead to making arrangements for the next "I quit" funeral.

Instead, I had enough emotional maturity to vent to my husband first. He, per usual, told me to calm down (which always makes me angrier). Instead I ranted to him that I had looked at this situation from every perspective and every angle (note to self, neither exists), and that she *must* be setting herself up to leave and take my clients like all the others had done in the past.

Not buying my sales pitch even one little bit, he gave me some Kingly advice, which thank God I actually followed. He suggested that I ask her *why* (novel idea) she featured herself in the company newsletter.

I thought, "Men are so naïve. I don't need to ask, I *know* why. She's building her platform and positioning herself to take my clients!"

However, through the years, I have been triggered enough times and learned enough lessons about jumping to conclusions the hard way that I realized that asking someone *why* they did something is, like Paris, always a good idea.

Working really hard to be somewhat coachable and walk my talk, I was still too angry to speak, so I quickly shot off an email. "Hey! I'm curious as to why you featured yourself in the company newsletter this week?" Without missing a beat, completely neutral, she immediately emailed me back, "Actually, I didn't, the graphics team did, and I just wanted to see what you thought of it. I'm more than happy to remove it!"

Oh. My. Gawd. The Paranoid Gangster had gotten it wrong. Again. Turning me into the ugliest version of myself, ruining my quality of life, almost destroying my relationship with my A+

team member, and making this situation seem so real when in reality none of it was true.

All I could do was stare at her innocent "happy to help" email in disbelief. She had no malice, no game playing, no manipulation, and no evil client-stealing agenda. And just like that, when the truth was revealed, the negative energy dissipated.

What did I learn? When the Paranoid Gangster self-manufactures pain, the damage is real. For a week I had been spinning on something that didn't even exist. I put my body, my nervous system, and my husband through an obscene level of unnecessary stress. I unfairly judged someone who had nothing but my best interest at heart.

As Queens, we have an opportunity to know ourselves well and be spiritually centered, so that we're able to respond rather than react to situations. Great decisions don't happen when you're in a state of trigger. And it's hard, if not impossible, to hear Divine Guidance over the Paranoid Gangster's suspicious gossip. This neurotic character shows up because we've been conditioned to believe that our only option is to be either the victim or the villain. We think we don't have a choice and things are just happening *to* us.

So let's set you up to be untriggerable. As a creator and a Queen, you always have a choice. From this feminine position you are capable of knowing the right response at the right time, and you have the ability to make excellent decisions for yourself.

Here's your opportunity to learn how to never let your Paranoid Gangster hijack another situation. And if she does come around stirring up trouble, you'll know how to push your shoulders back, oust her, and handle it like a Queen.

Becoming Untriggerable

AN EXERCISE

Step 1: Know thyself and where thy triggers come from

Triggers are unconscious reminders of past pain, and at some point, we were conditioned to develop a default response to shield those wounded places. Becoming aware of your own patterns of what your triggers are is the first step to being able to control your mind and master your emotions.

For some women, emotional upset triggers our defiant side with anger, rage, criticism, judgment, bridge burning, or domineering and punitive measures, to name a few. Women on the compliant side collapse into despair, guilt, anxiety, embarrassment, and an overall hopeless sense of "I can't have what I want." And in case you think the Paranoid Gangster is only for the defiant ones, remember that tantrums and tears can also be weapons of emotional mass destruction. Crying may look like weakness, and yet how many little girls learn that's the best way to get the toy they want? How many grown women feel that releasing the waterworks is the only way to get their partner's sympathy or their boss's attention?

Whether your Paranoid Gangster prefers to elicit pity or throw a punch, take a look at what situations trigger you into compliance or defiance as you jump to conclusions. Think about the last time you had a meltdown or a freak-out. What past betrayals, disappointments, and perceived failures swirled to the surface? Abandonment? Being made to feel wrong? Authority issues? Boundary busting? Not belonging? Feeling easily dismissable? Not good enough? There are only so many scripts out there.

Behind every triggered drama is a painful memory. Like that time your dad didn't show up for your fifth birthday party, leaving you to feel abandoned by men. So now, when your new beau doesn't text you back within fifteen minutes, you spiral into thinking he's lost interest, doesn't care about you, or has suddenly met someone else. "Men can't be trusted," the Paranoid Gangster confirms. And if you're not in check, she might even steal your phone and send him a slew of accusatory messages, ruining the relationship before it even had a chance.

Or if your biggest triggers are rejections and failures, this could be traced back to that summer at camp when you auditioned for the choir solo eight times and never got it, causing you to forever believe you don't have what it takes to achieve your dreams. (True story.) Perhaps now in adulthood, hearing no a few too many times immediately takes you out of the game with a tragically unnecessary detour of "it's never going to happen for me."

Once you're aware of these sore spots, you can program your brain to receive what used to be triggering events neutrally. Developing the belief that your good is consistently coming to you, and that as a Queen, you are worthy, capable, and always taken care of, is the core of being untriggerable.

Step 2: Take radical responsibility in all matters

The fastest way to get out of trigger is always, always, *always* to own your part. It's how you empower yourself. You don't need to take on other people's issues, but you do need to take responsibility for your own. This involves taking an honest (and at times very humbling) look at what you did to co-create this situation.

I know. This is when the Paranoid Gangster starts screaming, *"Nothing! I did nothing! It's all their fault!"*

Ahem. Please summon your Queen. Her honest assessment will empower you to feel safe to own your part even when you haven't done everything right. The story I shared about my trip to Sydney gave me a number of opportunities to take personal responsibility that were empowering.

First, I saw that I had never formally sat down with my rock star assistant and explicitly trained her on my preferences for how to interact with clients at this specific event. I realized that I was expecting her to read my mind as to what I did and didn't want to happen. What I judged as getting "too chummy" with the event participants, she had seen as "doing her job" and taking excellent care of our top clients on behalf of our company.

If you expect people to be masters in telepathy, you're going to be disappointed on a regular basis. As a Queen, you clearly communicate your expectations, and if you expect people to "just get it," you've set yourself up for defeat.

Personally I'm obsessed with this step because it shows me where there was an unconscious weak link in my life. And every time a link is strengthened, I get stronger. A lot of people think taking personal responsibility means focusing on where they weren't good enough, which makes them beat themselves up and feel even worse. Instead, use it as an opportunity to discover new solutions. Once a solution is put into place, you no longer have to combust over the same old trigger. This is how a Queen sets everyone up for continuous growth.

Step 3: Believe the best in others

No relatively conscious person wakes up saying, "I'd like to use the worst judgment possible today." No healthy person spends their time scheming, "How can I harm or take advantage of someone else?" while saying to themselves, "I'd like to speak in the most shaming, terrorizing way possible." The truth of who you are is what's also true in others. At our core, we all desire to love and be loved.

Whatever hurtful triggers surface, a Queen always gives the benefit of the doubt first. Assuming the best in others is kryptonite for your Paranoid Gangster. It stops the suspicious archetype from jumping to conclusions and taking over with a sinister view of reality. It keeps you aligned with the truth, which opens you up to receive new ideas that lead to the best outcome for everyone involved.

Step 4: Avoid shaming confrontation

There are two kinds of confrontation: healthy and shaming. When it comes to conflicts, most of us have been modeled communication that either shames ourselves or shames the other person. Because we're in fear, any possible "threat" sets off a downward spiral wherein we then think the only way to protect ourselves is to tear others down. The way to avoid it is to condition yourself that you can be there for yourself *and* confront others in a healthy way that leads to a powerful resolution.

For the most part, we've been conditioned to believe every action is either "right" or "wrong," with no in-between. And the wrong must be made to suffer with shaming confrontation: "What were you thinking!? Why do you still not get it? We've already discussed this." Or it can be more subtly disparaging, like "That's not how it's done. Do I need to just do it for you?" Ouch.

Healthy confrontation is possible. I've watched my husband communicate with other men. They are masters at confronting conflicts in the moment without letting resentment, trigger, or drama build up around it. Their implicit guy code has them directly state their issue without needing to ask for permission, dance around trying to be nice, or hit below the belt.

Since most men aren't interested in emotional theatrics, they stay focused on a quick resolution. A simple, "Hey, dude, why'd you do that?" leads to two mature men hashing it out, and ten minutes later, it's "Wanna grab a beer?" Women, on the other hand, haven't given themselves (or others) this same level of permission to honestly share their point of view, address the issues in the moment, and be done with it.

Due to our Injured Feminine Instinct, women stuck in compliance succumb to social expectations to "be nice," "be polite," "be accommodating," and definitely "never hurt anyone's feelings." Confrontation that might do otherwise is strictly forbidden, so the Ghost avoids speaking up altogether and goes into shutdown mode.

Meanwhile, the Bitch has shaming confrontation on speed dial. She's learned that the way to handle a trigger is to show her power with brutal or punitive communication. Assuming the worst of whoever set her off, she lets the Paranoid Gangster take her vendetta to the streets.

As you've probably experienced at least once in your life, this false sense of a power trip leads to nothing but an emotional mess and zero satisfaction. Relationships are blown to bits. Feelings are hurt both ways. All parties are left incomplete because no solution or resolution was ever created. In the end, nobody wins.

And that is not how a Queen does confrontation. Step 5 *is*.

Step 5: Be curious, not condemning

This one took me a while to get. Yet once you develop this skill you'll find it so liberating, easy, and empowering that you'll wonder why you ever defaulted to the lower-vibrational wording of the past.

Healthy confrontation starts with being *curious*, not condemning. I know it sounds almost too simple, but trust me, it's life-changing. Since you're assuming the best in the other person, choose to become genuinely interested in their perspective before letting the trigger set in. Release any prejudged energy of "I'm assuming you messed up again," and ask them, "I'm curious, why did you __?"

Make sure your mind isn't racing with defensive comebacks. Put yourself in the other person's shoes, really put them on. This will have you be *present* with them. Once you've heard their side (where I promise you'll learn tons), be visible by also sharing yours. Remember that *your voice matters, and so does the other person's*. You get to speak your truth. And you don't need to apologize for it. So do they. You both just need to communicate it in an empowering, loving way.

For me and my assistant, speaking my truth in love could have been communicated this way: "Thank you for doing such an amazing job handling your event tasks while also doing social media. In regard to the pictures, I'd prefer that our event photos only have clients in them, not mixed with team members." And since she is such a dedicated team member, I'm sure she would have responded with something like, "Of course! I'm sorry if this got mixed up this time, I was just trying to do what I thought you wanted. I will be sure to add this to our company procedures and make sure it doesn't happen again."

Boom! This would have *completely* resolved the predicament with zero emotional turmoil, pushback, or the need to summon the rage of a North Korean dictator. And just like that, we'd have two people communicating like conscious, considerate adults.

DEALING WITH DIFFICULT PEOPLE

Now, you may be thinking, "Okay, that's a great formula when you're communicating with a sane, loving, smart, and considerate individual. But how does this work for the manipulative, impossible, narcissistic person whose knack for dispensing black-widow-like venom is particularly poisonous to anyone with a remotely decent outlook on life?"

Glad you asked. Too often, because the Victim, the Martyr, or the Ghost has taken over, we feel like we're stuck with these toxic people and must learn to survive their nastiness. Society supports our list of excuses (particularly women's) for keeping these energy vampires around as we settle, convincing ourselves: "I have to have this person in my life because he's my child's father, she's my boss, it's my mother, it's my in-laws, he's not *all* bad, maybe I just need to give it more time, she's my daughter's partner, this coworker isn't going anywhere and I don't want to lose my job."

As a Queen, you *do* have a choice. You have the option of either changing your experience of the relationship, changing your proximity to the relationship, or even deciding whether you desire to have the relationship at all.

I've done the hard work of removing toxic, overly demanding, and dysfunctional people from my life because you can't apply logic to insanity. You can't expect a cat to bark, and you'd better not expect a narcissist to consider your needs and desires on a consistent basis. Healthy confrontation and curiosity will only work on people who are willing to grow and take responsibility.

The way out is to become truly unavailable to have unsafe, unsupportive, and unfun people in your life. Remember, the royal road is not an ordinary one. Setting these boundaries is not usually easy, and they may not even line up with what you've been taught are "good" values. It's up to you to reclaim your power and discover the solutions that will make you stronger.

HOW A QUEEN RESPONDS TO TOXIC PEOPLE

1. **Only own your part.** Assess if there is any truth to what's being said. Even if it doesn't feel good, own it. Whatever elements of the criticism or attack *are not yours*, do not take them on. This is easier said than done, but a Queen who's connected with Spirit has the ability to discern and refuse to engage in someone else's trigger.

2. **What other people say about you is not your business.** None. Whether others are crazymakers or conscious civilians, for the untriggerable Queen, whatever story they create about her has zero power to knock her off the throne.

3. **Remove the toxic people from your life.** You can ask yourself, do you desire to spend one more moment of your precious life managing crazy, unsafe, toxic, unwell, or emotionally abusive people? It's time to set new boundaries. Regardless of whatever excuse comes up because of who this person is, remember a Queen always has a choice.

4. **Focus exclusively on the love and positivity you're committed to bringing forth in the world.** There are 7.8 billion people in the world. Surround yourself with good-hearted, smart, amazing people who uplift and inspire, and do the same for them.

THE TRIGGER-FREE QUEEN

It's up to feminine women like us to commit to speaking up, speaking out, and speaking the truth in love and change the culture of both invisibility and shame that we've succumbed to. If you condition yourself to have faith that you can always get your needs met in this loving Universe, you've created a profound foundation for a trigger-free life. We all have what it takes to share our perspectives with compassion for everyone involved. Together, we're creating a world where no one is right, no one is wrong, no one is invisible, and no bridge is burned. In the age of Queens, each of us matters.

twelve

THE SEXINESS OF CERTAINTY

Queens, of course, have confidence, but certainty is a whole 'nother realm of power. This high-vibrational state of being can be likened to an unwavering faith; it's a feminine quality, to have a clear vision for what does not currently exist and a deep *knowing* that in the spiritual realm it is already done.

The power of this rare mystical art is not of the intellect; it is of the divine. Certainty is the highest form of showing up for your dreams and your purpose—which, as we've discussed, is a "double blessing." Cultivate certainty and you'll become the star of your show! You'll see your life transform into your own personal J-Lo world tour complete with oversized feathers of fun, sparkly diamonds of success, hot backup dancers in support, gold glitter of abundance falling from the ceiling, and boas of love for all.

The only way to let our dazzling light shine so that we can inspire and move populations of people is to become certain of the inimitable women we are and the fabulous outcomes we're meant to manifest. Refusing to self-abandon is the missing link to guaranteeing success and happiness. It's the key to living the epic life.

Asking yourself "How good am I willing to let life get?" on a regular basis will support you in cultivating certainty as you co-create with the Universe. Every time you ask this question you'll be immediately connected with the loving and unlimited nature of God that is available to assist you in bringing forth your biggest dreams, and those beyond your wildest imagination, especially the ones you desire so badly and fear are out of your league.

Unless we *know* in every fiber of our beings that our dreams *can* and *will* be brought to fruition and that we *do* have what it takes to achieve our goals, we'll find ourselves perpetually wishing, wanting, procrastinating, and making excuses to no avail.

Certainty puts an end to any slouching, recoiling, apologizing, or acting like you desire anything less. "Who, me? What will people say? Is this too much? Can I dream that big?"

All of those fears, insecurities, and doubts get totally wiped out when you have the unshakable confidence that comes with being certain. It's how you defy the conventional wisdom to "go with the flow" that is secretly keeping your life from ever reaching a crescendo.

THE STATUS QUO OF GOING WITH THE FLOW

Between the constant barrage of advice, to-do lists, and instructions on how life "should be" done, it's not easy to know when to move with certainty in the direction of your desire and when to let it go and practice *non-attachment.*

Trying to become spiritually healthy can be as frustrating and confusing as trying to become physically healthy. First, you're told soy milk is good for you. Then a study comes out: Soy disrupts your thyroid function, so you should drink almond milk instead. Next thing you know, oat milk is the new goat milk? And what could be more mystifying than the perfect diet. Keto? Paleo? Vegan? What happened to South Beach? To carb or not to carb, that is the question.

Similarly, the lessons all the spiritual greats have taught can look equally perplexing and contradictory if you're not solid in your Queenhood. Have faith, believe in miracles, "seek first the kingdom of heaven and all of these *things* will be added unto you"... or wait, am I supposed to surrender, take a vow of poverty, and not focus on the material world?

We all have big dreams, but when manifesting them seems too difficult, many of us become uncertain, unconsciously misusing our faith as a spiritual bypass for not living our epic lives. We tell ourselves, "Well, since it didn't happen, I guess this wasn't God's plan." Our past neurological webbing is wired to hope for the best, prepare for the worst, and accept the chips wherever they may fall. We learn to tolerate what we perceive as fate with lukewarm disappointment or, at worst, tragic melodramatic dismay.

THE ROLLER COASTER RIDER

Without certainty, we experience the journey of going for our dreams as a series of neurotic and dramatic ups and downs. This is how the *Roller Coaster Rider* leaves you nauseous. One minute you're flying high, confident that it's all going to work out for you, proudly announcing "I'm going to double my rates!" The next, you've dropped into bottomless self-doubt, you've started avoiding your inbox like the plague, and you're too scared to even send the invoice! One month it's "I'm *only* going to date someone deserving of me!" The next, it's "Well... maybe I should give this relationship *one more* chance." July was off to a strong start with a promise of "I'm going to lose twenty pounds this month." Until your girlfriends invite you to brunch: "Bottomless mimosas can't be that harmful."

The low point of this wild ride shows up as self-abandonment. The minute it seems things aren't going according to plan, the only focus is on the first shred of evidence that your dream may not happen, filling your head with nothing but a worst-case scenario.

Suddenly your excitement is replaced with thoughts of "I obviously don't have what it takes. This is clearly not going to work out. Who was I to think it would? Let's please dream a little smaller next time so we don't suffer the humiliation of creating this mess again!" Giving up on what's possible, assuming it just "wasn't meant to be," you find yourself whirling around in circles, with the uncertainty and indecision stopping you from ever moving forward.

This wishy-washy, insecure energy keeps women riding the steep emotional slopes so they never get off the coaster to cross their goal off the accomplishment list. You don't get to be ambivalent and fearful and still manifest your dreams on a regular basis. If you're timidly working on your TED Talk and "hoping for the best," and another woman is certain she's going to get booked on the biggest stage, you'll be cast aside as she steps into the spiritual knowing you haven't fully claimed.

A Queen takes a higher level of responsibility for her life's outcomes. She is not on this planet just to put a quarter in the carnival machine and see what plastic prize pops out of the chute. She is here for a purpose. We all are. A Queen's dance through life is highly intentional. She is fearless in her calling and has the intact intuition to discern the difference between a passing craving and a Spirit-led, on-purpose desire. This is how, even when all external signs point to "it's not happening," a Queen is able to, against all odds, fulfill her destiny.

THE ELEVENTH-HOUR MIRACLE

It was November 2008. I was still struggling in my new business. My dining room table was still my desk. I was still more or less friendless. And I was definitely still dreaming that "one day," I'd have a big life.

To my credit, I was working on all of the above. There I was, at *another* self-improvement seminar for female entrepreneurs. Not there to find a business bestie, I sat nameless and faceless in the back of the room, planning to just get the information and leave.

Watching the established experts present onstage, I wished that would one day be my life. "That *should be me* up there!" I thought. I knew I was a talented speaker. I was positive I was meant to inspire, entertain, and empower others. As I imagined the title of my signature talk, the Roller Coaster Rider tapped me on the shoulder and whirled me into fear. Instantly, I was insecure of my own speaking ability and plummeting into "What would I talk about?" and "Hasn't it all been said?" With the perpetual "What if I'm not good enough?" story blaring full blast, I succumbed to the lie that I had lifetimes of more work to do before I could ever get on a stage.

This is the same lie that has convinced too many smart, talented, ready-to-go-now women that "you need to get one more certification, one more degree, one more year of practice, and *then* you'll be ready."

Intimidated, indecisive, and shrinking in the back row of the conference room, I checked in with what I was sure was my intuition, which told me, "Next year, Gina, maybe then you'll be ready to speak onstage." But this wasn't really my intuition at all. It was only my self-doubt stepping in with a spiritual bypass to avoid the fear.

This time, however, promising myself I'd do it later wasn't convincing enough to quiet my inner Queen, who spoke louder and louder the longer the seminar went on. And then, despite my conditioned insecurities, the Queen broke free and made sure I heard what the next speaker had to say loud and clear. Though he spoke for three hours, the only thing I remember from his talk was "You can have what you want, and you can have it now."

Ping! That one sentence changed my life and began a

conversation with my inner Queen on an entirely new level. "Why are you procrastinating on your dream of speaking?" my Queen asked. "You don't have to wait another year to speak onstage. You could be up there now." Ding, ding, ding! My true intuition was lighting up like the pyrotechnics at a J-Lo grand finale.

Right then and there, I decided to get off the roller coaster. I was going to host my first live event in January, only six weeks away. That was what I desired: to stop waiting for "one day" or thinking that I needed to do more or be more. I was ready to put an end to procrastination that kept me as the nameless, faceless woman in the back of way too many seminar rooms.

GOOD-BYE TO PLAN B

The opposite of procrastination is making a decision. The origin of the word *decision* comes from the Latin "to cut." When you decide, you cut off any form of backup plan. You've now created a new thought at a new vibration that requires a new level of support. "Ask and it is given." Spirit receives the royal memo of your desire and now works on your behalf to bring to you all manner of resources supporting the manifestation of your choice. This is how you turn a "want" into a "must" and make your main dream or desire happen, with certainty, *no matter what.*

In that moment, I bent space and time by taking the action to host my first seminar in six weeks instead of twelve months! Queens have no time to hesitate. There's only one epic life to live here, people!

Clear that my debut event's purpose was to gather and support female business owners on their way to seven figures (not stopped by the fact that I had only just crossed the six-figure line myself), I searched for the perfect venue. To be on brand for Divine Living, it had to be a beautiful location, sufficiently high-vibe to uplift and inspire these rising female millionaires who were naturally attracted to elegance and style. A little research and a couple of site visits later, I did what I'm sure most first-time speakers do. I booked the grand ballroom at the Luxe Hotel in Bel Air. And with all the certainty of my beginner's naïveté, I swiftly signed the contract to save the date on this 350-person-capacity space.

Putting the five-figure deposit on my credit card, I simply thought, "My first live event is going to be spectacular! All these fabulous women will show up and fill this beautiful room! They're going to realize what's possible for them! Their lives will be transformed!"

Even though I had a small mailing list per industry standards, I was *certain* that the room was going to be packed. Undaunted that this was January 2009, the stock market had just crashed, the housing bubble had just burst, Bernie Madoff had just made off with countless people's life savings, and all anyone could talk about was eating dinner at home to save money, I held on faithfully to my big dream.

Having just learned that "thoughts are things" about ten minutes prior, and that I have the power to create my reality, I chose not to participate energetically in the global economic crisis and instead maintained certainty in my vision. Completely unfazed by the fact that I had never pulled together more than twelve people for a workshop before, I was confident that I was being spiritually led and that this event was going to be a massive success.

Along with my daily mantras and visualizations, I took all the entrepreneurial actions I knew to do so that tickets would be sold out. All day, every day, and right on through the holidays, you could find me hustling behind my laptop, sending out tons of marketing emails, calling everyone in my cell phone, showing up at networking functions, and praying.

When ticket sales were off to a slow start in December, I assumed everyone was just on holiday break and come January the ticket purchases would roll in. I'm not sure what your definition of "rolling in" is; mine was hundreds of email "cha-ching" notifications. Ahem. Cough.

Two weeks before the event, I had *four* women from Los Angeles registered and *one* from Ohio. This was embarrassing. Crippling. Somewhat devastating. And definitely *very* expensive!

The Roller Coaster Rider showed up and had a lot to say about what was going to happen next. And she wasn't the only one crashing my certainty party. Things looked so bad that even my always supportive, constantly believing-in-me husband, Glenn, totally well-meaning and trying to protect me, said, "Gina, what is it that you need to see before you cancel this event? It's clearly not happening."

No, no, no, *no*! I refused to be dissuaded. My inner Queen kept the faith, stepped up, and declared, "It *is* happening. I'm *certain* of this vision." In my mind there was no going back on my decision. Not only was this clearly my truth and my calling, I had also signed a contract with the hotel, and a Queen honors her word. It would be against my integrity to cancel. And I mentioned expensive, right?

As I hustled to get the word out even more to the women whose lives would be transformed by attending this event, friends and potential clients offered feedback that amid all the economic turmoil, this just wasn't the "right time" to be spending extra money on event tickets. Persuasive, but still I knew the recession wasn't it.

SOLUTIONS COME FROM SPIRIT

Having "tried everything," I didn't know *what* I could be doing differently! So after the most anxious and sleepless night of my life, I prayed and meditated. Certain that there must be a solution, I asked for guidance and opened up to a higher realm of consciousness.

In my meditation, I received very specific, practical steps on how to manifest this vision. I was not guided to give up on my dream. I was guided to course-correct from my original filling-the-room strategy. First, I dropped the ticket price. Next, I reached out to ten influencers in my industry and invited them to speak onstage that day as well, asking that they each bring ten people. That would get me a hundred people in the room. Not entirely embarrassing optics!

My divinely inspired efforts began to snowball and tickets started to move. Every day, I kept at it. Fast-forward to the morning of the event. I'm in the greenroom at the hotel, hair and makeup done, earbuds in, gospel music on repeat pumping me up to get onstage (every Queen has a preshow ritual). My husband walks in at 9:20 a.m., twenty minutes past our listed start time, beaming. I look at the clock, wondering why he's late to get this show going.

"What's going on? Why aren't we starting?!" I frantically inquired.

"We have to wait a little longer," he said, peacefully. "There's a line of cars around the hotel, and the parking lot is backed up because so many women are trying to get in and take their seats!"

Don't tell the fire marshal, but 354 women showed up that day. And the vision I was certain of was fulfilled. As a Queen, I was living my dream. I gave myself permission to unleash G-Lo, my inner glamour girl, as I owned the stage. I spoke from my heart, inspired the audience, and facilitated coaching breakthrough sessions. Lives were transformed.

The double blessing of this unprecedented success? The feeling of euphoria and abundance that was instilled in this newly created community of women, at a time when this message of unlimited possibility was so desperately needed. The participants became best friends, quit dead-end jobs, and formed joint-venture partnerships. Given the permission to go for their big dreams and the tools to bend space and time, many got out of settling where it mattered to them most. A number of these driven women also stepped into opportunities to be mentored, signing up for my programs so I could support them in pursuing their goals.

With complete certainty in my own quantum leap, not only did I manifest my onstage vision much faster than I had originally thought possible, but that day I made more money than I had *the entire previous year.* The beauty of this was not just the digits in my bank account but the expanded ability to share my gifts and talents as a coach with dozens and dozens of new clients who were now claiming what was possible for them.

WHAT YOU CAN BE CERTAIN OF

Before anyone out there decides to cultivate certainty around meeting and marrying their celebrity crush in the Maldives, I'd like to distinguish what you do *and* don't get to be certain of. (This should clear up some of the questions on practicing nonattachment.) If you're calling in your soul mate, you get to be certain that a loving, trusting romantic relationship with the right partner exists. You don't get to control *who* your soul mate is.

Being fixated on any narrow set of attributes or individuals only blocks you from meeting your beloved. Trust that the Universe knows what qualities in the right person will best contribute to your growth and the most fulfilling romantic experience possible.

It's a similar principle in business. If you're a female entrepreneur or have a dream of a side hustle, you *do* get to be certain of making your revenue goals, filling your programs and events to capacity, or selling a specific amount of products. However, you *don't* get to control who your clients and customers will be, where they come from, or what they end up doing with your product or service.

If you're an artist, influencer, or leader of any kind, with almost eight billion people in the world, you *do* get to be certain that your audience already exists. The people who will be inspired and uplifted by your work are already out there, waiting for you to show up. Yet you *don't* get to dictate exactly which human beings will be your fans and followers. As Queens, we have great powers, but controlling people is not one of them.

How to Create Certainty

AN EXERCISE

Step 1: Decide on your desires

Once we get that our dreams matter, walking around saying we don't know what we want is emotional laziness. The truth is, you *do know* what's meant for you! You've just been burying your desires under a blanket of endless limiting beliefs that say "I can't" or "It's not possible." A Queen doesn't cower and hide under the covers. Clear on her desires, she unapologetically claims every single one of them and creates full certainty that they can and *will* happen. So your first step is to get honest about what your truth is.

Is it moving to a new country and starting fresh? Moving to the top of your Multi-Level Marketing upline? Qualifying in a fitness competition? Living on a boat in the Caribbean? Walking the red carpet at glamorous events in L.A. and London? Being interviewed in the media about your work? Choose one specific desire and bring it to mind. Feel it, visualize it, connect to the why behind it, and write it down by using the following prompts:

I desire to _____.
I am unapologetic about my desire for _____.
I am ready to fully embrace my truth about _____.

Step 2: Commit to a no-excuses policy

Now that you're clear on your desire, it's up to you to create your own no-excuses policy about it. You have to feel in every inch of your body and soul that you are going to make this happen *no matter what.*

Take a moment to write down all of the excuses that have already come to mind about your desire. "It's too expensive," "It's too big of a reach," "It's not practical," "I don't have the resources or connections to make it happen," "But who else is going to watch the kids, feed my husband, water my succulents, and fold the laundry?!" Whatever specific reasons your brain has for why it won't work, write them down.

Now, in your full power and passion about your desire, cross every single one of these out. Excuses can no longer exist. And you cannot be available to let any one of these lame reasons get in your way. Your new strategy is to ask, "Who else can help with this? How can this work?" Solutions come from Spirit; get them.

Step 3: Cancel your backup plan

Without action, a desire is merely a wish. Certainty comes with making a decision and taking an action that cancels out any possible "backup plan" of giving up, procrastinating, or settling. For me, booking the venue was the step that officially made my dream of speaking onstage in six weeks a "must," lifting me into the miraculous space of manifesting.

Consider this: What's it going to take for you to create a "no going back" situation, where you *must* be fully devoted to your goal? What one specific action can you take today that will put your dreams in motion and guarantee your success? Is it enrolling in a program? Putting down a deposit? Getting an accountability partner? Signing a lease? Listing your house on the market? Clicking the "public" button on your dating profile? Take the action that will weave your decision into reality now.

Step 4: Be available to course-correct

A Princess naïvely believes that no is final. A Queen understands that no means not yet. The gatekeepers and decision makers won't always get our vision or see our greatness initially. It's up to us to keep the faith and make any necessary adjustments. Just because the doors to one opportunity are closing doesn't mean our certainty won't come to fruition in some other way and with some other person or resource we do not yet see. This is where a Queen has the courage to ask herself (and Spirit) more intelligent questions like:

> What is another solution?
> What else can I do to manifest this?
> Spirit, how else would you use me to create this?
> Please show me another way.

Remember that Queen Esther took three days in prayer and fasting to receive her strategy. The solution always exists, even if a small (or large) pivot along the way is needed. Allow yourself to keep asking the better questions, meditating and asking Source for new answers whenever your first door begins to close.

Step 5: Know that the eleventh-hour miracle is there for you

Keeping your full certainty before the clock strikes twelve is not for the faint of heart. In most cases, it's actually much easier to quit before time runs out to save yourself and your dignity. But that's not what a Queen does. A Queen believes in the true power of her miracle, and she does not waver.

Through visualization, repetition, mantras, and conscious language, she trains her brain to believe at the deepest level that her dream is possible. To open up to receiving what she desires, she does not speak out loud or even to herself any word that goes against the full manifestation of her purpose. Not one. When we're connected to the miraculous realm, infinite possibility is our reality.

Revisit this exercise daily. The more you anchor into these truths, the more confidently you'll believe that your vision is meant for you.

In my story, remaining certain that a way to manifest my vision *was* available even when an entire culture of economic doubt (and only five ticket sales) tried to convince me otherwise, required a tremendous amount of faith, confidence, and dedication.

I didn't let myself get distracted by the naysayers or my own *what ifs*. I never thought about a plan B. This level of certainty didn't just randomly appear; I consciously created it. I made the decision, cultivated the belief, and nurtured it and strengthened it daily. And this opportunity is available 24/7 for you too.

THE QUEEN OF CERTAINTY

Certainty is a skill set that every legend and icon has developed. It's how the greats made their masterpieces. Success has never been about being smarter or more talented. It's about being *certain* in one's singular mission. Certainty gives us that added spark and fervor that makes us unstoppable! Even if we don't know exactly how our vision will come to life, we know that with Spirit, a solution is always available.

As Einstein is understood to have said, "We cannot solve our problems with the same thinking we used when we created them." In other words, the neurological pathways we've gotten used to and the habitual thinking that worked for us in the past aren't going to take us to the next level. A higher consciousness is required. With the spiritual realm always a thought away, certainty puts you in a league of your own. Hire security and get out your sparkly bodysuits. Cue the spotlight and turn on the smoke machines. Moving forward, you get to claim every last detail of *your* sold-out world tour, down to the last feather boa. Queens have proven: You can have what you want, and you can have it now.

PART IV

The Fully
Financed Queen

thirteen

MANIFESTING A FINANCIAL MIRACLE

Money. It's the biggest story on the planet. Not only does every woman have a story, every woman has a "money story" too. Whether you're currently scraping by to pay your bills or trying to figure out which charity to donate your next million to, you may be surprised to uncover the countless ways that your life is influenced by your money story.

Growing up, I didn't know anyone who *didn't* have some sort of struggle or scarcity point of view regarding money. Every family on the block lived paycheck to paycheck, so I thought stressing about finances was the norm. Among the members of my church and neighbors in our subdivision, certain ideas were accepted as fact. "Money doesn't grow on trees. You have to work *really* hard for it. You must stretch every dollar. And *obviously* one doesn't go grocery shopping unless it's triple-coupon Sunday."

From a young age, I didn't realize how these stories and all their contradictions were being ingrained in my subconscious. On the one hand, I saw that money was good. It helped my parents pay their bills, provide a nice home for us, and take us out to dinner for special occasions. Yet my religious upbringing somehow implied it was bad. "Don't make money your God, it's the root of all evil, give what you have to the poor." And in society, I learned "Don't talk about money, don't focus on money, and downplay your fine things so people don't get jealous."

Like all conditioned beliefs, money stories are pretty much formed by age seven. So by the time second grade rolls around, most children's financial worldview is already set. That's a lot to process before you've even learned cursive!

As I became an adult entering the professional world, my finances confirmed my little-girl beliefs that money was mysterious. Invisible. Hard to get and stressful. And yet it was a key ingredient I needed not only to survive but to thrive. The only thing more frustrating and excruciating than not having it was the fact that I was working seventy-five hours a week and still earning less than enough.

My money story was programmed and affirmed: No matter how much I earned, it all went to bills, taxes, credit card minimums, and student loans. My battle with my bank account (plus the semi-regular insufficient funds fees) robbed me of any sense of freedom, quality of life, confidence, and the ability to live my purpose. I felt imprisoned. Every decision I made was constricted by my love-hate relationship with money. Every reason I couldn't do something I desired boiled down to a lack of financial power.

THE MONEY SLAVE GIRL

As we've discussed, archetypes are meant to be used symbolically, to illustrate our internal belief systems through character studies. The *Money Slave Girl* is not meant to have any historical or cultural meaning in this book. In my work around the world, I have found when a woman feels a complete absence of choice, as though she's chronically forced to overwork and underearn, that she must obey money's cold, hard, demanding rules and "just be happy" living off whatever financial crumbs she's thrown, this is what life looks like when the Money Slave Girl is running the show. It's important to note that "financial crumbs" are relative. For me, as a budding life coach *extraordinaire* in Santa Monica, $2,000 a month was scraping by and just meeting my needs; for other women, depending on where they live and what their circumstances are, that could be a life-changing amount of money. I also know many seven-figure earners who are engulfed by this archetype, chronically overworking, always stressed about their bills and fretting that there is never enough for their desires. The point is, the Money Slave Girl is a conditioned mentality that becomes your reality regardless of how many zeros are involved.

In the professional sphere, becoming a "slave" to the company you work for or to your own business can be obvious. Yet this archetype is often the mentality for creatives and service providers too—graphic designers, stylists, caterers, writers—who are always willing to make a deal, undermining their worth. And then there are those in the healing professions, like chiropractors, counselors, physical therapists, and nurse practitioners. Maxed out at their hourly rate, they think the only way to make more money is to take on extra clients outside the clinic, after work, or on weekends.

As an additional crushing blow, a woman in Money Slave Girl conditioning is constantly punished for not having more money. How so? Smart intelligent women are *expected* to have a padded savings account, pay our bills on time, dress on trend, keep the fridge stocked with organic free-range grass-fed whatever, have a monthly membership at the latest all-the-rage spin studio, donate to charities, drive the Alfa Romeo (okay, maybe this one is more of a desire than an expectation), and afford our kids' Baby Einstein extracurricular activities. So even though we're working ourselves to the bone, we're totally ashamed for falling short of society's standards for a decent human being. The feeling of "never enough" is so all-encompassing that there is no end to the high or low levels of "never enough" in sight.

With my Money Slave Girl setting the four-digit pin to my debit card, I felt so discouraged and defeated that I tried to avoid money altogether. But what I *couldn't* avoid was how directly it linked to the epic life I desired. The beautiful home I'd love to live in if I could one day move out of my parents' house, the ability to travel somewhere glamorous like Paris (or at that point even Pittsburgh would've been nice), to give to causes I care about, and to be generous with friends and family would all take cash I was getting no closer to having.

Can you relate? Have you ever felt that awful feeling of wanting so badly to give someone a meaningful gift or attend a loved one's special day but being too maxed out to do so? When I was in Money Slave Girl mode, my mantra was "I'd love to, but I don't have the money." Embarrassingly, I had to RSVP *no* to my cousin's wedding in Iowa because the $200 plane ticket was too expensive. In fact, every time a friend was getting married I would dread it, cringing as I checked off the cheapest item on the registry, which was *always* the salt and pepper shaker set.

WEALTH CONSCIOUSNESS 101

We are going all the way back to the beginning of my career, a few years before my miraculous debut speaking event in Bel Air from the previous chapter. In fact, I was still living in Detroit when I decided enough was enough. I was done having everything in my life be dictated by an absence of money. I didn't know how to transform this lingering lack yet, but I was determined to make it happen. From buying the Suze Orman books that told me to save my latte money to getting an accountability partner and trying to "live within my means," I was on a mission. I knew there had to be a better, more pleasurable way to enjoy life, and I was going to find it.

After a year of taking on extra therapy clients and hosting Esther Experience workshops on the weekends, I saved up enough to move out of my parents' house and relocate to Los Angeles. Along the way, I stumbled upon a topic I'd never heard of: *wealth consciousness*.

More than money management, wealth consciousness is the psychology of manifesting financial abundance. *Huh? Tell me more.* As I slowly picked up a book here and a life-changing audio program there, this new mindset helped me build up the courage to finally leave behind my Money Slave Girl identity that came in the form of being a "struggling psychotherapist" who always offered "sliding scale rates." Then, a few Tony Robbins *Hour of Power* cassette tapes later, I declared myself a life coach *extraordinaire* and started selling packages in the land of beautiful and wealthy people.

As the Universe perfectly designed, through a friend I soon met another life coach with whom I had a lot in common. And I was amazed to discover that she was charging $15,000 for her packages, more than half my annual salary at that point! Knowing that I was equally talented and just as educated, I saw that the Money Slave Girl had me undervaluing myself. So I took to my journal, tapped into Divine Guidance, and mustered up the courage to create my own $6,000 package. Hey, it was a start.

My big leap was off to a stumble. I went from being consistently broke to being *neurotically* broke. Those $6,000 packages sound sexy, except when you only sell one every four to six months. Not so sexy.

Working hard to crack this brand-new "wealth consciousness" code, I still felt stuck playing the "how am I going to get my next client?" game. I was in feast-or-famine mode, never knowing when or how I would find the next person to work with. Something had to give.

Down to $100 in my bank account, with all credit resources exhausted, *I did not know what I was going to do.* I didn't have a single friend or family member I could ask for money. I felt depressed and prayed for a miracle. Since I had hardly any clients, all I had was time, so I sat in my tiny Santa Monica apartment reading every personal development book ever mentioned on *The Oprah Winfrey Show.* In the middle of Alice Miller's *The Drama of the Gifted Child,* the phone rang. A friend of a friend called and offered me a free ticket to a "business event" in Orange County. With zero appointments on my calendar for the foreseeable future, I just said yes.

I put $20 worth of gas into my car and drove down the coast. I had no idea what to expect. Apprehensively, I stepped inside the conference center and stopped at the registration table. I was handed my event materials, a three-ring binder, and a thin green book titled *The Science of Getting Rich.* I didn't know whether to be thrilled or horrified. However, from the basics I had learned thus far about this mysterious wealth consciousness subject, I was willing to give it a chance.

Not there to make friends, I timidly proceeded to sit in my favorite spot, the back row. Looking around, I noticed, "These people are *happy!*" Largely because I hadn't left my apartment in weeks, it had been a while since I'd seen live human beings smiling, laughing, and high-fiving. Feeling like a fly on the wall in a room full of people buzzing and hugging each other, looking like they were up to big things in the world, I started to remember what it was like to be *this* excited about life.

Intimidated, I kept to myself, flipping through the pages of my three-ring binder. I was sure the room couldn't be more lively until a slick, silver-haired gentleman in a three-piece suit walked onstage to raving applause and a standing ovation . . . *at nine a.m.*

Bob Proctor began his lecture. He started preaching about the book in my hands, *The Science of Getting Rich,* written over a hundred years ago by a man comically named Wallace D. Wattles. Internally, I was freaking out. As much as I wanted to learn how to make money, I had also been taught that pursuing wealth was unspiritual, so I was terrified that these teachings on "getting rich" would pull me away from my faith. Sitting there, arms crossed, questioning everything, I wasn't sure if this was for me. And then he said something that struck me like a lightning bolt.

"It is not possible to live a complete or successful life unless one is rich. No man can rise to his greatest possible height in talent or soul development unless he has plenty of money."

"Is he out of his mind? Did he really just say that out loud... from the stage?" were the last words my inner Money Slave Girl ever uttered.

That was the moment my soul heard what it had known all along. With the Money Slave Girl freed and my Queen back on the throne, I was finally given permission to be spiritual *and* wealthy. For the first time in my life, I understood deep down that answering my calling, offering my biggest impact, and living my best life *would* require money. Lots of it!

Suddenly, my yellow highlighter was out and I was working in turbo mode. I was taking notes with underlines and soaking it all up. I learned that successful spiritual people see the world according to a different set of universal laws. One that proves almost everything I had been taught about money was false.

As Wattles puts it, "Every person naturally wants to become all that they are capable of becoming; this desire to realize innate possibilities is inherent in human nature; we cannot help wanting to be all that we can be. The desire for riches is really the desire for a richer, fuller, and more abundant life; and that desire is praiseworthy."

Mic drop! My mind was instantly opening up to mega possibilities. No one had ever told me that there's more than enough money in the world *for everyone*. Or that my desire for more money is connected to my desire for more growth. This was all about expansion! Of course, moral values must be applied, but now I finally got that there is also nothing spiritual about lack. Money in and of itself isn't bad and wrong, it's all about how we generate it and use it.

I realized, "Why have I been trying so hard to live on two thousand dollars a month when that's not even what I desire to learn how to do! I'd much rather live by what these universal laws are teaching me!"

This was the beginning of my money story transformation. In that moment, all the contradictions I grew up with fell away, and in their place I found the simple, loving, spiritual truth about an unlimited resource that Spirit gives generously to help us live our purpose.

Money Truth #1: Money Is Infinite

The first mind-blowing new truth I learned is that there's no limit to the amount of money, energy, or creativity in the world. Abundance is simply always there, always flowing and always available. You making more money doesn't mean there's less for someone else, contrary to what most of us have been taught. For example, if I make more money in my business, that doesn't mean that the restaurant owner in Seattle can't also make more money in her business. Because you get a promotion doesn't mean your coworker who wasn't chosen isn't able to find the successful path that's right for her.

Yes, money is unevenly distributed in most of the world, and yet, as women who care deeply about our planet and its people, we do not contribute to equality by actively denying financial support to ourselves. There is much work to be done in the healing of the planet, and you definitely have a big part to play, which you can't very well do without an abundance of financial resources.

Money Truth #2: Money Is a Tool to Fund Your Dreams

People like to blame money for the problems in our world. They say that it's the cause of greed and evil, when in truth it's only humans who have the consciousness to apply meaning and purpose to what happens financially. Money is currency and currency is energy, and all energy is neutral. Just as water is good when you're thirsty and bad when your roof is leaking, money is good or bad depending on our intentions around it.

For a Queen, money is essential for you to fulfill your mission. You have the power to create and share money based on spiritual guidance, and you are worthy of receiving everything needed to answer your calling, including financial support. The more you create that positive association with wealth, the less you will block money from coming into your life, and the more open you will be to receiving.

Money Truth #3: Money Has a Vibration

Everything has an energetic vibration to it, including money. Remember that "thoughts are things" and "you get what you focus on," so if you're constantly worrying about a lack of cash, that will continue to be your reality. Choosing instead to focus on abundance, fulfilling your dreams, and being of bigger service in the world puts you in a high vibration that attracts money and energy like a magnet.

Money flows where there's a purpose. That's why making big money isn't about being smarter or more talented. It's also not necessarily about you working overly hard to get it. Yet it is about you being clear on who you are and what your purpose with it is, to make sure you are energetically open and available to receive the necessary funds. From that place of complete *certainty*, your actions will create the results you desire.

BACK TO THE SEMINAR ROOM...

Three hours later, my world turned upside down with these new money truths, I reached a profound place inside of myself. I made wealth consciousness a decision. So much so that it became the decision of *decisions*. I had always *wanted* to make more money, and I mean really, really, *really* wanted to. However, the vibration at this event was so high that it elevated me to make this decision from a place of "must" for the first time on this subject. I committed that *no matter what*, I would learn how to make money like my life depended on it. Because my life purpose did.

I declared, "I will *never* again struggle financially!" Even though I didn't know *how* at this point, I promised myself I'd never again say, "I would love to, but I don't have the money." I was ending that lame mantra here and now. I swore to never let the illusion of lack be an excuse keeping me from living my purpose again.

Later that day, the next speaker walked up onstage. She was a super-cool multimillion-dollar business owner running numerous companies. I *knew* that I had to be around her. There I was, hanging on her every word, and when it came time for her sales pitch at the end of her talk, I had already told myself, "Whatever she offers, I'm a *yes*! She is my next mentor! I'm totally doing this!"

And then she announced the price for her package: $17,000. "What the f***, who has seventeen thousand dollars?! And if you *did* have seventeen thousand dollars, why would you even need a coach?!" To my inner schoolteachers' kid from Detroit, this was an astronomical amount of money. And yet, thanks to my new commitment to myself, I decided, "It's okay, I'm a great negotiator. I'm Sicilian, we bargain for everything! We'll get this payment plan down, no worries." Clearly, my wealth consciousness was soaring, because I did not have a job or a Publishers Clearing House sweepstakes check on its way with which to ensure monthly payments.

Too committed to my new worldview to let any sticker shock stop me, I strutted up to her on the break and introduced myself.

"Hi! I'm Gina! I'm your next student, I'm going to be in your program, just one question—do you offer a payment plan?"

"No."

Gasp! You rich bitch! Help a sister out! I thought if she would just let me into her program for free, I would be a great client and I'd pay her back immediately when I made the money. Did she not recognize the star power within me?! What was there to be worried about? Think of the testimonial! This made complete logical sense to me. Apparently, not to her.

Still, three hours earlier I had promised myself that I would never say, "I'd love to, but I don't have the money" ever again.

With the verve of someone who just slammed three Red Bulls, I walked up to her assistant at the program enrollment booth and filled out the order form: first and last name, full address with zip code, and all sixteen digits of my debit card with the $80 bank balance.

"You give me two weeks before you run this card."

As if one quantum leap for the afternoon weren't enough, another electrifying speaker later pitched *her* $10,000 package that I *also* unmistakably knew was for me. I know you think I'm straight-up crazy at this point. Remember, God is outrageous and the feminine way doesn't bow to practicality or in this case even probability. Plus, a Queen is all about taking a stand for the *and*, and that was exactly what I did.

Leaving the seminar with two programs purchased (funding TBD), my three-ring binder under my right arm and *The Science of Getting Rich* under my left, I was ready to dive right in. I had just two weeks before the programs would start and my card would be run. Eminem's "Lose Yourself" was ringing in my head: "You only get one shot, do not miss your chance. This opportunity comes once in a lifetime."

With my recently borrowed *8 Mile* attitude, I was determined. I started reading my new wealth consciousness books daily, doing everything in my power to manifest the $30,000 to cover the new training and support that would guide me to my epic life. I had no idea where the clients and money would come from. I didn't even have a website or a mailing list at the time! I needed a financial miracle.

Following the teachings from the seminar, audibly over a hundred times a day I recited, "I see myself with thirty thousand dollars in two weeks. I see myself with thirty thousand dollars in two weeks. I feel myself with thirty thousand dollars, I'm so grateful to have thirty thousand dollars in my bank account in two weeks! I see myself being coached by these coaches, I see myself around people who are up to big things in the world, I see myself finally having a life!"

The days went by and I maintained full faith. The mantras and visualizations continued: "I see myself with thirty thousand dollars in one week, I see myself with thirty thousand dollars in five days, in four days..."

Down to three days, my then-boyfriend, now husband, could not believe I was still pacing around the apartment, proudly singing my mantra as if rehearsing for the half-time performance at the Super Bowl.

"Gina, what are we gonna do with you if—"

"*Shhhhhhhhhh!!*" I cut him off. "There will be *no* thought other than the complete and total manifestation of thirty thousand dollars into my bank account by the deadline!" I was unavailable for defeat.

Two days before the deadline, I was working with one of my three existing clients who had bought one of those $6,000 packages.

It was his last session on marriage coaching (I clearly wasn't doing any kind of business coaching at the time). And as we were completing the session he said, "Gina, this has been great, my marriage is better than ever, I totally got what I needed. And I've been thinking... I'm wondering about having you coach my sales team."

Huh? I thought. *This is out of left field.* Hoping to sound like an experienced businesswoman, I went with, "What do you sell?" Logical question... and I definitely wasn't expecting to hear the response...

"Basement waterproofing." *Thud.*

Can we take a moment to pause here? Seriously, Universe? Do I look like a basement waterproofing sales manager?! *This? This* is my big opportunity?!

I'm back now.

"Ahem... how many people are on your sales team?" I ask.

"Ten." I didn't know what else to say. This was so far out of my wheelhouse.

Thankfully he broke the silence first. "So, what do I do? Buy ten of those six-thousand-dollar packages of yours?"

"Yes. That's exactly what you do," I calmly replied, as if I closed this level of transaction daily.

What? Did this really just happen?

Yes, this is how a loving, benevolent Universe works when you are in alignment with your purpose.

And in two weeks, one day before my deadline, not $30,000, but $60,000 was deposited into my bank account. This is the way the Universe responds when you're in high vibration and have a specific purpose. I never could have predicted this. And yet it happened because I freed the Money Slave Girl and claimed that a financial miracle was available to me. It's available to you too.

Manifesting Your Money Miracle: The Steps I Took

Without a shadow of a doubt, you too have the full capability to manifest *your* own financial miracles. Wondering how? Here's what worked for me. Since success is about repetition, I followed many of the steps for cultivating certainty that we discussed in Chapter 12. Here's a recap:

- I got clear on my specific desire and the purpose behind it, and set a deadline for when it needed to be manifested by. ($30,000 for coaching programs that started in two weeks.)
- I created a no-excuses policy and turned it into a "must" versus a want. (I wouldn't let the price stop me from saying yes to my desire.)
- I took decisive action not to create the excuse of "I'll do it next year." I became committed that my desire would happen no matter what. (Handing over my debit card info and signing the program contracts.)
- I worked myself into a white heat by visualizing my goal being already done and feeling all of the incredible emotions it would bring. (Reciting my money mantras one hundred times a day.)
- I was open to receiving my eleventh-hour miracle, not knowing how it would happen. Never in my own consciousness (or wildest imagination) would I have had the idea to sell ten packages to one person; that's where faith in spiritual guidance comes in.

As a Queen, you have the power to manifest the money for anything you desire. And as you'll discover in the following chapters, it doesn't always have to be so directly career-related or results-oriented. Remember that money flows where there's a purpose, and feminine wisdom holds that pleasure, play, and meaningful experiences can also have a purpose in your soul's journey. Being specific about the *what*, *when*, and *why* is the key. When you decide, hypothetically, that you'd like to honor your relationship and celebrate your anniversary by embarking on the Belmond Grand Hibernian train through Ireland in October for five days during the oyster festival, the Universe knows exactly how to guide your steps. Once you've selected your on-purpose desire, write the following mantra down in your journal and allow yourself to fill in the blanks.

Miraculous Money Mantra

I see myself manifesting _____ of money. I see myself with _____ amount of money in my account. I see myself bringing in _____ by _____ date for the specific purpose of _____. I see myself doing _____, _____, and _____ with this amount of money. I feel the emotions of _____, _____, and _____ that the fulfillment of my desire will bring. I see myself offering _____ in exchange for this money. I am open to receiving ___ amount of money that I know is coming my way.

YOUR ROYAL RESOURCES

For the woman who craves growth, the desire for more comes naturally. That's who a Queen is and that's who *you* are too. It's not selfish for you to want more money. It's not greedy. It's not in and of itself "materialistic." It's your opportunity to act and contribute at a higher level.

Start living by the money truths in this chapter and your next financial miracle is closer than you'd think. You will understand in your bones that money actually *is* unlimited for you and everyone else. You will see yourself as a creator of money, capable of manifesting your desires and bringing abundance into the world. No longer will you sit on the sidelines living vicariously through others.

Your choices are between you and God. Allow Spirit to lead you, and you will never stress about money again. Step into your Queenhood, and you will find the most benevolent way to be in your finances. Cultivate exciting new habits and actions, combined with a fierce no-excuses policy, and you'll be booking your private cabin for your luxury train ride across the Emerald Isle sooner than you ever thought possible.

fourteen

ALL THE QUEENS ARE DOING IT

The age of Queen is now. And by now you've probably noticed, it takes money to be one. If financial abundance comes from Source who, by nature, generously gives, then our only responsibility is to ask and be available to receive. The key is thinking big and asking for *more than enough*. *A Course in Miracles* says, "Our problem is not that we ask God for too much, our problem is that we ask for too little." We are Queens. It's time we stop playing around with baby amounts of money.

There's a bold movement of women around the world who are no longer willing to entertain the old story that money is scarce. Women are wising up to the truth of wealth as our birthright. We know that we were never meant to sacrifice who we are, oppress ourselves, put a limit on our desires, or sell our souls to survive. In this bold new era, we've accepted that "for such a time as this" it is our calling to contribute our highest value as we become feminine leaders on the international stage.

The power of this movement is undeniable. Women now control nearly a third (some say more) of worldwide private wealth, and in the United States, we account for nearly half of household breadwinners. Globally, we're starting companies at twice the rate of men, and more of us believe in the importance of having a positive social impact through our businesses. Our rising influence is both collective and authoritative, as this century saw women at the helm of the U.S. Federal Reserve and the International Monetary Fund for the *first* time in history.

No matter what our outdated conditioning may say, clearly wealth is no longer only for men or the elite few who were born in the right place at the right time. Opportunities, resources, and abundance are becoming more and more available to the masses. Women are learning the *truth* about money at a revolutionary moment. Each of us is a media outlet with access to the global marketplace, whether that's from the boardroom in our Chanel suits, or from the bedroom on our laptops in our pajamas.

Women are redefining what it means to leave a legacy. Money doesn't have to be the biggest story on the planet any longer. And it certainly doesn't have to be the reason to *not* fulfill your purpose. Everything is transformable and that's why we're doing this deep work together. All women deserve to have a healthy and vibrant relationship with financial abundance. When one of us heals, we send a ripple effect into the world that inspires others to do the same. And this unstoppable tsunami of women claiming their worth and using wealth with benevolence, pleasure, and intention is exactly what the world needs.

WOMEN AND WEALTH

After transforming my own money story, I've since guided thousands of women on this journey and found that we have so much in common. If you've ever felt icky about asking for the promotion or the sale, this chapter will support you in getting great at receiving the money you deserve.

Or if what gets you squirming is the idea of hiring help, booking a business-class ticket for your important transatlantic meeting, or even reaching for the top-shelf wine, you'll no longer have to do mental somersaults to justify the expense of treating yourself like a Queen. And if you're just *finally* done spending every month in a panic because you don't know how you're going to make rent and you're over drowning in deprivation because no matter how many pennies you pinch, hardly a dent is made in your massive debt, keep reading.

As a Queen, one of the most powerful relationships you'll ever have is with money. Each of us has a relationship with our finances and until we've done the work on it, we all need a transformation in this department. Most people don't walk around thinking they have a "relationship" with money per se, and yet every day we do this dance with our wallets, our debt, our assets, our monthly bills, our bank account balance, and our earning potential. And the worst part is that we may not even realize how much our conditioning is choreographing our every move. Of course, this unconscious mindset is a major obstacle keeping us from playing a bigger game in the world.

Developing the wealth consciousness of a Queen will free you from patterns of underwhelming paychecks, late nights at the office with a tub of hummus as your dinner date, feeling guilty when you spend on yourself, being ashamed to admit what's going on with your credit, and all the rest. Across all income brackets, the woman who's about growth always has the opportunity to expand into a more conscious, healthier, and wealthier dynamic. Being available for the continuous up-level is what this movement of influential women is all about, and now it's your turn.

UPDATE YOUR MONEY RULES

Just like everything else in life, our ideas and views about money are a result of our conditioning. This includes all the beliefs we pick up from Mom and Dad, Grandma and Grandpa, teachers, religious leaders, the crossing guard, ice cream man, and all the other authority figures around us before age seven.

Closest to home, the way our parents earned, spent, and spoke about money modeled for us the "right" or "wrong" way to care for our cash, setting our beliefs in stone. It's why your brain signals the sweat to drip at the thought of signing the lease on the car, because Mom was always hesitant and indecisive about making a big financial commitment. Or maybe your fourth-grade teacher's high expectations made you feel like you're "not good at math," an identity that lingers today, keeping you from getting into the details of reconciling your bank statements.

Did your father proclaim, "Renting is throwing money out the window"? Is the result that most of every paycheck goes into buying a fixer-upper in the boonies complete with a two-hour commute, because it's the only place you can responsibly "afford" to live?

We've all fallen prey to what the adults around us dictated, landing us either in compliance or defiance when it comes to our money rules. As we become aware of our conditioning, many of us find that we've either become exactly like our parents, reenacting what was modeled financially, or grown determined to do the opposite of what we observed in our society and culture.

We've heard that "you must save every penny for retirement," we are admonished to "save your latte money," and we get the antiquated memo that "men handle the finances," but these outdated and impersonal rules have gone uninvestigated for way too long, and by the way, they're unnecessarily ruining our lives and limiting our influence. Fortunately, the conversation has evolved. Women are waking up to the understanding that these stories aren't ours. Letting them go for good, we're liberated to live life as Queens in our full glory and impact.

Pour yourself a glass of champagne; the corset strings on your money rules are about to loosen. Once you see how many women like us have been living by seventeenth-century norms and our ancestors' regulations, you'll get why your money story is as old as a hoop dress caught in the door of a horse-drawn carriage. And on the other side of these rusty beliefs, you'll be thrilled with the opportunity to design your own personal, empowered relationship with money, on twenty-first-century, feminine terms.

YOUR RELATIONSHIP WITH MONEY

Let's get this transformation started! Now, as fun as it is to play in the pool of personal development, taking a deep dive into our money patterns and becoming aware of our unconscious programming about earning and spending can be highly confronting. It requires a Queen dose of willingness and personal responsibility. Like any significant psychological operation, it's a serious procedure that requires great care—and urgency. A dysfunctional relationship with money robs us of our true lives and destroys our potential. That's why we're rushing this generation of women into the ER and surgically removing any trace of what I call the *Money Monster* archetypes stat so that you can join the wealthy woman movement.

These monsters responsible for our financial wounds have kept smart, capable women from playing big for long enough. Rest assured that their hold on you ends here, darling. To guide you in becoming aware of who they are so that you can recover fully from this lifesaving operation, I've broken down the top Money Monsters for you here. Most women I've worked with identify with more than one on the list on the following pages, so don't feel pressured to limit your level of woundedness. Having identified with 80 percent of these, I would know.

THE BIG THREE MONEY MONSTERS

The Abuser

I named them Money Monsters for a reason, and the *Abuser* is no different. Sadly, I understand this abusive dynamic with money only too well. Our heated romance was of the love-hate variety. I knew I desired money to afford my expenses and also to enjoy the finer things in life, so there was the love part. Then *bam!* I'd get hit with an overdraft fee. Slapped with a parking ticket. Any unexpected bill felt like blunt-force trauma, requiring paramedics to rush me to the financial emergency room. I'd be left in bandages feeling wounded and bruised, hating and avoiding money at all costs while desperately and secretly craving its support and attention. I so badly wanted it to be there for me as a trusted life partner. Then voilà, a paycheck would show up and I'd feel like "Wow, maybe money really does love me! Everybody has an off day, maybe I really can trust money again!"

I'd be back in the honeymoon stage for all of twenty-four hours, and then the phone would ring. It was the creditors calling to collect and *wham*, back to the ER.

I didn't realize I was the one unconsciously creating this endless cycle with my not-so-fabulous financial affairs. I thought I was doing everything right. The truth is, having a loving, supportive, and abundant relationship with money was something I knew nothing about. I thought it was *supposed* to be stressful. Hard. Crushing. That this was just "the way it was." The only people I assumed had it differently were celebrities, oil sheiks, and investment bankers, and since I was a psychotherapist, I held an unconscious belief that having a powerful and plentiful relationship with money was for *other* people and not me. I never challenged this notion and remained dutifully hope-addicted to the fantasy that somehow, "one day," my income bracket would change.

The Gambler

If your relationship with money feels as predictable as hitting triple sevens on a slot machine, you might identify more with the *Gambler*. You don't have to consider yourself a financial risk taker to have this Money Monster's all-or-nothing dynamic be a defining feature of your cash flow. I certainly didn't. And yet as I transitioned out of being a therapist, freed the Money Slave Girl, healed my Abuser monster, and raised my rates (I told you, ladies, it's a process!), the Gambler was the next archetype to show up for me.

The early days of my coaching business were total feast-or-famine. I'd go so long without bringing in new clients, I'd be fearful and starving financially. Then finally one program package would sell, and *boom*! The Gambler would urge me into feast mode, paying off bills, scheduling overdue teeth cleanings, and filling myself up wherever I had gone empty until the money dwindled back down to zilch, leaving me in a hunger once more. Like all hope addiction, this mindset swirls your life like a slot machine. You keep feeding it in hopes of winning big.

This excruciatingly stressful pattern is common with entrepreneurs, entertainers, sales professionals, real estate agents, and stockbrokers, just to name a few. Weeks and sometimes months go by without any money coming in. Then all of a sudden, a house is sold or a gig gets booked, and we're on top of the world once again! The Gambler takes over and is speedily putting upgrades and celebratory purchases on credit cards, because under no circumstances are they available to look like the underearning Money Slave Girl. "Life's short, buy the shoes," they think. And yet, when the mind is programmed for feast or famine, at some point the bank account drops down to nothing again.

Why does this unstable cycle keep repeating itself? Deep down, the Gambler, like all of these shadowy archetypes, has us fear that we're never going to get what we want. So they convince us to try to grab it all now, setting us up for mayhem later. (Sound familiar? Yes, the Gambler is in cahoots with the Saboteur.) Sometimes this conditioning has been modeled from a gambler or daredevil parent who lost it all and never recovered it. Other times, it's simply low wealth consciousness, thinking that our dreams are too expensive and there won't ever be enough, that blocks money from coming into our lives consistently.

The Frugal Fanatic

Although the Gambler's fear-based defiance causes much damage, there is also such a thing as being so overly responsible and tight that you lose touch with authentic spiritual guidance. That's where the *Frugal Fanatic* comes in. I've seen this Money Monster present with women who make $25,000 a year all the way up through women worth $250 million. I can't tell you the number of trust fund babies who are so proud of their Costco card they will announce over brunch at the country club that they got your wedding present there, on sale.

With plenty of anxiety and loving their money in the bank, the Frugal Fanatic will convince a woman she's being smart because she's doing everything "perfectly." She's bought her practical home, and it's the exact percentage of her income her financial advisor told her to spend. She's created color-coded Excel spreadsheets identifying and tracking how much of her paycheck is going into savings, investing, the kids' college fund, vet bills, the mortgage, and paying the plumber. Whatever money she earns is already allotted to these preordained obligations, where it remains untouchable to the nickel. No out-of-the-box expenditures, concerts, shopping trips, sporadic Sunday Funday splurges, opportune business investments, or impromptu weekends in Palm Springs allowed.

Turning us into human spreadsheets, wasting precious evening hours researching online endlessly just to get the best possible deal, the Frugal Fanatic blocks us from hearing our intuition, discovering our true desires, and developing our money-manifesting potential. Instead of enjoying the grander possibilities in the moment, we save everything for the retirement we assume we'll live long enough to experience. Although it's certainly wise and highly recommended to save, invest, and plan for future security, and a Queen of course knows where her money is at all times, being so tight and fear-based with our finances is to deny and deflect the flow of abundance. No matter how compelling the Frugal Fanatic's fantasy fiction, true power is not found in an annual return on investment, and pleasure shouldn't be squeezed into column Z of "if there's enough left." At the end of the day, there is no magic number that will quell this Money Monster's all-consuming sense of scarcity. Financial relaxation is a distant hope as long as the Frugal Fanatic's in charge.

ALL THE MONEY MONSTERS

You've likely spotted the Abuser, the Gambler, or the Frugal Fanatic at some point in your life, though it could be that one of these other archetypes has played a more prominent role in your story. Being honest with yourself about which of these you can relate to and why is the first step to removing them from your consciousness for good. Scalpel, please.

The Money Slave Girl

Willing to work endlessly hard for the basics, as if it is her only option.

The Avoidant Princess

Afraid to look at her finances, doesn't know how much she makes or what her expenses are.

The Dinosaur

Defers to men's or experts' permission on how to earn, invest, and spend money.

The Victim

Feels at the mercy of "outside forces," including penalties, broken agreements, and bad investments.

The Overextender

Feels vulnerable receiving, and thus is always overspending on others.

The Authoritarian Dictator

Lives by a rigid, punishing set of rules for how to interact with money.

The Sugar Baby

So used to being supported by others that she hasn't taken responsibility or given herself permission to earn.

The Trust Fund Baby

Depending on her family's money, feels locked in with their values.

The Diva

Entitled, gets easily frustrated when fantasy plans for making money fail.

The High-End Escort

Finds and stays in less-than-ideal jobs or relationships for money or perks.

The Martyr

Must sacrifice herself financially in the name of her cause or family.

The Saboteur

Afraid she won't get what she wants, blows up her credit or consistent employment.

Whichever archetype best describes *your* relationship with money, none of it is the real you or your truth speaking. It's all going on in your unconscious conditioning, and we are going to surgically remove that diseased thinking here and now.

It's intense. *I know.* It's humbling, eye-opening, and sad to see how we've let other people's programming take us so far away from the epic life the Universe designed for us. Some women, not yet ready to claim their full power and responsibility, will do a spiritual bypass at this point, not allowing themselves to feel the travesty that has played such a major role in this one precious life we've been given. Let yourself feel, *deeply*. Cry, get angry, hate the fact that you've been ripped off, misguided, and, perhaps even though it was well-meaning, lied to.

When I went through this process of awakening to what was actually going on, I felt devastated that I had wasted twelve years on the "unlived life"—time I'll never get back. I became aware that for over a decade my financial dysfunction robbed me of my birthright: to live freely, abundantly, and on purpose. I felt gutted.

Which is why today, I don't take one day for granted and live life to the fullest. I take radical responsibility over my thoughts and choices, especially when it comes to money. Knowing that I am the creator of my own experience, I use this life-changing realization to make sure my relationship with wealth remains as strong and healthy as possible.

WHEN WEALTH CONSCIOUSNESS CLICKS

When a smart, capable woman wakes up to what's possible financially and develops a close spiritual connection, there's no stopping her from fulfilling her Queen purpose. This movement is catching on with women around the world across a wide array of professions who are daring to transform their money stories and serve in a much bigger way.

Sydney-based executive Jessica was just twenty-six years old when she was already feeling the corporate burnout. Although she was seen as successful and most definitely on the prestigious path, she still felt boxed in and bored. She started wondering how else she could make a great living and comfortably support her dream of being a mom too. She wanted the freedom to live and work from anywhere she desired, the time to spend with her husband, and the meaningful fulfillment that came with helping others on a more personal basis.

In 2011, she had started running her own wellness blog and online health store in addition to holding down her successful corporate position when she found my startup business accelerator program. We realized that Jess, taken over by Little Miss Perfect, had a belief that she had to have a "good job," even if it didn't make her happy. Working on her wealth consciousness through the exercises and events in the program, she turned that mindset around 180 degrees and affirmed that she could in fact create real financial abundance doing what she loves. She took the leap, completed her corporate chapter, and dove full-time into launching her brand-new online business. In year one, she made $140,000 and traveled to Paris, L.A., and Miami. By year two, she doubled that and crossed Saint-Tropez, Tuscany, and Cabo off her bucket list. A few years later, she now has a seven-figure business, a highly ranked podcast, and a large virtual team, and she just bought her second home in Bali, where she, her husband, and her son now spend half of their time living.

You do not have to be a corporate career blazer to join this movement. It's for every woman. Emily was a twenty-eight-year-old nanny wondering when her real life was going to start. A Midwestern girl, she had a dream of getting a lifestyle brand off the ground, but thus far she hadn't made any money from it. What was stopping her? Deep down, we uncovered Emily's belief that coaching wasn't a "real career," that it was only a hobby and that she needed to have a steady job if she was going to make any sort of "real money." You could say her old-school money beliefs were running the show. Giving her mindset a twenty-first-century makeover, she was able to quickly come around and declare that creating content, consulting, and inspiring people is indeed a real profession. This changed everything for her. As I coached her on wealth consciousness, her perspective changed and her self-worth blossomed. She suddenly had new energy to take action on her dream business, and in her first month of offering services, she made $442. Every month from there her income went up exponentially, amounting to $500,000 in sales in her first year! She too proceeded to hit seven figures. I'm pretty sure the people she was nannying for weren't paying her this kind of "real money."

It's amazing what women discover about themselves when they update their money rules. Mel is one of hundreds of women I've seen take a completely new direction as they step into Queenhood and thrive. Mel was a personal trainer going door to door in New York City, working long hours just to bring in $1,500 a month. Mel was barely making her rent each month, let alone living any sort of glamorous lifestyle. She had already taken the leap of leaving her corporate management gig in Boston, which, though it paid better, also had Mel working sixteen-hour days. You could say she was used to the grind, and indeed, this small-town Idaho gal had a classic Money Slave Girl money story: We have to exhaust ourselves just to make ends meet. When I started working with Mel, transforming this story was one of our first big tasks. Mel created a vision of pleasurably creating wealth and found her new calling as a business coach. Her motivational, management, and sales skills took off as she owned her new sense of self-worth. Less than ninety days into my program, Mel had her first five-figure month and today, her business continues to soar so quickly I can't keep up with her latest stats.

Take it from Jessica, Emily, and Mel: Every woman has what it takes to create wealth on her own terms. You are strong enough to fully recover from this surgery and emerge more financially free than you ever thought possible. Transforming a money story is very personal and is meant to be individual and unique to you. We're about to get intimate and personal, putting your existing mindset under the microscope and finding your version of financial freedom. Get ready to remove any belief that is not serving you and transplant it with the money mindset of a Queen. They did it, and so can you.

You're Invited: Join the Wealthy Queens

AN EXERCISE

Step 1: Admit that money buys happiness

Where did we as women get the ridiculous notion that money doesn't buy happiness? It is all it actually does! Of course it doesn't buy *all* happiness. It doesn't take away the grief when you've lost a loved one, though it does buy you a plane ticket so you can be there for your family, and it doesn't eliminate the heartache after a breakup, but it sure is nice to be able to support yourself after a split and treat yourself to a "new you" cut and color at your favorite salon. Collectively, let's stop saying money doesn't buy happiness because the more we tell our brains that, the more we condition ourselves to repel rather than attract money.

Money buys all kinds of happiness. Don't you feel happy when you can pay your bills on time with complete relaxation? Aren't you thrilled to stroll through the grocery store and add whatever you fancy to your cart without needing a calculator? I cherish treating myself and the people I love with something special, and so do most women I know.

There's no longer any superiority in saying "I don't need money to be happy." Consider the astronomical numbers of people living in poverty; of course money would bring them more joy and happiness. And no need to deflect on them; remember that money is currency and currency is energy. When you get an influx of money's energy, it buys choices and it buys happiness. So let the abundance flow!

Step 2: Get clear on your limiting money beliefs

To get clear on your beliefs, it will help you to get your thoughts about money out of you and onto the page. We do this exercise at my live events and it's always liberating and revelatory for the women in the room. There are a few ways you can go about it. If you're the more linear type, I recommend that you write down on the left side of your journal all of your mother's beliefs about money. On the right side, do the same for your father's. Truth time. While looking at what you've just written, be honest with yourself about which ones you've been taking on and circle all that apply to you.

If you're more of the creative type, get out a piece of paper or poster board and select an archetype that you feel is primarily in charge of your money story. Close your eyes and ask that Money Monster to reveal itself to you, then draw out what you see. Next, ask it what message(s) it has for you. Draw or write out any words, feelings, or phrases that come to you. Do this for as many of the archetypes you feel would reveal any of your unsolved money mysteries.

If you're an overachiever, do both.

Step 3: Create the money mindset of a Queen

It's up to us to reprogram our minds to receive the experience of money that's right for us. Maybe you've had the belief that you have to work really hard for money and do things you don't like to get it. Replace that with the belief that you can be paid really well for doing what you love with pleasure. Say to yourself, "I have a great relationship with money, I am financially rewarded abundantly for my efforts, and I do not have to slave away or overwork for money."

If you have a belief that money is scarce and that no matter what you do you're always in lack, you can reprogram your mind with mantras of "There's always enough money and I live in financial abundance." Write these down, and make it your new daily commitment to recite or rewrite them ten times daily.

Step 4: Exit avoidance to clear your energy

Princess-style avoidance can be a major energetic block to transforming your money story. More subtly avoidant, if you don't know the balance on your credit cards, when payments are due, or how much exactly you make in a year, then you are living in a fantasy and the Universe cannot support your expansion, explaining why you've been feeling or sending out repellent vibes about money.

A Queen is never in avoidance about her finances. Calling in your Queen and finding out exactly how much you make, how much your expenses are, and how much your desires are will reboot your relationship with money from an energetically clean place.

Step 5: Make your own money rules

Now you're ready to get out of financial compliance or defiance and into alliance with money. A Queen lives by her own rules and values. Not her parents', not her social circle's, not her knitting club's, but hers. Just like a healthy relationship with food, she designs her own balance between doing what's best for her in the long term and enjoying her life in the present. Her decisions are wise and well-informed, not tight, fear-based, and austere. Her expenditures align with her own feminine spirit, not masculine rules of what's practical.

What's healthy for each of us at each season of our lives is different. One woman who was always told, "Don't waste money on rent" and discovers that the story about "wasted" cash is not her truth can make a new rule that says, "Renting is what's right for me right now and I'm comfortable with it." For another who heard, "You don't have what it takes and you won't be able to own a home," decided that wasn't true for her, and found that she did in fact desire home ownership, the new rule might be that she *does* have what it takes and will make it happen no matter what. And we've said a lot about the perils of making your savings account Source; however, a woman may also arrive at a place in her life where she joyfully and pleasurably adds to her retirement account, because that's what she's been guided to do.

It's exciting to be a woman who is taking time for herself to sit down and consciously choose what her money beliefs are. It also takes a lot of courage. There is no right or wrong way to do this. Close your eyes and say a prayer. Ask your Queen to guide you.

Step 6: Become financially untriggerable

A Queen doesn't make financial hits, disappointments, or losses mean she's a failure. I remember launching a $99 sales program that only five people bought. I was tempted to think this meant that nobody liked me, that I couldn't sell higher-priced programs, and that I should pack up and move to Cyprus already. But when I meditated on it, that wasn't the message I received. Instead, I was guided to offer private one-day intensives at the Ritz in Paris that had a significant five-figure price tag, and I sold out seven openings in five days. The Universe was conspiring on my behalf and guiding me to think bigger for myself; it wouldn't allow me to sell an info-product because I was meant to be changing lives with a high-end intensive offering.

No matter what unexpected bills or layoffs cross her path, a Queen remembers that everything is happening *for* her. When losses come, she knows she can absorb them. When higher-than-anticipated expenses come, she knows she can manifest the funds to meet them. If she doesn't get the promotion, she doesn't take that to mean she's not meant to succeed. Maybe she's meant to work at another company at an even higher level! Seeing her finances not as they are but as they could be is how a Queen stays open to receiving her next big success.

Step 7: Open up to the flow of abundance

We've talked about how developing your femininity will make you great at receiving; this is important to apply when it comes to financial abundance too. Everyone says they want more money, but when we're the ones feeling unworthy or uncomfortable, we cut ourselves off from receiving.

Open up to feel worthy of receiving the amount of money that's right for you. Wake up to the ways you may be unknowingly blocking yourself from the flow of abundance. Fear and doubt are common blocks. In my own journey, as long as I felt money was okay for other people but not me, I was too intimidated by wealth to receive it. I had to go into visualization and meditation to familiarize myself with what it would *feel* like to experience an abundance of money. Through practice, I became more excited than anxious about money, thus putting out a more open, attractive energy.

Holding this higher level of wealth consciousness is knowing that that there is no shortage of money and energy on the planet, and honoring that truth with your behaviors and actions. Once you've done your work, surrendering your finances to Spirit will have you feeling more confident, in control, and consistently taken care of than ever, regardless of how much you have in savings.

Lastly, cultivating active gratitude is necessary to being open to receive. If you don't appreciate what you're already receiving on a daily basis, the flow of abundance that's already coming your way gets squeezed to a trickle.

WEALTH IS FOR YOU

In the age of Queens, it is time for us women to give ourselves permission to make, earn, and spend on our *own* adult terms, according to our feminine values. Knowing that money is a resource that comes from Spirit, we trust that it's there to fund our purpose and our desires. Creating financial freedom is not so much about reaching any particular number, it's about the essence of money being supportive, consistent, and abundant.

Welcome to the movement with the most promise to change the world. Your Queen is already at the bank opening up a new account for your million-dollar mindset. She is also developing a personalized financial playbook and creating an unstoppable action plan for manifesting the moolah you deserve. It's your turn to recognize that you are a creator. Honor the truth about money and operate from a core belief that "there will always be enough." As you transform your money story into a beautiful, fun, and plentiful journey, creating financial miracles will become your new normal.

fifteen

MONEY SHAMING IS THE NEW WITCH BURNING

The plane tickets were booked. My dream was coming true! Finally, my then-boyfriend, now husband and I were going to Capri for a long overdue, true vacation. With my budding business off the ground, some money in the bank, and my first team member hired, I had finally been able to manifest the extra money to get to the motherland. I felt elated, researching every last detail, picking out a fabulous Renaissance-inspired hotel, reading about the best terrazzas for sea-view dining, and making plans for our daily scoop of gelato and evening strolls through the piazza. A week before takeoff, I realized I had forgotten something. It was something vastly important to my ultimate dream experience. Suddenly, all my prior excitement over our Amalfi Coast getaway was stained with a twinge of regret.

"What's wrong, Gina?" Glenn asked.

I was reluctant to reveal my truth. My disappointment was real, but so was this audacious desire. I revealed, "I made the money to cover all the bills of this vacation, but I haven't set aside any for shopping." *Cringe! Did I just say that out loud?!* I immediately felt engulfed with shame and shallowness for admitting it.

"How much money do you need to shop?" he asked.

"Twenty grand" poured out of my mouth faster than I could judge it as "too much." (Yes, I was shocked too.) I thought for sure he was going to sign me up for Shopaholics Anonymous right then and there. Instead, his reaction took me by surprise.

King as ever, without missing a beat, he said, "Then go make the twenty grand."

What? He made it sound so easy. Just go make twenty grand in one week. For *shopping.* Is that even legal?

"Okay, I can do that," I thought. "But wait...what if other people find out? Is it really okay to spend money this way? I know other women do this but is it actually allowed?"

I plummeted into a downward spiral imagining what the finger-wagging "responsible" onlookers in my industry would say. I thought of my clients, my audience, my family, and my mentors. I heard their voices echoing in horror and disgust: "Who does she think she is, dropping twenty thousand dollars at Valentino in Capri?" "How materialistic of her." "That's so selfish. How irresponsible!"

I could hardly contain the bottomless supply of judgments swirling to the surface. The more I considered them, the more sure I was that this would, in fact, be career suicide. "I'm supposed to be all about deep and meaningful topics like women's empowerment, spirituality, and personal development," I thought. "If I'm caught, will anyone ever hire me for transformational coaching and mentorship again?"

No, no. If I was going to do this, I had better keep it *top* secret. You would have thought I was about to mastermind an illegal *Ocean's Eleven*–caliber heist.

THE SECRET SPENDER STEPS IN

The *Secret Spender* had overtaken me. Internally, this archetype is a rebel, because nothing is going to stop her from spending money on what she wants. Sneaking around, hiding things, lying about where she's at or what she's bought, the Secret Spender prefers to mask her purchases at all costs. This typically has nothing to do with an overspending binge or buyer's remorse. This is straight-up "I want it, and I'll have it, and I don't want to tell others about it for fear of the judgment and criticism I will get from those who have a different opinion."

The rules for how a "good woman" earns, makes, and spends her money are no longer codified and legally enforced, and yet I knew my Capri shopping trip would entail breaking protocol within my "helping, healing" profession. Unless you're some sort of celebrity or kept woman, you don't spend that kind of money on yourself (and certainly not on your wardrobe). Maybe no one would lock me up or institutionalize me for my little spree, but the judgment? Who could bear it? Not me.

I had thrown all my weight into the world of psychology and spirituality, a community that deemed such material things "not important." If I were an editor at *Vogue* or an A-list actress, no one would bat an eye at my luxurious tastes or question my right to enjoy them. I wondered, "Why is it socially acceptable for a famous singer or a model to spend this amount on clothes, but not for a speaker, mentor, and women's empowerment coach?" Sure, I knew multimillionaires in my field of transformation, and trust me, they weren't wearing khakis from Target or flying in economy class. But none of them ever spoke about the Gucci silk blouses hanging in their closet, or how they all had private chefs managing their nutrition and drivers delivering them to their mansions. Not publicly, at least. In their teachings, financial abundance was discussed as a by-product of their devoted transformational work, not something anyone serious about being of service should aspire to achieve. Meanwhile, the few fashion-forward girlfriends I did have who would happily accompany me to Rodeo Drive would rather get their teeth whitened than hear about the life-changing breakthrough I got at therapy that week. I didn't see a single place where I could belong, where I could be *all* of me.

THE FEAR OF BEING TOO FABULOUS

Something deep was triggered inside me: the fear of the consequences of nonconformity. I pulled up the roots, finding traces of my ancestors (yes, we're going that far back). I knew very well that for so many billions of women before me, the penalties for stepping outside the social bounds, wielding one's own feminine power, and pursuing one's own desires have been dire. As we discussed in Chapter 3, countless women have been accused, tried, and exiled for all kinds of threatening activities such as speaking her mind, looking too good, living with passion, making up her own rules, being too smart, claiming to have her own direct relationship with God, trusting her intuition, or, of course, the cardinal sin of putting herself first.

In order to squelch the power and individuality of women, those who were different were called "witches" and branded as being "of the devil." These women were judged to be heathens and forced into submission. It's no coincidence that in modern times, the *W* has been replaced with a *B*, rendering the same effect. We've all seen and heard too many of our sisters publicly shamed and emotionally or literally killed for their strength of character, independence of thought, spiritual practice, or audacity to stand out.

The cellular memory of the pain has yet to fade. That's why, deep down, we suspect the same dreadful fate should we defy the roles society sets for us. No matter how far we've come as a gender, the flames of judgment are still licking at our feet. And all too often, it's other women who are holding the matches.

THE AUDACITY TO DREAM BIG

I had done way too much work on my mindset and my business to get to the point where making $20,000 in one week was actually doable, so I wasn't going to let this haunting herstory stop me. "It's not a criminal activity to walk into a store and purchase clothes," I told myself. Besides, I hadn't spent that much on clothes in my entire life! I was ready to make up for lost time. If the price tags were what they were, it meant that people, women, were buying them. "Who are these women?" I wondered. "If these beautiful clothes are okay for them, why not for me? Why does this whole thing feel ever so...wrong?"

Feeling completely alone, I settled for a shadowy double life. Just like my ancestors who managed to survive the witch hunts, I let my Secret Spender hide my truth.

What other option did I have? The thought of being exclusively all about serious endeavors like personal development and wearing cardigan sets for the rest of my life felt painfully boring, and yet the alternative of going full *Real Housewives*, dripping in Chanel and lounging poolside all day with an umbrella in my drink, sounded completely empty. Living in an either/or world felt hopeless. I could choose a life of integrity, following my heart, helping others, and eking out enough income for a mere existence (but not a penny more), or I could walk the heathen, rebel path of making (and spending) plenty of money, at the cost of my morals, my relationships, and my hard-won "good woman" image.

MONEY SHAMING IS THE NEW WITCH BURNING

This, my sisters, is the new "stake." Often, we ourselves are the ones leading the inquisition. Yes...you, me, *us* women. We are

the ones saying, "She went to Ibiza for *how* long?" "She remod-
eled her kitchen *and* upgraded all of her appliances?" "She's paying *how much* to send her kids to boarding school?"

Price tags are nearly more scandalizing than leaked nudes. But
when you zoom out, you quickly see how arbitrary these numbers
are. It's like when you're out to dinner with a group of friends. As
long as everyone is ordering off the menu within the same price
range, it's fair game, right? Let's say you're at a nice restaurant in a
cosmopolitan city; you wouldn't feel too weird or think poorly of
someone else for ordering the chicken or the salmon dish. But who
would dare order the seafood tower with caviar? Cue the death
glares from every corner of the table. "Oh, I would never!" Most of
us shudder at the thought. The subtle consequences of such outrageous ordering may be only verbal, passive-aggressive, or entirely
unseen, and yet we'd all rather settle for an average dinner than risk
violating our implied "thou shalt not order the lobster" agreement.

Think about it. Which choices do you make because that's what's
"sensible" and socially acceptable for you within your circle? How
many desires do you deny yourself because your friends or family would be aghast to discover what you actually spent on those
Louboutins? Or because your purchase would open up a Grand
Canyon of buyer's remorse, and you'd wind up giving the shoes
away rather than be constantly reminded of your sin? Or are you
only indulging in your desires during late-night online romps with
the Secret Spender, thus making sure nobody sees the real you?

Although nobody thinks it's off limits for men to talk about
and actively pursue fine cars, expensive watches, another round of
golf, and the creation of wealth into the millions and billions, you
wouldn't want to be seen as one of those women who's "all about
the money," would you? I know. Me neither.

What remains as true today as it was in the seventeenth century is that a lot of people squirm with discomfort when a woman

dares to play a bigger game—with her career, contribution, self-worth, and wallet. Seeing a woman say yes to a "big" purchase triggers our own secret desires and jealous judgments.

Either we want what she has and, thinking it's not possible for us, pout in envy and inferiority, or we're so unconscious and self-punishing about our own desires that we declare her depraved for having hers. When we are desperately afraid there's not enough to go around, there's nothing like the anxiety of "will I get mine?" to fuel the bitter fire of judgment. Just like a good old-fashioned witch hunt, when the effect limits our freedom, everyone suffers.

Thankfully, the days of us women dedicating our full existence to making sure everyone else is perfectly comfortable with 100 percent of our choices are officially over. Although we may not be able to stop our nosy aunts or overprotective fathers from making disapproving or even downright mean comments about our choice of red-soled stiletto, Spanish island getaway, or exceptional entrée with the caviar add-on, we can stop judging ourselves and each other, here and now.

FOCUS ON YOUR DESIRES

In my case, I recognize how fortunate I was to be able to out my Secret Spender to my man, who has never deemed my desires wrong. When Glenn asked me, "Why that amount?" I found that I was crystal clear on my vision. I saw myself walking into the Valentino boutique and purchasing the pieces I truly loved without basing my choices on the price tags. This, I knew, was one experience I desired to finally give myself as a Queen.

Knowing I wouldn't be alone in figuring out how to make it happen, I didn't go into overwhelm when Glenn casually suggested I go earn what basically used to be my annual salary in seven days. Instead, I asked Infinite Intelligence for the solution.

HOW CAN I?

With a clear purpose and a hard deadline, I went into meditation, asking the right questions, knowing that anything is possible. "How can I make this happen in one week?" Arriving in a miraculous instant that very afternoon, the divine guidance brought blessings far beyond the spectacular new contents of my closet. At the time, I offered a $2,000 info-course that was the self-study version of a live program I had taught for over twice that amount. The online version included all the same audios, videos, call replays, and worksheets, without the feature of coaching with me live.

Guided to be of bigger service, I saw a way to sweeten the deal, enrich the content, and bring in the sales I desired. I got the idea to create the Queen's Golden Coaching Circle, which would include a full year of monthly group calls with me, just for the women who purchased the online course. Normally, I would have charged about $500 a month per person for group coaching like this. This week only, I marketed that the first ten determined women who purchased the program would get their entire year's membership in the coaching circle for free!

Irresistible, don't you think? Precisely ten women did too. Not eight, not eleven. Exactly ten, and by Friday. It's these types of experiences that prove the power of the mind. Alignment is always a sign of you being divinely guided. Manifesting this money showed me just how supportive the Universe is when we're clear and available to receive our big desires.

Taking off for Capri with the designated shopping money in the bank, I felt liberated. I was on the flight journaling about what I wanted to experience on the trip. And what came up? I desired to feel *free*. Free to shop without the Secret Spender stalking my every purchase. To express myself for who I really am.

Free to demonstrate my passion for luxury and fashion *and* spirituality and purpose. Free to inspire other women to do the same.

THE POWER OF LIVING YOUR TRUTH

Before I said yes to my Amalfi Coast dream, I didn't know the full power of living my truth, *all of my truth*. I couldn't see it. As always, fear makes us self-obsessed. I was so scared of what people would say about my fashion foray that it never occurred to me that (a) my desire was *not* unique and (b) it was connected to God's plan.

Not once did it cross my mind that plenty of other women would love to go on a luxury shopping spree on the Isle of Capri too. I wound up feeling inspired to share the details of my *la dolce vita* trip in my newsletter to my entire mailing list.

The feedback I received? Hundreds of women shared how they too longed to experience the paradise of the Amalfi Coast. A woman from England wrote in to tell me that although she has no interest in travel, she was inspired to finally order new curtains for her kitchen. Another woman emailed to say that Italy wasn't her thing, but a yoga retreat in Costa Rica was now confidently back on her vision board.

Women from all over the world wrote in every single day appreciating me for sharing this genuine part of myself. Thanking me for demonstrating how to create a life we all desire and actually *live it*. Grateful for my showing them what's possible, for all of us. Right then and there, the Divine Living brand was born. Before then, I had only talked about the inner world of Queen; as a result of stretching myself in this way, the Universe gave me the opportunity to embody my brand and create the visual context that complements this deep work. And ever since, I have been honored to make a difference in the lives of thousands of women, inviting them into a space where they too can live their truth internally and externally at the highest levels.

SLAYING THE SECRET SPENDER

It felt so good to overcome the luxury stigma and no longer have my desires or purchases remain in hiding. I had tried to suppress my love for beauty, fashion, and lifestyle for far too long, when they were always an essential part of my vision of Queenhood. And I see now that it doesn't matter what your exact "taste" is; a Queen's purpose-led desires call for money. Maybe in your dream scenario, you would spend $20,000 on a different experience. That's your right to choose. If your idea of a fun and meaningful $20,000 looks like taking a six-month sabbatical to hike the Pacific Crest Trail, and your ideal shopping spree is a trip to REI to stock up on fleece for life, enjoy it and stay warm!

The whole point is for you to get honest about what lights you up and give yourself permission to express it fully and freely! Sometimes those delights will come in the form of Prosecco in Positano. Other times, they will be in your ability to write a check to an orphanage that will stay open as a result of your contribution, or to go on a month-long meditation retreat in Dharamsala where you get the idea for your next passion project. Part of the blessing of being liberated is that we no longer have to live in an either/or world. We feminine women get to take a stand for the *and*.

Starting now, you too are free to live by your own value system in a much bigger way. In choosing to do so, you get to remove the maximum price tag that's been set on your life, your contribution, and your happiness. You now know that money always flows where there's a purpose. It's time for women like us to thrive.

The Money Shaming Solution

AN EXERCISE

The end of money shaming begins with getting honest with yourself. The more you give yourself permission to make, use, and enjoy what money will buy, the less you'll burn yourself (and other women) at the stake. No longer experiencing guilt over money flowing freely in and out of your life, you'll become one of the change makers, here to help humanity evolve past financial fear and shame.

Becoming aware of how you've been limiting yourself financially is the first step to releasing your judgments of yourself and others. What desire are you denying because of the financial cost? What specific decision are you currently making from a place of "I shouldn't spend *that much* on [insert true desire]"? What dreams are you compromising on or putting off for the future to please that voice that says, "You'd better be reasonable"? Is it an upcoming trip where you're settling for using points so you can have free accommodations rather than staying at the boutique hotel that caught your eye in *Travel + Leisure*? A milestone birthday party menu for your bestie that got demoted to a taco night? Support at home or at the office that you're convinced you should just handle yourself?

Then notice:

- Did you know what you desired but didn't even look into it because you prejudged it as "too expensive"?
- Did you spend valuable time taking action on the lesser desire?
- How does this scenario feel? Usually, somewhere along the lines of normal, reasonable, responsible, practical, and "right." And you're probably feeling "good" about your sensible approach to life.
- Now, let's imagine for a moment there are no consequences or limitations to your desires. How would you

proceed differently with that trip, party, or support hire? What choice would your Queen make if she were living her authentic truth?

- Visualize the ideal scenario, then *feel* into it. How does it feel to make decisions from the feminine place of Queen? Usually, actual "feeling" words such as *powerful, exciting, relieving, joyful, peaceful, fulfilling,* and *uplifting* will instantly fill your space.

- From that place, write down one action that you will take on behalf of your truth. Your intuition will always guide you to the right next steps.

Now, notice how you feel. That flutter of "Oh my God, am I really doing this?!" can too easily turn to fear if our old money stories are allowed to resurface. Women are so conditioned to never make a mistake and always "get it right," especially with money, where the scarcity view programs us to be tightly guarded. Empower yourself to feel more excited than anxious. Affirm the truth of abundance, work yourself into a state of certainty, and keep your vibration high.

Remember, your inner Queen is always guiding you to your truth and daring you to live your best life. The old-school rules of only considering what's "practical" and "reasonable" are leading you astray to a bland existence, and yet it's hard to see it that way because we've all been brainwashed to wear these labels like badges of honor.

When Your Truth Triumphs

I'll share with you my personal experience of doing this exercise. When I wrote this, I was at JFK Airport waiting for my flight home to Los Angeles. I remembered that I would be returning to New York City the following month for a few weeks and still needed to book accommodations. I asked my husband how much it cost to stay at my favorite hotel. He told me a nightly rate range that triggered an internal judgment of "I shouldn't spend *that much* on a hotel for two weeks."

So instead, I spent the next forty-five minutes perusing fine, yet frankly uninspiring options on Airbnb that fell neatly in my "I can justify this amount" comfort zone. I made a selection. I was feeling responsible, practical, and dare I say proud of myself for being so reasonable. Then I went to create this exercise and knew I had to walk my talk. So I went through this process, and *wow*!

First, I realized I had so thoroughly denied my true desire that *I didn't even look into it at all*. Can you relate? I just assumed that what my husband said about the price range was true and that it was too expensive. Next, I spent valuable time looking into what did not inspire me. Finally, I justified my wasted time and subpar choice as an accomplishment to be proud of.

Following the exercise through, I asked myself, "If there were no consequences or limitations, where would I stay for those two weeks in New York City?" Of course, my favorite Upper East Side hotel immediately popped into my consciousness.

This time, I quickly skedaddled onto their website, entered my booking dates, and…what did I discover? They were actually $7 less per night than the uninspiring Airbnb option *and* they were offering a "book two nights and stay the third night free" special!

Women. Our Queens know better. Follow your desires. Seek them out. Take action on behalf of living your best life. Don't money shame yourself or others. It's an old, outdated, and unnecessary way to live. On the other side of playing small is playing *big*. Your Queen within is applauding your courage to live your truth. Mine is enjoying a Grey Goose martini at the Lowell Hotel.

sixteen

PRIORITIZING PLEASURE

Life is meant to be lived from a state of pleasure. I know…scandalous as it may sound, it's true! This *is* Spirit's way. I'm not saying one should indulge in frivolous activities like daily day drinking (anyone who's done that more than one day in a row knows it's anything but pleasurable).

I'm talking about a completely uplifted and renewed approach to life that starts with femininity at its finest. One where you're invigorated and vibrant because you're working *with* the way you are naturally designed. Prioritizing pleasure will open you up to receiving and give you that irresistible spark of inspiration and joy that is essential to manifesting your vision as a Queen.

Pleasure is defined as "enjoyment or satisfaction derived from what is to one's liking; gratification; delight." Think about how powerful you are when you feel enjoyment and satisfaction *according to you*. Bring to mind something that instantly makes you feel gratification and delight right now. There's clarity, enthusiasm, wholeness, peacefulness, and a fun dynamic here.

If it takes you a moment to recall your last great encounter with pleasure, it's because we've been taught to allow these experiences only *if* all our work is done (which it rarely is) and only *if* there is enough time and money left over.

Do you know that only 1 in 100 Americans even know what they want? It's because humans have disconnected from the feminine wisdom of pleasure, and instead we worship rules that aren't from the spiritual realm. When we put our faith in human-made things and lack consciousness rather than embracing the abundance of the Infinite, we get stuck. We become convinced that we have to work (overly) hard, stay in a job or marriage we don't like, and put off any notion of consistent fun for retirement, presuming we'll even live that long.

As far as the Injured Feminine Instinct is concerned, pleasure is another element that's associated with weakness. It's seen as a sign of indulging when one should be dieting, playing when one should be working, and getting a massage when one should really be finishing those dishes. In our productivity-obsessed culture, pleasure is seen as lunatic or careless behavior.

We live in a world that glorifies constant hard work. And because this mentality is what we are familiar with, it's what we've come to rely on as the only way to get our needs met or get ahead in life. It's rare to even hear a woman utter the word *pleasure*, as if it's been deleted from our vocabulary. And the outcome of declaring this word indecent, selfish, and only to be saved for later is a collective culture of underwhelmed, unfulfilled, and, to varying degrees, depressed women.

Statistics show that 67 percent of the American workforce is burned out in their job or looking for a new one. This soaring misery index can only exist in a society where people prioritize practicality over play, unaware they can have both.

Work isn't the only area where this shows up, as six out of every ten couples report being unhappily married. And taking it one step further, when it comes to pleasure and relationships, studies show that about 75 percent of all women never reach orgasm from sex with their partner, and 10 to 15 percent of women will go their entire lives without having one at all.

For most women, the barrier to pleasure encircles our entire existence, keeping us from having the thriving career, developing the soul sister friendships, enjoying the delicious dining experiences, embarking on the extraordinary adventures, and living in the magazine-worthy homes we would ecstatically select if we lived in a world where anything was possible. Which we do.

THE PLEASURE WARDEN

When a woman doesn't prioritize pleasure, simultaneously she doesn't prioritize her authentic self. That's when you know the *Pleasure Warden* has stepped in and removed most traces of enjoyment from her existence. Locked up in an overly busy routine of tending to others and obligations, we feel unworthy of taking time for ourselves or guilty when we spend money on anything that's simply for our own delight.

When femininity is falsely imprisoned, it's not just our hair and nails that suffer. More importantly, it's a woman's emotional, inner life that gets neglected. The Pleasure Warden withholds permission for all forms of self-care, self-consideration, self-reflection, and self-expression, which is why women with this archetype in control are convinced that any focus on themselves is selfish. The experience of just *being* a woman, connected to her femininity, feels entirely alien. And agitating.

Ready to relax? The journey to becoming Queen will dramatically transform your relationship with pleasure. Physical, emotional, spiritual, and taste-bud-related joy is no longer something you'll have to suppress, sneak, steal, or devour *now* before they take it away. The epic life does not have to be monklike unless that's genuinely your choice. The definition of "most fabulous" is completely up to each Queen to design.

MANIFESTING YOUR MOST PLEASURABLE LIFE

When I was a brand-new life coach hustling to line up the next client, European summer vacations seemed like a dream so far in the future that a time machine would be required. Taking a Saturday off was hardly an option. That is, until I flipped through a magazine and saw a story about Paris and Nicky Hilton summering in Saint-Tropez. What? I'm not even sure I knew where it was or exactly how to pronounce it (I also didn't know "summering" was a verb), but after a quick Google search, I was sold. On the beach? In France? *That.* That was what I wanted. Now. Not in twenty years, not when there was enough time and money left over. Now.

This was a daring concept for me. More than a stretch. Because believe me, I was tight. When it came to allowing pleasure in my life, just getting an inexpensive manicure felt as triumphant as having your heels actually touch the floor in downward dog.

Historically, I always made just enough money to cover my basic needs and only allowed domestic travel, self-care, and beauty treatments if there was "extra." And yet I just couldn't shake this South of France fantasy. Visions of my Saint-Tropez escapade were popping up in my meditations daily. And soon enough, I found myself watching Brigitte Bardot movies and brushing up on my French.

Once I got clear on my desire, I let myself look into the details. I ran the costs to figure out exactly what it would take to get me to this chic seaside fishing village. At the time, my $60,000 check from the basement waterproofing company was freshly in my bank account, minus the $30,000 I invested in coaching programs. When Glenn heard what I was intending to do with a portion of those earnings, his feedback was, "Gina, what about putting that money in savings and investing in the business?" *Of course!* I assured him that I intended to do those things to grow my business; however, as you know, a Queen takes a stand for the *and.*

"I'm not going," he protested grumpily, "because I'm not going to be a lifestyle junkie." Ouch. "Maybe he's right," the Pleasure Warden piped in. "If I just work really hard this year and fill up the coffers a bit more, maybe enjoying *moules frites* next summer is a better idea."

My Queen wasn't having *any* of this stifled thinking. She reminded me that he had just heard the term *lifestyle junkie* yesterday, when some guy accused him of being one. Evidently, he was so pissed about it that he needed to stay home from this amazing adventure just to prove that guy wrong.

Well, Glenn's temporary travel ban had no jurisdiction over this Queen. I was going. Flights were purchased, a petite hotel room was booked, and soon enough, I was packing my little pink bikini in blissful anticipation of my five-day sojourn *en France.*

In this high-vibrational space of honoring my desire and allowing life to be pleasurable *now,* I connected to the *why* behind my glamorous voyage. As I tapped in and asked Source, an even more audacious idea arrived. "I'm going to get a new client while I'm there!"

Ignoring the fact that I had forgotten about 90 percent of my high school French and had no idea where or who the ideal client would be, every day I remembered my vision and felt how amazing it would be to work with an international client.

The time came to cross the Atlantic and land in Nice, and after the mini road trip along the Côte d'Azur, there I was walking the cobblestone streets in this picturesque little pastel-colored village. I sunbathed on the beach, strolled through the Place des Lices market, gazed at all the stunning sea-view villas, window-shopped the beautiful boutiques, and definitely enjoyed *moules frites.* "I'm in total bliss!" I remember thinking. "The weather is warm, the sky is pink, the wine is pink…this place is perfect!"

Filled up with pleasure and completely relaxed in my body, on my second to last night on the Riviera, I was sitting at the bar at my hotel, waiting for my table for one, when I overheard a couple of interesting-looking people speaking English. They turned out to be from L.A. We wound up having a fabulous dinner together and during our conversation, the woman asked me what I did for a living. I told her I was a life coach. She started to ask me some rather detailed questions about my work, and then revealed, "I've been looking for a life coach, how can we work together?" Boom!

Prioritizing pleasure to the max, I had completely forgotten about my original intention and the request I had made to the Universe before leaving. When she inquired as to the price of my coaching package, I did not hesitate to say "Twenty thousand dollars." Yes, my rates had gone up like *that* day.

Right there on the bar stool in Saint-Tropez, my first $20,000 coaching package was sold. Prioritize pleasure, ladies! It works. Naturally, it was a double blessing. Confidently pursuing my desire didn't just make me money. It gave me the gift of living my purpose *and* fulfilling my mission, which can't be done without clients. As the Universe was well aware, my new coaching client needed me as much as I needed her. She was a top-performing medical equipment sales representative in her late twenties. For several years since her mother's passing, this young superstar had been channeling all her anxiety into her job, and had developed a drug habit to cope with her grief after hours. As a result of our work together, she got connected with Spirit and no longer needed to get her high from drugs. She transformed unresolved heartache in her relationship with her late mother and became at peace again in her body, giving her the sense of freedom she'd been seeking all along.

As for Glenn? He didn't miss many trips after that. It became clear to both of us that what the world convincingly categorized as "lifestyle junkie" behavior was actually a part of a grander plan. Leaps and bounds beyond playing it safe, after having denied myself for so long, allowing pleasure was the ultimate way to grow my business, serve others more powerfully, and enjoy life. As long as I was tending to my spiritual connection and keeping the Pleasure Warden at bay, I could have faith that following my desires would always lead me in the right direction.

WHEN PLEASURE LEADS TO PURPOSE

Most people see these pleasure-based pieces as "selfish." As Queens, we know they are the keys for us to live out our bigger purpose. Not everyone has your exact combination of interests because no one has your exact calling. And the benefits of claiming your personal desires always extend far beyond any one gratifying, delightful life experience.

God put those big, outrageous dreams in you for a reason. It's called the epic life, ladies! It's up to you to give yourself permission to think bigger and become available to live your grand purpose, which includes a life of meaning *and* pleasure.

It takes a certain level of spiritual development and emotional maturity to create faith in your truth. However, spiritual development doesn't need to take a long time, it needs only a fierce commitment. If a Queen is asking better questions, she'll find there's nothing slow-moving about the Universe.

Whereas other women think a small side of pleasure is the most they're allowed from life's menu, a Queen wonders, "How can I bring more pleasure into all areas of my life? What if losing weight didn't have to be a depriving journey? How can I live somewhere fabulous that inspires me, even if I'm a single mom with three kids? Am I sure my boss wouldn't let me set my own schedule and work virtually? What if it were possible?"

If you're concerned that giving in to this pleasure theory might have you go off the deep end into binging, overspending, and self-sabotage, fear not. A Queen is as committed to answering her highest calling as she is interested in living her ultimate lifestyle; the latter is there to support the former. With that in mind, a Queen checks in spiritually to identify the driving force behind her desires. She asks, "Is this ego-based? Am I only doing this to keep up with the Kardashians? How will I feel after this desire is fulfilled? Will I be inspired or weakened?"

Knowing if a desire is truly spirit-led or fear-based, a Queen spends time with herself daily, to connect, listen, commune with God, and strengthen her intuition. She is also specific about the *when* and is certain in the *why* behind her intentional choices. Every Queen must hone her own spiritual ear. As you get stronger you will become attuned to listening to your body, understanding your heart, and tapping into what's true and on-purpose for you.

Your Path to Prioritizing Pleasure

AN EXERCISE

Your life is good, yet it has the potential to be epic. Exciting. Fulfilling. Abundant. And it starts with you prioritizing pleasure. Time to give yourself the gift of exploring what's possible. Take out your journal and follow along with these steps.

Step 1: Determine where you crave more pleasure in your life

All work and no play makes for a very boring Queen. It's time for you to get clear on some of the main areas of your life that could use some spice. Whether it's the ho-hum dating life exclusively comprised of swiping left, the social calendar that revolves around stopping by your local bar Mojo's every day after work for an appletini and the same conversation with Jed the bartender, or the motorized neck massager from Costco that remains your greatest self-care splurge to date, get clear on what's most important to you at this moment and write it down. Check in spiritually to confirm what your true priority is. Ask Spirit to show you where prioritizing pleasure will make the biggest difference in your work and your overall well-being. As a Queen, you can transform what you look forward to the least into one of the most fulfilling and rewarding experiences in your life. Wherever you are weakest, you are meant to become the strongest.

Step 2: Discover how you can make this area more pleasurable

Now that you've prioritized one top area, here comes the fun part! Let's brainstorm some ways in which you could add pleasure. Could you swap one of your weekly treadmill sessions for a hip-hop dance class? Turn up the heat in your relationship with a surprise boudoir shoot or a tantra yoga class? Organize an out-of-the-box ladies' excursion to New Orleans for New Year's? Set up shop with your laptop in a sexy hotel lobby? Home-swap your place so you can spend an otherwise sweltering July in the city enjoying the breeze at a lake house in the mountains?

When it comes to pleasure, it's not always about the price tag. Sometimes it's taking a Tuesday afternoon off. Or taking a nap. Preferably something you're passionate about. As a new entrepreneur and foodie, I used to love strolling into Williams Sonoma (my *Breakfast at Tiffany's*) at the end of the week to treat myself to a fancy new carrot peeler. Pleasure does not have to be expensive, and we usually don't need to wait for "extra money" to come in to enjoy what is already there for us.

Step 3: Skip the future tripping!

A lot of women will find themselves on cloud nine about their totally meant-for-them desire. Then *ping!* Paralyzing fear sets in. They say, "I'm going to think about it." Which isn't about "figuring out how" so much as it's contemplating every possible reason why this can't and won't work (aka future tripping) and ultimately being paralyzed from ever moving forward.

One of my awesome team members, for example, had a desire to join a coworking space. Then she second-guessed her desire and started spinning. She was unaware of all the options, different locations, and different prices. She started to wonder, "Is this really important? How am I going to afford this? What if I move?" She was freaked out about finances when she didn't even have the data. Future tripping's superpower is that it keeps us from exploring how to manifest our dreams. This team member hadn't even looked into the options!

Skip the spin by getting intimate with the details. Sometimes you'll be amazed at how you can afford your desire, like I was last chapter when I researched room rates at my favorite New York City hotel. Pick your top priority and honor your desire with a little research and thought. Look into any of the tangible elements of making it real. What are the options? What are the costs? Who can help you with it? How quickly can it be manifested? (Don't forget your power to bend space and time!)

Step 4: Manifest unapologetically

If a desire is spiritually guided and on purpose, it's meant for you. If your desire is already within reach, take action now. Ask for the time off from work, book the eucalyptus wrap at the spa you've been longing to try, be the ringleader and send the group text with prospective dates for the girlfriends' trip to Tulum.

For those desires that are a bit more of a stretch, now is when you tap into your spiritual superpowers to bend space and time, train your brain to think like a Queen, cultivate certainty, and manifest your financial miracle. Remember that a desire has to be a "must" for you to bring it into being. When a woman taps into that white heat and decides that pleasure is possible for her *now*, the epic life becomes her reality.

ON-PURPOSE PLEASURE

Say good-bye to feeling ashamed, confused, or unsure about your right to experience the emotional and delightful joys of life. Yes, you have incredible accomplishments that await you on this epic journey. And yet you were not created *only* to give. You are meant to receive too. On the path to your purpose, your desires matter. They're here to keep you vibrant, youthful, inspired, and motivated on your journey. They're meant for you to celebrate your successes, with all the captivating wow-factor of your little-girl dreams.

When we reward ourselves for doing great work, stay in high vibration, and take action toward our dreams, we set ourselves up to get bigger and bigger wins. At the same time, we take our hits in stride, because we've filled up that bank account of self-care and self-esteem that nobody else can fill for us. For the woman who works hard on a daily basis, your job is also to treat *yourself.* Not just that one vacation once a year combined with your birthday. How can you live this one life that we've got, love yourself, and encourage yourself to do more of this at a higher level?

For Queens, productivity is a priority, but so is play. Making space for your femininity, you get to design your schedule so that some form of pleasure is a daily occurrence. And while on some nights that might be your favorite cup of tea and a book by the fire, on others it might look like spontaneously taking the day off to go to a movie matinee. Queens know that often in life, the invisible benefits of fun, connection, and unforgettable experiences take us leaps and bounds beyond the extra five hours at our laptops. The days of being exclusively practical and masculine with our time and money are over. Permission for pleasure has arrived.

PART V

Queens Do
Come True

seventeen

BORN TO BELONG

For most of my childhood, I didn't feel like I belonged, *anywhere.*
Sure, I had some friends in elementary school, but I wouldn't
say they were close by any means. Same for my awkward middle
school and high school stages. I always had a couple of gal-pals
that I spent more time with than others, but I wasn't an integral
part of a cool group of friends that I was excited to see every day.
Can you relate?

My experience within my church community was similar. I
had some "friends" there, but somehow I still felt like an outsider.
Was it because most of them went to the church school and I went
to public school? Not sure. Then came college. Lord. We've discussed how I couldn't have felt like I belonged anywhere *less* than
in Kalamazoo, Michigan. I wasn't into rave parties, and sitting on
freezing-cold aluminum bleachers during football season, having some dude named Drew offer me a sip from his thermos that
reeked of peppermint schnapps, wasn't my idea of a grand Saturday afternoon.

Looking back, I can see that my Injured Feminine Instinct was
in full effect. I wasn't good at receiving close intimate friends and
thus never had the experience of belonging to a squad who went

to the mall together on weekends and burst out laughing at the same inside joke in the middle of third period.

As I fled to D.C. the summer of my junior year, *it* happened, again. I'll never forget the day I was sitting in the office of the first lady in the White House, reading something in the press clips about the "religious right." In Washington, and because I was a Democrat, they were, relatively speaking, the enemy. Oddly, though I grew up in a fundamentalist Christian church, I didn't see myself as part of or belonging to the "religious right." And then it hit me, you can't be a Democrat *and* a born-again Christian. And vice versa: You can't be a born-again Christian *and* vote blue. But I was! And I did. And that made me an enemy in both camps.

Then this alienating pattern got transferred into family dynamics. I fell in love with a man, and for reasons far too intricate to get into here, suffice it to say I found myself in my own *Romeo and Juliet* story. My family and community at the time was *not* having my choice in romantic partner. The intense efforts they went through to get me to comply with their rules and give up my soul mate or be exiled left me in a state of shock. Again it seemed it wasn't safe to be the real me, the full me, and the true me anywhere. Nowhere did I belong.

Lastly, because how you do one thing is how you do everything, this same misfit pattern spilled into my career as well. I loved being a psychotherapist, but for me the transformational process doesn't fit into a forty-five-minute-once-a-week session. I was forced to either be constrained with my work or give up my license. My soul chose the latter.

There I was, new to Los Angeles, new to life coaching, new to working for myself, and feeling utterly alone, overdressed, and out of place. *Again.*

VOLUNTARY ISOLATION

The *Loner* repeatedly fabricated this experience that my full self didn't belong anywhere. This archetype convinced me that I had to only show parts of who I am to be accepted or spend the rest of my life in a party of one. "You're better off alone," the Loner fictitiously maintained. This feeling that no one liked me or accepted me in my totality (orphaned and exiled) was excruciating. I became depressed and fearful and felt unsafe to be my full self out in the world. So I went underground, internalizing my self-manufactured shame.

Our conditioning is to worship the values of responsibility, self-reliance, and conformity, so we've dissociated from the feminine wisdom that appreciates the power of the collaborative collective and cherishes diversity, open-mindedness, and acceptance.

Part of the way the Loner wields power is in persuading you that pretty much everyone else has the perfect Norman Rockwell–painted family or fits into an entirely cohesive "it girl" social tribe. Except for you. Through this sneaky, obviously false logic (considering the global population), the Loner stalked me for years, keeping me isolated and self-identifying as a misfit.

A driven woman who's been infiltrated by the Loner long enough will inevitably disguise feelings of being the outcast with a false sense of purpose. In my case, the Loner subconsciously tricked me into feeling like I *finally* belonged within my "party of one" business, where *I* was the star. My business turned into the only place where I belonged.

Under the influence of the Loner's runaway ambition, I quickly learned that life was about work, not fun. Since I got my safety and significance only from career achievements, being "distracted" by any form of play and socializing was simply not going to happen.

I proceeded to judge the other women who were constantly out on the town or hosting meet-ups as "foolish." "Look at them wasting all this time at brunch; don't they have a career ladder to climb?!" And when jealous feelings would start to creep up, the Loner would jump to remind me, "They won't make it as far as you." The *Loner* and I knew we were going places, but sadly, I fell under her spell of believing that I had to do it *myself*, and help wasn't available through connections or fun. Apparently solo sixty-hour workweeks were the only way to get ahead.

And of course nobody batted a false lash at my long hours. It's normal for many of us. Modern-day women have become so overly self-sufficient and "comfortable" behind our laptops and cell phones that we no longer give ourselves permission to go out, connect with people, be in a community, and have fun. Not only are we uncomfortable asking for help, we're uncomfortable asking for *friendship*. At best, we work hard, we work out, and we work some more. We're there for our significant others or our families, yes. But the mentality becomes that being part of a larger community is superfluous and not worth our time, when it's just a deep-seated fear: "Who would want to go to brunch with *me*?"

"You'll get to make awesome friends later," says the Loner, "once you've made your money and established yourself." It sounds logical, though deep down, we're in pain because we know it's not our truth. It's the Injured Feminine Instinct all over again.

Ironically, men have historically been better at blending work and play than women. Think about the amount of business that happens on the golf course, the number of deals that get cut over steak dinners or negotiated at the cigar lounge afterward. Plenty of successful men don't think they have to do it all by themselves or spend eighteen hours a day at the office to be productive. And yet we think the way to make it in a "man's world" is to listen to the Loner, to isolate ourselves and get as much work done as possible.

To the degree that we've squeezed all the joy out of our lives, we've cut ourselves off from our feminine instinct for connecting. Working as hard as we do in isolation is not juicing up our ovaries. Nor is it making us more successful.

A Queen knows what actually fuels her higher consciousness and supports her creative abilities. She understands how to leverage the network around her to bend space and time. She knows to make *joie de vivre* a top priority.

FUN WITH FRIENDS IS FEMININE

Fun. It's the simple act of enjoying life. Being playful is one way to experience pleasure. It's one of the greatest gifts we can give ourselves at any given time, and yet, in depressing Lonerville or workaholic isolation, we have grown to place it dead last on our to-do list.

Cyndi Lauper had the right idea. But the truth is, girls don't just *want* to have fun, we *need* to have fun. We crave connection. It's wired into our cells. Our bodies literally thirst for it.

A recent landmark UCLA study shows that women under stress are prone to seek friendship. When "fight or flight" is triggered, our brains release oxytocin at higher rates than men, which the UCLA researchers contend is what naturally compels us to reach out to our community for help (if the Loner isn't standing in our way).

You could say we're physiologically rewarded for bonding. And for amusement too. Our brains respond to laughter with a rush of endorphins, adrenaline, and dopamine. These uplifting hormones and neurotransmitters are proven to reduce stress, boost serotonin (happiness levels), increase energy, improve memory and concentration, and contribute to sounder sleep. And in case the Loners reading this need more convincing, know that it's not only *joyous* to be in a community, we actually have *more power* in groups too.

THE MAHARISHI EFFECT

Ever been to a near-empty spin class versus one full of fifty high-vibe people all going for it? This past Tuesday night, I walked into the cycle studio to find, in what normally is a packed class, only about nine other enthusiasts on their bikes. The instructor was awesome, the playlist was great, and yet the vibe was still . . . *empty*. It felt like I had to do so much more work than usual to make up for the obvious gap of missing spinners. It hadn't dawned on me before how much being present in a community with the shared goal of accomplishing this spin class together lifted my energy and motivation, literally on a physical level. Now in this sparsely populated class, my commitment to staying in the saddle was dropping by the minute. Thirty minutes in, I unclipped my shoes and walked out. And I *never* leave early.

The vibration that we awesome humans create when we get together and align our glorious intention is proven. The Transcendental Meditation organization has funded countless experiments to measure the impact of groups of people focusing on a shared goal. They call it the Maharishi Effect.

The Maharishi Effect had a record victory in 1992. At the time, Washington, D.C., was statistically the most violent city capital in the world. Even as the crime-fighting budget increased to $1 billion annually, the rate of violence went up a whopping 77 percent. Enter Maharishi's Yogic Flyers, volunteer expert meditators on a mission to bring peace to this tumultuous metropolis through the power of their collective mind. Locals were skeptical.

Echoing their disbelief, the chief of police appeared on TV and declared that only twenty inches of snow could slow the violence. And it was summer.

For eight weeks, the Yogic Flyer meditators arrived by the hundreds from all over the country, gathering, closing their eyes, silently reciting their mantras, and visualizing decreased crime. For the final two weeks of the experiment, four thousand of them were working in harmony.

Meanwhile, an unbiased committee of sociologists, politicians, and police officers came together to vet the data. Plotting the numbers on a curve, they confirmed the results with astonishment. As the number of meditators went up, the number of violent crimes went down. The correlation was unmistakable. At the time of maximum Yogic Flyers, the crime rate was down 23 percent! Astonishing, and relatively inexpensive. The meditation cost $8 million, compared to $166 million spent on the police budget for the same two months.

Boom! This is the feminine power of community and collaboration. When you're surrounded by others who share your same beliefs and hold the same vision of what's possible, you access abilities you didn't even know you had in you.

THE LITERAL UPLIFT

I stepped into my biannual, level 1 yoga class. Same room, same instructor, every six months. Like clockwork, I confidently walked into the empty studio, rolled out my mat, attempted a half moon stretch, and then gently folded my legs in lotus position, closed my eyes, and went into a pre-class meditation until the instructor and my fellow beginners arrived. I heard a voice welcoming the arrivals, and it didn't sound like the teacher I was familiar with. As I opened my eyes to see who this substitute must be, I noticed that the entire class was packed, with no familiar faces. I quickly scanned the room to see what looked like cast members from a Cirque du Soleil show and realized I was in an advanced level 3 vinyasa flow. In the front row. *They must have moved rooms!*

I was dripping sweat before the first warrior one. Barely surviving warrior two, I proceeded to "rest" in my rather tight downward dog, thinking, "What have I gotten myself into?!" I wanted to leave, but that'd be disruptive and rude. Lord help me. Deciding to do my best and go with it, I pedaled my feet and awaited the next line, which was *supposed* to be "walk or jump your ankles to meet your hands." For me it's usually a waddle anyway, and in a room of beginners, I'm okay with that. This time, however, the teacher said, "Float your feet to the front of your mat." *Huh?! Float?! How far? Antigravity forces, I'd love some assistance!*

Bracing myself to slog forward leg by leg, I took a deep inhale, then exhaled, and...felt a strange sensation. It was as if someone or something mysteriously lifted my hips and floated my legs forward...to the front of the mat! It actually happened!

Since I had never pulled this off before, my hypothesis is that being surrounded by the high-vibe individuals in that room who also had a single intention to float to the front of the mat, beyond my own limits, I was lifted with them. Their collective energy literally moved me forward. Where I had gotten used to slogging, I could have been floating all along.

COMMUNITY GOALS

It's not just fitness. In all of life's arenas, community is where the quantum leaps are. Prioritizing community actually helps you go further, faster. Friendship and connection contribute growth and fulfillment to your life. Not to mention endless resources and opportunities.

I've seen firsthand the incredible opportunities that arise when a woman aligns herself with other high-vibe women. Take one of my entrepreneur colleagues, for example. She recently had her business totally plummet and was holed up at home, stressed, angry, and scrambling frantically trying to close the next deal. One day, she finally got out of her slump and left the house to meet a friend, who turned out to be working with a company who needed her exact skill set in that moment. The meeting resulted in a $100,000 contract that saved her year. She could have easily found herself dangerously close to shuttering her business, not knowing how to find the next client. Instead she decided to stop isolating. A Queen must not underestimate the power of leaving the house.

Outside your comfort zone, meaningful connection happens all the time. For Patricia, her first women's retreat with me brought blessings far beyond what she had expected. She had been dating this sweet man for about four years and they had just discovered that he had Parkinson's disease. Frantically researching, looking for more information to help her boyfriend, and trying to get some follow-up doctor appointments booked, she subtly mentioned it during lunch at the retreat. Little did she know, she was sitting next to Brynna. Remember the woman who worked at the naturopathic integrative clinic? The doctor of that clinic specializes in Parkinson's; he was even in the process of writing a book on it! Right then and there, the two women were connected and appointments were set.

Whereas a woman going it alone might have spent many isolated nights online Googling the options, getting mixed messages, and not knowing which review to trust, just like that, while she was enjoying a women's retreat in New York City, having lunch with her community at a beautiful restaurant, a world-class resource to support her significant other's health had appeared.

These kinds of resources rarely show up because we spend twenty extra hours trying to figure out a solution by ourselves. And yet when we put down the technology and place ourselves in a high-vibe vortex of like-minded women, we attract such opportunities effortlessly.

OUTGROWING YOUR CIRCLE

For many women, feeling like we don't belong has to do with no longer having much in common with the people we know. By becoming Queen, we become conscious to the energy around us and typically find that who we surround ourselves with could use some curating.

Outgrowing your circle can be painful, confusing, and rather heartbreaking. Many women come to me wondering what they can do to get their lovers, friends, and family members to be more on board with their new growth and abundance mindset. They try to "help" these loved ones: introducing them to self-help books, podcasts, coaches, therapists, healers, seminars where you walk on fire, anything to enroll their inner circle in their new high-on-life perspective. And yet, no matter how much transformation the familiar circle has witnessed, many won't budge an inch from their set neurological pathways and established way of life. After most efforts have failed and hope addiction ceases, my clients come to me conflicted and feeling guilty over having to "leave people behind."

This is where spiritual surrender is quite useful. You're not God and you don't need to play Savior in anyone's life. It's not your responsibility to take on other's stories, stuckness, or screwed-up lives. Not everyone needs to "get you" and your dreams. But you do deserve to find a community that *does*.

COMMUNITY OF QUEENS

As the years went by, I started to crave connection. I'd see smart, soulful women on social media gathering in groups and clearly having a blast. They were getting together in person frequently, hosting chic dinner parties at each other's homes, going on girl-friend getaways to Cabo, and creating cool business collabora-tions. I came to realize, *"That's* what I want. That's what I'm missing!" A community. More fascinating friends who all know each other. Women where there'd be a mutual love fest, where we'd really get each other, support each other, and have real fun! I got my journal out and wrote down my new intention.

Cultivating community and fascinating friendships is a priority for me. I see myself enjoying deep connection with my soul sisters and experiencing laughter, joy, and fun with them.

Lastly, I created the following mantra and repeated it daily: "I have the world's most fun, interesting, smart, feminine, and spir-itual community. We travel together and see each other in person regularly. Everyone is up to big things in the world and we all feel loved and accepted in totality."

Have I mentioned there's nothing slow-moving about the Uni-verse? Less than one month later, I received an invitation. A new friend invited me to a holiday party she was hosting at her home in Los Angeles.

Here I was, having manifested my intention, surprised to immediately be concerned with those big little-girl worries, *but will I belong when I get there?* Going alone to a party where all the entrepreneurial "it girls" I'd been stalking on social media would be under one roof was intimidating. The Loner tried to convince me of the many reasons why I shouldn't go, but none were compelling enough to override my new intentions. I was determined to find *my* tribe. I took myself to the salon, dressed in holiday bling, and was on my way. Once I arrived, I *instantly*, and I mean lighting-bolt-flash fast, clicked with Ashley. We started talking and it was *easy* and the conversation was nonstop! We laughed, and she gave my husband a nickname he will *not* stop using: Dr. G Money. We got real with each other real quick. She asked me what were some of my intentions for the new year, and I vulnerably shared, "I'm craving friendship. Real female friendship." She whirled her hand on her hip, and with the confidence only an ultimate ringleader would have, she said, "Well, Gina, you've met the right woman!"

She proceeded to inform me that she was known as the "connector" in their group. (See how the Universe delivers when you set an intention and show up!) Ashley more than stuck true to her word. She too was working on writing her first book, so we started meeting at her private club and became writing buddies. At first, our word counts were definitely lacking because we couldn't help but dive into juicy conversations sharing hilarious stories as we got to know each other. We seemed so similar in *so* many ways until the DJ at "our office" that came on every day at four p.m. started blaring beach club music. Ashley reached for her headphones to play seriously depressing Beethoven, where I was lit up and the words flew out of me and onto the page. Maybe you had to be there, but the point is, the Universe delivered me a soul mate of a sister that I'm deeply grateful to call my friend. She's also been in nonstop introduction mode! Of course like attracts like, so the ridiculously smart, loving, generous, successful women she's connected me with are all major inspirations in addition to being *fun*.

YOUR FASCINATING FRIENDS ARE WAITING

Craving your own community of Queens? You too get to attract friends who want to have the same deep conversations and epic experiences that interest and delight you. Friends who inspire your curiosity and have you ugly-cry-laughing into the night! These women are waiting to meet you! As a Queen, you have no reason to hold yourself back from what's important to you.

Every Queen deserves to belong, be supported, and have fun on a daily basis. Whether you feel like the Loner who never fits in or have a handful of friend groups that you've secretly outgrown, it's time for all women to make thriving in community a top priority. You need and deserve to have fun with friends. It's time to be a star among stars. Trust. Your intuition, your purpose, and your inner Queen are leading you to the community where you belong, every awesome part of you.

eighteen

A ROYAL ROMANCE

Through my many years of reckless relationships, codependent crushes, and hopeless hookups, finding my soul mate felt like *Mission: Impossible*. If only I knew then what I know now. I would've saved a lot of money from splitting lame dinner-date bills, spared my ego a few "he never called" hits, and enjoyed life up to age thirty-one a lot more. The lessons I learned in attracting my King (and now husband, Glenn) changed the trajectory of my romantic life.

Whether you're stuck trying to find "the one," currently recovering from a blowout with "so not the one," or feeling blessed to be with your beloved, I'm delighted to share with you the insights that have served me in creating a healthy, loving, and supportive and long-term relationship with my King.

UNFULFILLING PATTERNS

Up until my early thirties, all I knew was that I wanted to find my man and get married. My Princess programming had me believing in the fantasy that the "perfect" person (aka Prince Charming) was going to appear and sweep me off my feet and into our fairy-tale life. He would be a thirty-six-year-old Italian rock star, with green eyes, dark hair, a house on Lake Como, and no previous marriages or children, and he would be the primary breadwinner in our family. The total package, right? Not exactly.

Being a Naïve Princess about men and relationships made my whole dating experience a very unfun and unfulfilling process. We're going back to the beginning of my "local loser rock stars from Detroit" saga. I remember going shopping with my mother and hearing her say, "Gina, you have such great taste, you better marry a wealthy man!" She never said, "*You'd* better become wealthy." It's not that she was trying to hold me back. And she definitely wasn't trying to suggest I didn't have the capability. Like all mothers, she just wanted the best for her daughter and thought that manifesting through a man was the most probable option for me. She guided me toward getting good grades, going to college, and being able to support myself. I wouldn't be where I am today if she hadn't always modeled for me how to make life happen.

This "marry a rich man" conditioning runs deep. And all throughout my manhunt I kept an eye out for one, but sadly, I was more attracted to the bad-boy musicians. Looking back, I almost wish I *had* taken my mother's advice...think of all the enjoyment I'd have had if *I* were the one being wined and dined.

In addition to being the Naïve Princess, I equally (and unfortunately) was also great at being the Ghost during my single years. Because I was invisible to myself and apparently anyone I was attracted to, I was stuck in a cycle of chasing the front man for the band, or being pursued by someone I had zero chemistry with; usually his name was something like Adam and he worked in Accounting for one of the Big Three automotive companies. Either way, the whole never-ending and never-fulfilling story was a snoozefest.

I decided to do something about this and turn my love life

around. "When the student is ready, the teacher appears," and that was when, while visiting Los Angeles, fate invited me to a dinner party where I met Katherine Woodward Thomas, bestselling author of *Calling In "The One"* and America's foremost expert on attracting your soul mate. I was instantly mesmerized by her unmistakable feminine essence, and I sensed a wise knowing in her soul. That night she shared that one of her workshops was coming up and I immediately enrolled.

Fast-forward a few weeks and there I was (again) at a personal development event, but instead of sitting in the back of the seminar room, this time I entered a historic house and was seated in a circle on the floor on oversized pillows, journaling about my future Prince Charming rock star that this renowned love guru was going to help me land. She angelically entered the room and opened the weekend event by asking, "What's your pattern with men?"

Huh?! I never thought about *me* having a pattern. I just thought I couldn't find the right one, or that I needed to stop trying to meet him backstage.

So elegantly, Katherine explained, "Everyone has a pattern. Some women go after emotionally unavailable men, married men, narcissistic men, obsessed-with-their-work men, or guys that are broken birds and need to be saved or fixed. Others go after weak men they can easily control."

I thought deeply about her question. Reflecting on my personal development journey thus far and newly aware of my money story, I could not believe that I was repeating the same pattern with my *man story* too. The dynamics were almost identical! My conditioning was that I believed that men weren't there for me (just like money), that they didn't support me, and that they'd never cherish me. I also didn't think I could trust them to have my best interests in mind or that I could rely on them. Worst of all, just like money, I believed they would never choose *me*.

And that was when I realized that my pattern was set up for defeat. The mediocre musicians were unavailable to me emotionally, romantically, and financially, and yet *I kept chasing them*. In trying to force what I wanted so badly to turn into a picture-perfect relationship, I made it all about them, and trust me, so did they. I was showing up for their gigs, supporting them from "behind the scenes," believing in them, and cheering them on. You name it, I did it. Talk about Injured Feminine Instinct. There was no receiving in sight. All femininity had exited out back, right next to the roadie named Big Ed.

At the time, I was convinced that I had "tried everything" to call in my rock star romance. I was about ready to give up on love completely until a deeper discovery at Katherine's retreat, found through her profound methods, shattered my illusion. I realized I was trying to marry who *I* wanted to become. I was living vicariously through these performers, when actually I desired to be the rock star in my own life. I wanted to be onstage (speaking, not singing...trust me, it's much better this way). I wanted my man to *come to my gigs!*

No wonder these poor guys were repelled. I wasn't into them or there for them at all, *and they felt it*. Once I stopped projecting my big dreams onto anyone who recorded in the *8 Mile* studio, I started to rewrite my list of relationship "must-haves" and created a new vision for what my soul yearned for in a romantic partner.

Excusing the Naïve Princess from giving notes on my dating life was a process. At first, my list started with all of the typical marriage-material qualifications. In no particular order, he had to be good-looking, fun, trustworthy, and emotionally available; earn a good living, treat me well, not get annoyed at long brunch lines, and have a solid spiritual connection; and be strong, smart, and all-around great at being a man. But the new number-one quality? He had to "claim" me. I wanted to be pursued and claimed by a King of a man. Not a hero, not a monk, nothing macho, and please, Universe, no more jesters. I was only interested in meeting a *King*.

I became obsessed. Studying anything I could get my hands on that would educate me on what a man who embodies this empowered masculine archetype is became my full-time hobby. What drives him? How is he wired? What does he base his decisions on? What are his desires? What is he repelled by? What is his purpose?

I discovered that the *King* is certain in his vision, known to provide *and* protect and to be generous, supportive, and giving. He encompasses the most glorious elements of all the masculine traits we discussed in Chapter 3, as well as a healthy respect for feminine values. Reading about the King, I understood why the purpose of the masculine is to be *in service* to the feminine.

The more I learned about this empowered archetype, the more some of the boxes on my matrimonial checklist seemed superficial. The more I read about the healthy relationship dynamic between Kings and Queens, the less I showed up as the Naïve Princess who had been leading me astray.

As shocked as I was to say *arrivederci* to the "Italian rock star" qualification, I was beyond surprised to discover that "makes more money than me" was also not my true value. *What?!* I wasn't supposed to be fixated on marrying a wealthy man? This Katherine woman was *good*. It was an *Aha!* moment that came from the heavens.

I discovered that what *was* most important to me in my partner, and remains so, is that he knows his vision, is true to his word, is emotionally safe, cherishes me, secures corner table reservations at chic restaurants, has his own spiritual connection, and enjoys life in the same ways I do.

This was my vision of the ideal relationship, where I'd be loved and supported to bring my work forth in a big way. Your vision for the ideal relationship might look different. Every Queen gets to design her own. I saw myself traveling the world with my soul mate. Together, we'd impact lives globally and enjoy our contribution and success.

THE KING AND I

I'll never forget that Saturday morning. Having just moved to California, I flew back to Detroit one last time. I had arrived early to the Birmingham Community House to get ready to host my first Esther Experience seminar on Queenhood.

It was eight a.m. As I was setting up the registration table, I looked up. I wasn't expecting to see *him* standing at the door. There he stood, Dr. Glenn A. Sisk, this good-looking man in a sports coat and slacks. "I think you're in the wrong spot," I informed him. (Queen tip number one: Don't ever say that to a King.)

Having seen the advertisements for my event, he proceeded to inform *me*, "No, I'm not. I'm a King, and I haven't been with a Queen. I want to know how this Queen thing works."

Compelling; however, I stood my ground. "You can't be here. This event is for women only."

Somehow, he convinced me to let him stay. "Fine," I said. "But you have to sit in the back of the room next to the recording guy [who happened to be my boyfriend at the time] so you don't distract the women." (P.S.: My boyfriend apparently decided on his own accord to sleep in that day, so he sent his assistant instead.)

As the ladies walked in, I had candles and red roses on every table plus special handouts created to accompany the day's content. And yet any compliments on the decor were drowned out with murmurs of "Who's the good-looking man in the back corner?"

I was so irritated. He was distracting from my presentation before it even began!

I chose to ignore the hushed chatter, excited to present my material. Soon enough, I was speaking and coaching and the room started to open up. These incredible women were making greater sense of their own life journeys, taking in awareness after awareness and loving every second of it.

When we got to the part in Esther's story about communicating like a Queen, a woman in the front row raised her hand to ask about a delicate issue she and her husband were experiencing. As I was coaching her through the scenario, another participant exclaimed, "I'd like to hear a man's perspective on this."

I quickly dodged that remark with lightning-fast, catlike reflexes and continued with my teaching until another woman made the same request. After clearly failing to avoid the clamor for the man in the room to speak, I finally gave in and asked Glenn if he'd like to share any words of wisdom from the perspective of a King. He rose eloquently to the occasion. Jaws dropped as women hung on his every word. As soon as he was done, the pleas began: "Will you talk to my husband?!"

Only partly triggered by the interruptions of this spontaneous guest speaker, I was thankfully able to stay in my empowered feminine, deliver *my* content, and complete the day. As the women started funneling out that evening, thrilled with their breakthroughs, I walked around to all the tables to collect my evaluation forms, so interested to see the feedback!

That was when Glenn came up to me and asked, "Would you like to go to dinner and 'debrief' the event?"

I was already on a slippery slope of being annoyed and intrigued by him all at once. I felt a bit flustered and perplexed. But before I could think it through I found myself saying yes, and we were on our way to the steakhouse down the street.

Though to the best of my ability, I had just been in Queen mode all day, the Naïve Princess took control once we got to the restaurant. Even though my vision of my Kingly soul mate had matured, a few fantasy-based specifications still lingered, and he didn't quite fit them. This man had been married before. He had kids who were my age! So as much as I liked him and was looking to attract my soul mate, according to my conscious, "practical" mind, he couldn't possibly be the one. And as far as the Naïve Princess was concerned, there was *no way* that I was going to marry a blond-haired, blue-eyed chiropractor from Michigan!

For most of dinner, it felt as if I were sitting back, watching it all go down. He's into her, but the Naïve Princess isn't having it. He told her right then and there that he loves everything about her. She replied, "You know *nothing* about me." Then, sometime over dessert, I got lovingly knocked out of observation mode to receive a message from the Universe. Like a rolling window shade, *the veil lifted* and I heard, "He's the one." I quickly reached up, grabbed that veil, and pulled it back down. *The hell he is.*

Clearly, he was pursuing me and I didn't want to hurt his feelings. I said, "Look, I'm sure there's a great woman out there for you. But I just moved to the West Coast..." This man was not taking no for an answer. Still thinking I had control of the situation, finally conceding to just buy myself some time, I said, "I leave for California in the morning; I'm going to need to journal about this first, so don't call me, I'll call you."

Thinking the twenty-five hundred miles was enough of a buffer, I flew back to the Golden State and was having the best time setting up my new life. There I was, happily going to the farmer's markets, visualizing calling in my soul mate who, anytime now, would be arriving on his yacht to invite me for sunset drinks.

A few days went by and although I didn't see a yacht, I did notice a lady in a 1982 station wagon pulling into my driveway. She got out of her car with an enormous floral arrangement of white peonies. In a high-pitched voice, she asked, "Are you Gina?" I nodded. She waddled over to me with this stunning bouquet, said, "Don't lose the card," got back in her delivery ride, and drove off.

Now waddling myself under the weight of this George V–sized arrangement, I put it down and opened the small enclosed card: "To a rare and beautiful Queen, Your loving King, Glenn." *Greaaaaat.*

Then I opened up the big envelope. The card read: "The Ladies' Indulgence Package at the Four Seasons"...which was basically about eight different kinds of spa treatments for an entire day; one included a rose petal milk bath. Confused with the multitude of emotions flowing through me, all I remember feeling was *pissed.* I'd told him I needed to journal first.

"Well, it would be really rude not to pick up the phone and thank him," I reasoned with myself. Perplexed, trying to stand my ground and search for what a Queen would do, I came up blank. I'd swing from "I'm not calling him!" to "Okay, I'm totally calling him."

Finally, the Naïve Princess picked up the phone and snapped, "Well, *that's* one way to get a girl to call you."

To which he calmly responded, "Would you have dinner with me next Saturday night at the Four Seasons at eight p.m.?" I was so confused. He is in Detroit. This hotel is in California. Wait, is he flying across the country just to have dinner with *me*? I wasn't expecting this at all. I thought I was just thanking him for the flowers and spa certificate.

My hand shaking while holding the phone, before I could even collect my thoughts, I stuttered, "Sure."

"Dress appropriately," he replied, and hung up the phone.

Excuse me?! Who is this man who thinks he can tell *me* how to dress?! I had about $250 in my bank account at the time, and I'm pretty sure I spent $232 on a dress to wear on that date. I walked into the hotel lobby and there he was, standing tall and confident, impeccably dressed, already waiting for me. He escorted me to the bar, where we enjoyed a martini before we were seated for our reservation.

He ordered the tasting menu for both of us: "This way we don't have to make a decision and can just spend the time with each other." (Yes, we were *that* in love, as much as I didn't want to admit it.) Dinner was beyond fabulous; we laughed and couldn't stop talking, went for a walk on the beach, and then returned to his suite, where the fire was lit on the patio. A voice inside my head would fluctuate. *This is heaven.* I sighed. *This is* not *happening. He's really great. He is not "the plan."* And so the roller coaster went. He stayed in town for just a few days and then *thank gawd* headed back to Michigan.

"Whew. I officially dodged that bullet!" my Naïve Princess reminded me, and I needed to get back to the serious business of calling in my soul mate who matched the checklist I had worked so hard to create, which included no divorcés or Michigan zip codes.

The phone rang about five days later. "I got us tickets for Andrea Bocelli, will you meet me in Vegas?" Whaaat?!

This guy was out of his mind. Head shaking no, heart racing, I was about to inform him to go solo, and then I heard, "I would love to!" burst out of my mouth *once again*.

He booked us a dinner reservation at a stunning restaurant before the show, and I don't know what it is about me and restaurants, but the *veil lifted again*, and this time, I accepted that this really *was* my soul mate.

THE KING-AND-QUEEN DYNAMIC

At the time of writing this book, fifteen years later, this romantic partnership continues to be the easiest area of my life. Sadly, too often I hear people say that "relationships are hard work" and that you "have to sacrifice" just to keep it together. I'm happy to report that this hasn't been my experience when the empowered masculine and empowered feminine do their dance.

Of course, Glenn and I have our issues. And we grow through them knowing that relationships are teachers.

Here are a few of our values and guidelines for keeping our relationship alive and healthy and our connection strong and open.

Personal Responsibility

Neither one of us is looking for the other to "complete" us or be the one to make us happy. We're both deeply committed to personal responsibility for our individual levels of joy, our life choices, and their results. When things are great, and when things aren't so great, our commitment is that each of us owns our part in any situation. Even if our responsibility is only 5 percent (I also learned this from Katherine), owning our part completely is the only way to receive the lesson the Universe has for us.

Address the Issues in the Moment

Anytime a trigger or issue comes up, we reconcile it right away, often regardless of who else is around. I'm not saying this is what you need to do, but it definitely works for us. We're so committed to laying zero bricks of resentment between us that we voice our disagreements, frustrations, and feelings instantly and until they're resolved. Knowing we're both committed to a solution, healthy confrontation allows us to move on quickly, avoid passive-aggressive remarks, and go back to enjoying each other's company.

Unlimited Do-Overs

The Do-Over is another favorite habit that instantly fixes problems. Whenever either one of us says something hurtful, we own it *and* ask for the chance to say it differently. We established this habit early on in our relationship and it never fails to serve us! When asked, the other must immediately say yes (rules of the game) and allow us to rephrase using conscious communication.

Here's how it works. Let's say his college friend Tom is supposed to stay with us for two days, then wants to stay for two weeks, and I "go along with it" to be nice. I Ghost my feelings, and resentment builds up. I get angry and complain, "I'm so sick of your friend being here. He's so annoying. *He's a mooch!*" Seeing Glenn start to get mad at my blow-up, I take a step back and say, "Wait, let me do a Do-Over," and he agrees to hear me out. "I want to share with you that I said yes when I wanted to say no. I didn't really want Tom here more than a few days, but I was trying to be compliant and didn't want to disappoint you. So I've been building this resentment up. What I'm realizing is, in the future, I need to speak my truth and to have that be okay with you." And just like that, the secret is out and both parties win.

Fun and Flair

Glenn and I thoroughly live by the "work hard, play hard" motto. If we're not careful, working together almost all day, every day can lead to life feeling dull and routine. This is why having *fun* is a top priority in our marriage. It's what pushes us through most of the "hard work." And the best part? We do it just about every day whether in large or small doses! Monday through Friday we find opportunities for impromptu date-night dinners, concerts, or beach walks with our furbabies Lily and Oscar. The weekends could include spontaneous getaways, Sunday brunch, or couples massages at the spa nearby.

Then when it comes to *flair*, this is like our second nature. We're conscious of celebrating each other and affirming our love in thoughtful and beautiful ways. Whether it's spontaneous small "just because" gifts like flowers from the market or reservations at our favorite restaurants, we find fun ways to keep life fresh and still feel like we're dating. He's always reminding me of his love for me, and I tell him what a difference he makes in my life on a regular basis.

Beating Boredom

It hasn't all been champagne and roses all the time. In rough patches where we focused more on work than our relationship, there was definitely a "going through the motions" feeling of taking each other for granted. It's really important to keep the focus on being "in love" versus just loving your partner. Of course, in any relationship, especially long-term ones, it's easy to fall into the latter. Prioritizing the connection, raising your standards, and being unavailable to sink into roommate status will keep you sharing oysters at sunset, laughing through the main course, and dancing the night away.

Protecting Our Playtime

Setting boundaries may sound unsexy, but in fact, it's about holding the container for pleasure, play, and intimacy to thrive. For example, one of our boundaries is that we're highly present with being productive during our "work hours," but once six p.m.

hits, it's laptops shut and we're done. And we do not allow professional discussions during "our time." This ensures we're connecting as a couple in love, not just as business partners, which can easily become the feeling even for spouses who *don't* work together! If our love isn't nourished through quality time and connection, soul mates can turn into platonic roommates whose main points of interaction are about as sexy as asking the other to do the dishes.

Another important boundary I recommend to clients is "don't make your man your journal." Yes, he is there for you emotionally and can be a great sounding board; however, if most of your interactions are you venting and processing your emotions, this can put tremendous strain on your relationship, muddling your dynamic and numbing the vibe.

Sexual Magnetism

It's mutually agreed that both of us are unavailable to *not* have great sex and often. It's a very rare occasion if one of us is interested and the other is "not in the mood." Because we prioritize our relationship, spend time being present together, and allow each other to embody our roles as Queen and King, bringing a lively balance of empowered masculinity and empowered femininity into the relationship, the energy between us is consistently magnetized. Having a healthy sex life is an essential element for any successful person, especially Kings and Queens. In that space of total love, intimacy, trust, and play, sexual expression is a beautiful dynamic between us.

Royal Romance on Your Terms

These are just a few of the many values that Glenn and I live by in our marriage. But your relationship does not need to look like mine. As a conscious Queen, you now have a glorious opportunity to rewrite the rules of your relationship and co-create something truly fulfilling for you and your darling. Whether your relationship has a permanent address on cloud nine or has fallen into a status quo slump, I invite you to write down some of your new Queenly values and romance rules. Here's to you and your beloved!

FOR THE SINGLE QUEENS LOOKING FOR LOVE

Your true soul mate *does* in fact exist. And the process of getting clear on what matters to you in a relationship doesn't have to take you as long as it took me. Every woman gets to consciously create her own list of what's important to her. This is all about you getting real with yourself. What does being with your soul mate feel like? How do you desire to be treated? How do you and your future partner spend your time together? What values do you share in common? Summon your inner Queen and write down your new vision for your relationship in as much detail as possible.

Be the woman who is the aligned match to the partner you seek. After becoming clear on the vision for your dreamy relationship, cultivate *certainty* and train your brain to be open for love.

THE ROYAL ROMANCE

The more you step into Queenhood in all areas of your life, the more you will be open to receiving the trusted, romantic love that you desire. Women are the gatekeepers of relationships, and we no longer need to subsist on scraps of love any more than we need to live off baby money. We are certain that the Universe holds all of the possibilities for our highest selves, including our most fabulous and fulfilling romantic partnerships.

A soul mate relationship is captivating and it can also be *easy*. That's not to say there won't be arguments or blow-ups, but now you know how to handle these dynamics in a way that will enhance your life purpose much more than distract from it. Remember, the masculine was designed to be *in service* to the feminine. Let your royal romance be a reflection of your epic life.

nineteen

THE NEW FEMININE LEADERSHIP STYLE

All women are leaders. Whether you're leading yourself, your family, your community, your department, a Fortune 100 company, a Girl Scout troop, a book club, or a nation, you have a leadership role that only *you* can fulfill. People are looking up to you whether you realize it or not.

You, my dear, have a responsibility to carry out, so let's make it the most exciting ride of your lifetime! For this to happen, culturally we have a lot of work to do because not enough women have been taught to see themselves as leaders. Since we've been trained to take our cues from men, masculine leadership, in its strengths and weaknesses, is what has predominantly been modeled. Through this conditioning, we have grown accustomed to a style where everything is black or white, logical and linear, and unemotional. Consider the classic "Thanks for your years of service, but due to necessary budget cuts, your position is no longer needed. Today is your last day." Ouch. And to make matters worse, the darker side of masculine leadership uses fear, domination, oppression, and punishment to force people into submission. "How could you possibly screw things up with our most important client? That's it, you're off this project."

For hundreds of years, this type of leadership was viewed as the only "strong" and "effective" way to get things done. In the process, just like feminine women, empowered feminine leadership became invisible, leaving us asking, "What does it even look like? How do I do it?" And wondering, "Am I being too much of a pushover? Too rigid? Is it okay to have high standards? How can I say no and not have them quit? How can I motivate people to do their best without being too pushy?"

As a female entrepreneur, I've needed to fulfill a multitude of leadership roles, and after making almost every mistake in the book, I think I've finally solved the mystery as to what feminine leadership really looks like and how it can be achieved. It's my great honor to share with you in this chapter the humbling, sitcom-worthy, yet ultimately empowering lessons I've learned. It's up to Queens to redefine what it means for a woman to be influential and powerful, together.

A NEW STYLE

About a decade into growing my women's empowerment company, I was still searching for that sweet spot of alliance when it came to leadership. At the time, I was busy with numerous projects, programs, and my online luxury magazine that I was deeply excited about. I had a heavy travel schedule and hundreds of new members enrolled in my courses that needed significant attention. To support our growing numbers, I hired two new high-level team members, which also meant taking on the responsibility of two significant salaries.

Though early on I noticed a number of red flags, I ignored them, hoping for the best and chalking up my underwhelm to their newness. Plus, I needed the help and didn't have time to start the hiring and training process all over again. Queen tip: This is *never* a good reason to keep anyone in your life, let alone a team member.

I had to go out of town for a magazine photo shoot. I had asked that while I was away, my new leaders create a training to help my clients use effective marketing to grow their startups. I was excited to see what creativity flowed through them. When I returned home, I asked to be shown what they had created. They directed me to an iPhone video they had filmed for my program's Facebook group.

To my complete shock, I saw these two "high-level" team players I had hired to represent the luxury brand of Divine Living like I had never seen them before. One was wearing a black bra with a skimpy white tank top and multicolored leggings, flopping around the ponytail on top of her head and *twirling a hula hoop.* I'm pretty sure she was also visibly and audibly chewing gum. The other one, meanwhile, stood in the foreground, filming them in selfie mode.

Hoping this was in draft form and hadn't been posted live to the group, I asked what was going on. They shared their thinking that this was a great way to show our clients, *who had paid five figures* to be in the high-end program, how to stand out online and get attention so they could attract their own clients. So they went ahead and posted it to the group in full confidence.

With my blood boiling and smoke steaming out of my ears, setting off every alarm inside my beating heart, there weren't enough fire sprinklers in all of California to put out my anger. This is *insane*! WTF were they thinking? I had worked with a top New York City advertising agency, investing serious sums to establish our online aesthetic. My clients had also invested to be in this program and trusted me to deliver at a world-class level. In that moment, Miranda from *The Devil Wears Prada* had nothing on this Sicilian slayer.

DICTATOR DIVA ARRIVES

My inner *Dictator Diva* had hijacked the situation. She's the arche-type who leads with fear, having us lord power over others to dominate and scare people into submission, doing unnecessary damage to everyone's confidence. Erroneously, the Dictator Diva convinces us that the only way to "motivate" people and get them to do what she wants is to point out the huge error of their ways.

It's a common strategy that's been modeled to us in the oppres-sive legacy of masculine leadership. This can be a bit harder to accept or even realize when *we are the ones communicating this way*. Our true nature is not to be Dictators. Yet it's how we can show up in the world if we've received false programming about power.

For example, if you had a father (or any other adult in your life) who strictly ruled with Dictator rigidity, criticism, and severe punishment, you learned there's no room for alliance. Either everyone was compliant in fear of going against what he said, or else they would be defiant, talking back, rebelling, and doing the exact opposite of his demands.

If everyone has the same core operating system of wanting to love and be loved, how does one become a Dictator? People who grow up in this punishing environment view berating people as normal, since it was normal for them. It's an explanation, not a justification for demeaning behavior. After hearing thousands of client stories involving this programming, I've come to realize that, ironically, a lot of these Dictators were, in a warped way, expressing their love language.

Dictator parents are typically so hell-bent on their children being good citizens and getting it "right" that they think they're doing them a favor by instilling high standards and a sharp sense of right and wrong. And of course, what we know about conditioning is that this false programming gets passed from one generation to the next.

I know that was the case for me. When I was growing up, church elders created a mentality that everything you did was good or bad, right or wrong, the latter being a "sin." So once I became an adult, in my overzealousness of wanting to provide the best for my clients, I thought I was being responsible by setting the bar high and making sure expectations were met. I thought this was what "leaders" do. I unconsciously believed that people would perform better if their errors came with consequences and that this would help them get it right in the future. Can you imagine?!

Sadly, since at that time in my career the Dictator Diva had the microphone, I called everyone into the boardroom and played the punishing authority-figure role perfectly. I let them know how inappropriate and off-brand their video was, modeling to my clients how to be "tacky and wacky" rather than engage in any form of the meaningful or elegant marketing that our company represented.

If you're wondering why I didn't simply get more specific and ask for what I wanted in the future or straight-up fire them, it's because I haven't shared with you the pendulum swing I did, crashing into the Victim.

THE VICTIM'S VEIL

Failing to see that a Queen always has a choice, I let the situation victimize me. Upon reflection (and a lot of deep coaching from my own mentors), the only reason I shifted into Dictator Diva was that it hadn't even occurred to my inner Victim that I could let these underperforming team members go. I was so angry that I was paying people who were so off-brand, yet unconsciously I felt I was stuck with them.

When the *Victim* casts its veil, we are blinded to having options or the power to create a solution. Feeling stuck, we turn to fear, failing to see how to set up the proper systems and boundaries to protect ourselves. The unfortunate patterns keep repeating themselves, the ultimate self-fulfilling prophecy.

This time, I was so bored with this recurring theme of mine, I couldn't even bring myself to call and complain *one more time* to one more friend about my inept "team dramas." So I sat down, prayed, and asked for a miracle. I asked to be shown the solution. I was done needing to be right and didn't even care about what was fair; I just wanted out of this painful and expensive pattern.

When you get humble, Spirit provides the truth. Once I became available to see my part, Spirit revealed to me what I was previously blocked to, and though it wasn't an easy pill to swallow, it was freeing at a level I never imagined. Spirit showed me that I was being a Dictator and a Victim. I was mortified. "Gina! You're supposed to be a 'leader' of a women's empowerment company who teaches spiritual principles, and *this* is the way you talk to people?" The last thing I wanted was to be seen as this mean, oppressive ogre of an employer.

In my shame and humiliation, I did the classic pendulum swing from defiance (Dictator) to compliance (Victim). I declared I would never call a team member "wrong" for their decisions again. No matter what.

A free-for-all ensued throughout my company. If someone showed up late, my response was, "Nice to see you! Thanks for coming in to work today. Traffic must have been a beast, so sorry about that!" Sloppy work was commended with "This looks fabulous!" Misspellings all over the place? "Hey, no one's perfect, everyone has an off day. Let me take care of that for you!"

Glenn would look at me in astonishment and say, "No, you need to set boundaries, and speak up." I was terrified to not get it right. My Injured Feminine Instinct had my senses off everywhere. When it was appropriate to set a boundary, I was letting it slide, and where I was being more strict, I needed to be more understanding.

This vicious cycle was frustrating for all. I deeply wanted to create a thriving company culture, yet nothing I did was right. Effective leadership where everyone could shine seemed so elusive. And all the books on the subject were so impossibly dry and boring that I was getting dangerously close to closing down my business and opting for my waitressing-in-Cyprus exit plan.

HOW QUEENS LEAD

Future generations of women can hopefully skip a few gray hairs on this one. Queenhood frees you from the teeter-totter between compliance (Victim) and defiance (Dictator) in all areas of life—from the bedroom to the boardroom to the presidential podium. Whereas masculine leadership is all about the *I* of the Dictator, feminine leadership is all about the *We*.

A Queen considers herself *and* others, as well as the whole. She doesn't discount her own preferences or expectations in fear of upsetting those involved. Nor does she lead from a place of "it's my way or the highway." Ultimately, this conscious leadership model is about taking care of whomever you're in charge of: your children, your team, your daughter's Brownie troop, your bridge club, *and* yourself.

Stepping into feminine leadership in my business, I realized I had to take responsibility for making sure my own expectations were clear and that systems were in place to support my team members in doing their best work. Looking back on the hula-hoop debacle, I understand that my team members were only doing what they thought was best. How did they have access to posting in the client Facebook group anyway? It wasn't their job to set up a system wherein other more experienced team members would be able to approve their work. It was mine.

This applies with family or in any group of people. As Queens in charge of our own experience, we get to have our preferences, and there is nothing "right" or "wrong" about them. I had to accept my own expectations for how I'd like my brand to be presented and my company to work together, knowing that those standards would be attractive to some and repelling to others. In alliance, I got to focus on those for whom my preferences were an energetic match. (And I got better at spotting those who weren't.)

INTUITIVE LEADERSHIP

A feminine leader listens to her intuition above all else. It allows for quick discernment and excellent judgment calls. As Queens, we develop this deep trust within by bringing questions to Spirit on a regular basis, reflecting on the outcome of following the guidance, knowing ourselves, and being in tune with our bodies. The amount of time that we invest in our spiritual practice and feminine rituals can save us days, if not years, that would otherwise be lost to overthinking, invisibility, or speaking in ways we'll regret.

Knowing the massive power of this practice, I now even train my team members to rely on their intuition as well. For example, one time my fabulous A-player of a community manager approved a client post in our Facebook group that didn't quite fit our guidelines. Thankfully, by this point, I was finally in alliance in my leadership style and untriggered by the error. I assumed the best, remembering that she wasn't trying to do anything but do a good job. So I went to her with an open mind and asked, "Just curious, why did you approve this post?"

"I was working too fast, and I suppose I thought it was harmless," she replied.

I went deeper. "Did anything in your intuition at any point hint that this wasn't a post to approve?"

She said, "It's funny you bring that up...my intuition did alert me that this wasn't appropriate, but then I talked myself out of it and came up with a logical reason why I should go ahead and approve this post."

I affirmed that her intuition was right on. She has the wiring in her to discern when something's off. She walked away feeling empowered rather than wrong and allowed herself to make better, intuition-based decisions moving forward. In fact, she's now been training new team members to trust their intuition as well! This is how true feminine leadership works!

WHEN LEADERSHIP FEELS FABULOUS

Know Who You Are as a Leader

Queens have clarity on what they value, stand for, and desire. So much of my struggle came from being unconscious about what I was creating. I hadn't visualized or set intentions for what my ideal team dynamic would look like, I was just making it up as I went along.

Essential as it is, vision is one of the elements of leadership I see women spend the *least* amount of time on. We're so focused on keeping up, crossing tasks off the to-do list, and doing-doing-doing that we don't stop to check in on what we are creating and whether it matches the level of life experience we desire.

Creating conscious intentions empowers you to lead in a way that reflects your personality. Since I'm clear now that much of my personal value system is linked to lifestyle and living, one of the ways I approach new hires is, "Would I desire to have dinner with this person?" Yes, they need to have all the solid skills for the position, *and* hosting fabulous team dinners is a big personal preference of mine, so I give myself permission to lead with that value in mind.

Your vision does not (and probably will not) look anything like mine, and that's perfectly fine. The most important part is that *you* consciously create it and stand by it. The more visible you are in living out your vision, the more the right people will naturally gravitate toward you.

Have the Support to Fulfill Your Vision

Well-meaning and hardworking women can do the work to get clear on their vision. We can have it all written out in detail and create elaborate Pinterest boards full of images. And all too often, the only reason we don't rise to the level of leadership we're capable of is that our default mode is, "I have to do everything myself." It's just one more way we've cut ourselves off from *receiving*. In this case, from receiving support.

Leaders delegate as much as they can as fast as they can.

As I learned this truth, I got in the habit of asking, "Who else can do this?" I even added a sticky note to the top of my computer asking the question to make this new motto second nature. In adopting this new mentality, I became unavailable for a number of tasks that I realized made no sense for me to be doing in the first place. I became "unavailable" to clean my house, take my car to the car wash, do certain administrative tasks for my business, and run unnecessary errands that would take hours out of my day. Not because I'm above doing anything, but because I knew that to grow as a leader, I'd have to master the art of delegation.

To start, hiring a housekeeper once a month was a big step. I immediately started to see the benefits of how it freed me up *and* assisted the person desiring income. Whether our dreams and projects are big or small, every feminine leader deserves to be well supported. For one woman, maybe it's a matter of help around the house or with the kids to free up time to pursue her vision. For another woman, perhaps it's spending $10 extra to have groceries delivered or laundry done so that she can carve out time for a fitness routine. And for another woman, it might be as simple as asking your boyfriend or husband to make dinner reservations and put gas in the car.

And for any woman still holding on to the concept that she can "handle everything herself," let me kindly remind her that I don't know a successful woman out there who *doesn't* have support in one form or another! It's up to Queens like us to transform the mindset of thinking that we can't delegate, that we have to change every diaper, fix every typo, and spend endless amounts of time looking for the best deal. We only have so much time, and we also only have so much attention. It's time to stop doing unnecessary work and learn to delegate so we can actually focus on living out our life's purpose.

Be Compassionate Yet Unapologetic

Taking on the responsibility of being the leader means you get to design the experience around your preferences and the boundaries that support you to do your best work.

Women often fear that making rules is Diva behavior, though in actuality most people crave clearly defined expectations so that they can know with confidence how to do their best work too. It's the masculine container that allows the feminine to be creative, fun, and playful!

A clear guideline I have for my remote team is to be available for work Monday through Friday, nine a.m. to six p.m. Although they do have flexibility on certain projects, we've found that for us as a team to be the most productive, being reachable during those hours is best. That being said, I don't dictate every moment and track every hour; I let them use their (now very well-trained) intuition to decide when it's appropriate for them to take a longer lunch or work eight a.m. to five p.m., for example. They enjoy the structure and it allows them to frame their projects and plan their days accordingly.

Create a Success-Oriented Culture

As a feminine leader, you must set the tone and establish a culture. A culture provides the environment to support you (and those you're leading) to function. Whether it's a culture for your household, family, career, team, or friend circle, you get to design what this ideally would look like for you. What do you all believe in? What's the mission? What principles do you function by? What are your non-negotiables and expectations? Rituals? Communication styles? Ethics? How do you set everyone up for success so that the group can consistently thrive?

Envisioning and sharing the culture invites others to quickly learn, adapt, and live by it too. Intention and energy goes where there's a purpose. And naturally, everyone is wired to want to "fit in." Once everyone has clear and established guidelines, it is *that* much easier for everyone to fit in and thrive.

In my company, I desired to create a culture where everyone would feel empowered and where A-players and self-starters would take it upon themselves to push themselves for growth. I didn't want to create a culture that relied on me being a Dictator or the one constantly pulling everyone along. And for that to take place, I knew that wouldn't happen if anyone was afraid that they were going to do it wrong, get in trouble, look like a fool, or even disappoint me or the team.

So at Divine Living, we set up a company culture where we

follow feminine principles. That means that when something falls through the cracks or when errors and mistakes are made, the *only* experience we typically have is *"Awesome*, what a great learning opportunity! We're grateful that the Universe has shown us how we can improve this system to get it better next time and grow!"

This is how we set everyone up for success.

Hold Yourself and Others to High Standards

Queens have high standards. They expect the best from everyone around them—significant others, students, children, pets, coworkers, and friends included.

They set their expectations high and also demonstrate the courage to address when their standards aren't being met. For example, say that your husband, child, team member, or family member didn't behave in a way that you prefer. You, as a Queen, get to lovingly, directly, and unapologetically communicate your expectations. For the team member who has gotten a little comfortable with her position and is dropping into B-level status, this can look like "I'm noticing that this hasn't been the amazing work that I'm used to seeing from you, and I would appreciate you bringing more wow-factor before you submit it to me." Or let's say you have higher expectations for how enjoyable talking to your mother should be. You can let her know, "Mom, I know you love me, and I appreciate your concern about my marriage, and yet I'm not enjoying the dynamic of you bringing this subject up unless I've initiated it first. If I want to talk to you about it, I'll bring it up."

WHEN LEADING WITH LOVE IS THE NEW NORMAL

Your fellow Queens are recruiting *you* for this new style of leadership. The outdated masculine model that excludes our feminine values no longer works. Female leaders have an important yet fabulous opportunity to show others, often for the first time, what it looks like to lead with love, communicate compassionately yet unapologetically, and create win-wins on a regular basis. As Queens we have the audacity to put ourselves first while creating the best possible outcomes for everyone around us. It's up to us to model what it looks like to say no to being "busy" and say yes to actually being successful. Every time we give ourselves permission to set a boundary, establish a higher expectation, and hire someone to pick up the kids on Wednesdays, it gets easier for us and for the next generation of women to bring about a spectacular new normal to management style. Your invitation to lead the feminine way has arrived.

twenty

FINALLY FAMOUS

From the time I was eight years old, *Fame* was my favorite TV show and my reason for living on Thursday nights. I'd watch Debbie Allen play Lydia, the ballet teacher with A-list expectations in her leotard and leg warmers. As she pounded her wooden staff on the dance floor, her message intimidated as much as it inspired. "You've got big dreams. You want fame. Well, fame *costs* . . . and right here's where you start paying—in sweat!" With that, she'd start the show and ignite my aspirations. Instantly, I would see myself in those performers. The fact that I never desired to be a professional dancer didn't matter, we shared common ground: We all wanted to be *famous*.

I was preparing for it, twirling around in my orange tutu with silver sequins, performing in every school play they would let me in, and tirelessly auditioning for the chorus solo (which, as we've discussed, *never* happened). No matter how many times I was rejected for a starring role, still the little girl within had certainty and excitement that when she grew up, she'd make her way to the spotlight.

And then she did grow up. She became an adult circulating in the spiritual and personal development arenas where to say out loud that one desired fame would quickly lead to exile. And yet, as I've observed after twenty years of working with all types of career women, I don't know *one* who doesn't crave whatever her version of fame is in a big way (though I'm sure almost nobody cares to be swarmed with paparazzi or have their grocery-run outfit pictured in *People* magazine). Little Miss Perfect is proud to proclaim, "I seek to contribute and make a massive difference in the world," but under no circumstances will she give herself permission to desire fame, let alone say it out loud, even when both are equally true.

So let's get this straight. Almost every woman desires *her* definition of fame, yet no one can safely admit to it? It's not like saying you want to audition to be the sixth Kardashian sister. For driven, spiritual women like us, being lit up about fame is because we're lit up about growth and contribution. And a lot of people have much to gain by limiting that growth, keeping women in line, and making sure their lives stay small and predictable.

At the core of this fear-based culture is our conditioning to believe that "more for me equals less for someone else." Not only is this a myth when it comes to money, it's also false when it comes to *attention*.

DESIRES NEVER DIE

As hard as we try, denying what's natural and attempting to control our instincts won't kill our original desires. Like water, they always find their way out, though in distorted ways. We see this in women all the time when the Martyr has ripped up their permission slip to be the star. (Remember, the Martyr is the archetype who spends her life giving up what she wants, wearing her sacrifice like a badge of honor.) And yet forbidding herself the spotlight won't eliminate the star power in a woman, it'll just distort her sparkle so she appears needy and attention grabbing.

This happened recently to my client Veronica. On a coaching call, she told me about an old pattern she fell back into during a glamorous trip to Las Vegas with her husband and his group of friends.

"I found myself acting like an idiot," she recounted. "I know that I'm smart, and I know I'm successful, probably more successful than some of the men on the trip. Yet there we were with our college friends, watching the choreographed water and light show outside of the Bellagio, and suddenly I was showing up as ditzy arm candy."

Young, blonde, and beautiful, Veronica told me that in high school and college, she felt like being "arm candy" was what was expected of her.

"I just felt like that's what people wanted from me, so I really turned it on. It's frustrating because I've done so much personal development work on it. And then, for seventy-two hours in Vegas, I completely let go of my power."

"What'd you get out of it?" I asked her.

"Attention," she replied frankly.

"And that's how you're used to getting attention?" I asked to confirm.

"Yes," she admitted sheepishly.

Knowing this was out of character for Veronica, I continued, "Let's look at this from a compassionate angle. Why were you looking to get attention from these men?"

"Wow, that sounds horrible." How brave she was to be this vulnerable and transparent in front of our coaching group. "I guess I just like the validation and reassurance, male or female. I just like attention."

"Okay. Can you give yourself permission to enjoy the attention?"

"Yes, I can, but I want the attention to come naturally because of who I'm authentically being. I don't want to have to play a ditzy game to grab it."

Veronica, as we can see, like many women, enjoys receiving attention from others. Perfectly natural. Yet she feared the serious social stigma of being seen as the woman who "wants attention." So she was "sneaking it." In total defiance, grabbing for the attention. Like a little kid sneaking a cookie before dinner. If the child was given permission, she might realize she didn't even want it. But because she knew it was strictly forbidden, she got caught up in the game.

I shared this analogy with Veronica, continuing, "From what I've learned from being around you, I don't even think it's about attention for you. I think that you are at a place on your journey where, as a young woman, a mother, and a wife, it's time for you to get into alliance and grant yourself permission to be the star of your life! A star's purpose is to give off light and heat as it dazzles and shines. There's a passion in it. It's very generous."

"That actually makes my heart quicken a little bit," Veronica replied, understanding for the first time that her desire for attention was about full self-expression, growth, fun, and contribution. In that moment, she made the audacious decision to show up as the superstar she is, granting herself carte blanche to shine and share her personality, passion, enthusiasm, femininity, and flair, and to receive attention and recognition in exchange.

THE BLESSING OF FAME

The age of invisible women is officially over. Our ongoing anonymity serves no one. The more visible and famous we women are, the greater our potential for creative fulfillment and making the grand contribution this world needs. Having the courage, confidence, and tenacity to be a Queen publicly isn't being "hungry for attention." It's the generous act of shining your light. Whether you dream of being acknowledged in your community, being a household name, or anything in between, fame is for you.

You've waited your whole life to be a star. Permission granted. Welcome to a world where your vocabulary no longer includes "I'm not good enough" or "That's not possible for me." We don't need to be concerned with the trolls and the haters, because we're committed to the bigger vision and surrounded with our powerful community of Queens. We don't have to waste precious energy constantly wondering what people think of us, because their judgments have no power over a Queen.

Every day brings the opportunity to focus on what *is* possible. Continue to grow and learn the lessons that empower you. Being famous doesn't cancel out being a human being. We get to be famous *and* make mistakes. We get to be the star *and* get it wrong sometimes. The only way to reconcile this is to focus on your truth. On your desires. On doing your spiritual workout every day, honing your intuition, and becoming unapologetic about who you are. A Queen.

ACCEPT YOUR CALLING TO PLAY BIG

The age of Queen allows for the masterful blend of masculine and feminine energy. Through this powerful combination we can see things not as they are but as they could be, and we can also see them through to completion.

The Dalai Lama said, "The world will be saved by the Western woman," and he was right. It will be saved by the women who have power and soul plus the ability to be visible, write checks, speak from the heart, and do it all in alignment with spiritual values.

Empowered, feminine women no longer have time to sit around and talk about feeling insecure, not being ready to play

big, or not knowing enough to get involved and make a difference. Stay committed to your greatness. Continue to make your
purpose your priority. Hire your mentor to ensure your victory.
Do the exercises in this book as many times as it takes to create
new conditioning. Transform your money story and train your
brain to accomplish your mission. Call in your soul mate and
enjoy the love that makes life worth living. Call in the community
you crave and experience the friendships you deserve. And above
all, let go of all of the conditioned, false, and limiting archetypes
that are no longer serving you. There is no more hiding it. Your
time to be Queen is now.

Who do you think has been prepared to radically shift humanity's experience on this planet? *We have.* With the international
marketplace at our fingertips, advancements in technology, and
greater access to education, no previous generation of women in
history has been more empowered to model feminine leadership
full of love, healing, and transformation on the global stage.

Being Queen is about changing the world. Ultimately, that is
what we are doing individually, and collectively.

Your Divine Assignment is waiting to be claimed. Now it's your
turn to be the inspiration. To do what all the legends and greats
have done. To drop "Oh no, not me" and replace it with this:

*Yes, here I am. Yes, yes, yes. Dear God, please use me. My
life is available. For such a time as this, I know I have been
called, and I am choosing to be of service now, to be seen,
and to declare that I am good enough and I'm here to make
a difference. Amen.*

Thank you for saying yes. Thank you for showing up and
having the courage to go for it. Thank you for stepping into the
unknown because that's what we wise women do.

THE WORLD IS WAITING

The Universe is in love with you, my darling. It is so generous and is not done giving to you. In every moment of Queenhood, you have the power to summon Divine Guidance to lift you up and add the sparkle of infinite possibilities to your life. Spirit is already flowing through you, ready to abundantly support you in ways that you didn't even know to ask. Your divine destiny has been predetermined and preplanned; just don't block it. Open up to receive your full glory and get comfortable being the leading lady of your life.

A luminary knows that her unique purpose *must* be fully expressed in the world. It's intended to be shared for both the giver and receiver, continuously creating the double blessing. People on this planet are suffering, and *you* are needed now more than ever. The challenges you've overcome, the lessons you've learned, and the plot twists you've mastered have all prepared you to make the ultimate difference in the lives of others.

You are as worthy of a calling as Queen Esther, and your "for such a time as this" moment has arrived! Yes, *you* are ready! Every powerful word you speak, every positive post you make, every soothing smile you share, every time you unapologetically over-dress, every day you say yes to having your life be used, the ripple effect of your love and influence expands. That's why you're here, darling.

Every woman has a story. As Queen, you have the audacity to make yours epic. Treat yourself like the miracle that you are, and you can expect miracles. Expect greatness, expect support, expect abundance, expect fascinating friends, expect your soul mate, expect center-stage opportunities, and expect people to write you saying, "You've changed my life. Thank you for showing up and inspiring me! I didn't know what was possible until you came along." You never know whose life will forever be changed as a result of you sharing your gifts and talents.

As a Queen, enjoy the new blessings of wearing your crown. Your most fabulous life starts now.

THE END

ACKNOWLEDGMENTS

After reading hundreds of acknowledgment sections in other books, I'm humbled, grateful, and honored to now be writing my own version. In this moment I understand more than ever why so many of them sound the same. It really does take a village. The way this book has come about was only because of all of the angel messengers that have crossed my path along the way. As I breathe deeply... I'd like to thank:

My parents, Bob and Connie Ratliffe, who instilled in me my faith in God and that anything was possible. Thank you for your love and all you've provided and given me so that I can be the woman I am today.

To my fabulous agent, Wendy Sherman, you truly were an answer to many prayers. I'm so grateful your feminine instinct immediately sparked to this project and saw the possibility for this book to be a reality. You've made every step of this journey an absolute pleasure. You truly have been an angel.

To my smart and elegant editor, Krishan Trotman, I'm so blessed to have had your love, passion, excitement, and vision for this book. Your unbounded enthusiasm to get this message to change the lives of women has warmed my heart through every page. To my publisher, Mary Ann Naples, what they say about you is true: You're a genius who has heart, soul, depth, and a great personality. Michelle Aielli, your zest and tenacity are rare jewels to encounter and your take-charge leadership style brings dazzle everywhere you go. Michael Barrs, I appreciate your innovative ideas and hard work. Amy Schneider, your copyediting skills are in a league of their own. I don't know how you do what you do. However I'm most grateful for your laser attention to every detail. And to the entire Hachette team—Carrie Napolitano, Odette Fleming, and Lauren Ollerhead—thank you for your dedication, professionalism, and big vision for this book. You've been an absolute dream to work with, and I could not be more proud of the final results we've created together.

To those who've been with me from the beginning: Marianne Williamson, my original Queen mentor, you've shaped my life in countless ways and I'm forever grateful. Katherine Woodward Thomas, your wise feminine guidance from the early years lives in me to this day. Darlene Winter, I thank you not only for the years of friendship, but for the red-pen feedback that only you could give. And to Jen Sincero, thank you for your constant belief in this message, your friendship, and for being the first person who thought I was funny. This adventure would never have been the same without you.

To those I didn't even know to ask for, Steve Dennis, your profound belief in this message and advice regarding the process brought me much needed support and peace. Jennifer Racioppi, your generous and wise counsel has been a bright guiding light from the valley to the mountaintop and every step in between. I thank you for holding the space for all of it. Natalie Berthold, thank you for continuing to, through love and beyond-your-years wisdom, bring out the truth and the best in me. And to Ashley Stahl, whose writing companionship brought joy every minute I wrote words on the pages, and whose friendship has truly been a divine connection.

To my team: Kendall Dekreek, your unparalleled energy,

guaranteed fun, hilarious suggestions, countless hours, and unending passion for this book have been the greatest source of commitment, support, enthusiasm, and drill sergeant-ness an author could ask for. Rebeca Arango, after hundreds of thousands of magical words together, I'm surprised to find myself at a loss for how to adequately thank you. Your wit, writing skills, professionalism, dedication, and all-around genius work in this process have been beyond any gift I could have anticipated. To the entire Divine Living Team, who give so generously daily to get the message of Queenhood into the lives of women around the world, I can only do what I do because of your incredible skill and support.

To all of the precious, brave, and amazing clients I've had the privilege and honor to be on this journey with for over two decades, you continue to teach me, inspire me, and renew my own commitment to Queenhood.

And to my beloved husband, who has believed in me and supported me every step of the way, I'm the luckiest woman in the world to experience the power and depth of being loved by you.